THE
LAST
PIRATE

THE
LAST
PIRATE

A Father, His Son, and the Golden Age of Marijuana

TONY
DOKOUPIL

Doubleday | New York London Toronto Sydney Auckland

All rights reserved. Published in the United States by Doubleday, a
division of Random House LLC, New York, and in Canada
by Random House of Canada Limited, Toronto,
Penguin Random House companies.

www.doubleday.com

DOUBLEDAY and the portrayal of an anchor with a dolphin
are registered trademarks of Random House LLC.

This work is based on "My Father the Drug Dealer," which first
appeared in *Newsweek* (July 2009).

Jacket design by Michael J. Windsor
Jacket photograph courtesy of the author

Library of Congress Cataloging-in-Publication Data
Dokoupil, Tony.
The last pirate : a father, his son, and the golden age of marijuana /
Tony Dokoupil. — First edition.
pages cm
1. Dokoupil, Tony. 2. Dokoupil, Tony—Family. 3. Dokoupil, Anthony,
1946– 4. Journalists—United States—Biography. 5. Editors—United
States—Biography. 6. Marijuana industry—United States. 7. Drug
trade—United States. I. Title.
PN4874.D63A3 2014
070.92—dc23
[B]
2013034094

ISBN 978-0-385-53346-1
ISBN 978-0-385-53347-8 (eBook)

MANUFACTURED IN THE UNITED STATES OF AMERICA

1 3 5 7 9 10 8 6 4 2

First Edition

For my children

Main entry: Do•ko•u•pil
Pronunciation: Da-ko-pull
Function: verb, past tense
Etymology: Czech
Definition: to buy it all, as in "I bought it all"

Author's Note

This is a true story. To tell it, I researched it. I pulled court documents, troweled newspaper archives. When I thought I had every relevant record, I hired a lawyer to come behind me and make sure. I also reported this story, traveling to five states and into interviews with the DEA agents who investigated the case, the former head of the Organized Crime Drug Enforcement Task Force who prosecuted it, and more than a dozen former smugglers and dealers, most notably my father himself, who showed me the sights in Miami and New York. Although this is in practice a work of journalism, the sources were often very happily unsound during the years in question. Where memories differed or broke down, I deferred to the written record, my father's version of events, or the most plausible version, in that order. Most of the sources were also friends and family, so I've repaid their generosity by altering their names and on occasion other details so their past lives may remain past. The only names I haven't changed, in fact, are those of the three feds, who are proud of busting the biggest pot ring of the Reagan era, and of my father, who is proud of being part of it.

Contents

THE
LAST
PIRATE

Prologue

Digging Holes

My mother tucked me into bed, changed her clothes, and walked outside to find a shovel. She searched the perimeter of the house, a mansion in the mountains outside Albuquerque, and decided on a spot near the foundation, a few steps from an old pine tree. She paused there, poised between one era of our life and the next, looking warily toward the tree line. On a cloudless southwestern night the stars throw off enough light to read a newspaper, and my mother could see she was alone.

She thrust the shovel blade into the ground and turned up the soil. Nothing.

She thrust the blade into the ground again.

Nothing.

She was almost forty at the time, still youthful, straw-haired, stylish, neither fat nor thin, a fresh golden cake color.

After a few feet the dirt was a little darker than the topsoil and she felt a change in the air. She scanned the horizon one last time, aimed the shovel, and stomped hard. She turned up the soil and saw the first flashes of white: pieces of a large Styrofoam cooler, no more than three feet down.

My mother removed the lid. Plastic baggies, dozens of them. They were filled with what looked like crustless sandwiches gone rotten. For an instant she thought bugs had chewed through everything, which they sometimes did, but when she opened a bag and then another she found what she expected. Each bag had $5,000 inside, moldy but still usable, and there were bags down as deep as her arm could reach.

The following morning my mother took the wheel of a rented motor home, two thousand miles to go before we reached home in Miami. I was seven, working a flap hat against the summer sun, responsible for radio stations and refilling the water bowl for Captain, our flatulent black Lab. We had been doing a lot of driving lately, my mother taking advantage of the long hours behind the wheel to draw me out about grade-school crushes and playground fights.

We hit Florida's Redland region to pick up a pair of collectible cars, which Mom loaned to the makers of *Miami Vice*. We hit Long Island in pursuit of other coolers stuffed with cash and buried behind a house in the suburbs off I-495. But by far the richest prize was the one in Albuquerque, half a million dollars dropped into a hillside at my cousin's house. Sure, my mother loved the open road. She also knew you couldn't take more than $10,000 on an airplane without telling the authorities.

The man who buried the money began to amass it in his mid-twenties, selling a few baggies of pot. By his late twenties, he sold bricks of Mexican reefer every weekend, sometimes from the window of a Good Humor ice-cream truck. By the time he was thirty, he moved hundreds of pounds a month in the trunk of an old Buick, crisscrossing the mid-Atlantic states under the guise of delivering concert tickets. When he'd saved enough money, he flew to Miami, uninvited and alone, to knock on the door of a former car mechanic who imported tons of Colombian marijuana. He pitched himself as the most reliable black marketeer on the East Coast, "the best there is from box to box" (drugs to cash). He drove mobile homes packed with weed out of Key West, secured a fleet of pickup trucks from New England, and began to transport acres of South American mountainside up the I-95 "reefer express."

This was the late 1970s, I should add, which was also about the same time that he decided to start a family. He became a father the year he graduated to loads of ten and twenty thousand pounds of marijuana, transported on freighters and tugboats from the extreme northeastern edge of Colombia to sailboats near the Virgin Islands and ultimately to New York City wholesalers, vacation markets, and college towns along the East Coast.

In the years that followed, he buried nearly a million dollars, invested more than half a million more in a Yukon gold mine, and prepared the paperwork of escape, should he ever have to hit the reset as a card-carrying union welder and avid user of the Monmouth, New Jersey, library system. At his peak in the mid-1980s—which was also the peak of the drug war, and an impossibly late date for pot smuggling—he broke a weeks-long national dope panic, a drought that *New York* magazine dubbed "Reefer Sadness." In a single load he supplied enough marijuana to levitate every college-age person in America and send them sideways to the store for snacks.

By that time the Old Man, as he'd come to be called in the business, ran stateside operations for one of the most successful marijuana rings of the twentieth century. In careers that spanned the drug war from Nixon to Reagan, the Old Man and his friends slipped every major counter-narcotics operation, and came within one week—one idiot with a lead foot and a Ferrari, in fact—of getting off forever. In all they hauled and sold hundreds of thousands of pounds of marijuana, and the Old Man distributed at least fifty tons of it, an environmentalist's nightmare of plastic baggies, enough bud for thousands of part-time dealers, and millions of left-hand cigarettes, pinched and passed between friends.

At a certain point he grew into a "marijuana millionaire," as the press dubbed his kind, and the Old Man decided he needed to start acting more like a drug dealer. He bought a succession of inky-blue Mercedes sedans, a thirty-five-foot cruising yacht, and a hundred-acre swath of pristine Maine forest, dotted with lakes and capped by a dome of powder blue sky. He moved from Connecticut to Miami, the Wall Street of American weed, where he paid cash for a three-bedroom home south of the city and doted on the son he'd always wanted.

Together they toured the real pirate forts of the Caribbean and had a pillow fight beneath the gilded ceilings of the Plaza Hotel in New York. But perhaps their most blissful adventure came in late 1986, when family and friends gathered for a kind of retirement bash in the U.S. Virgin Islands. During the previous two years the gang had pulled off massive deals, netting the Old Man and his partner a million-dollar payday.

What followed was not your average cake-and-wine send-off but a weeklong bacchanalia culminating on an eighty-six-foot schooner near St. Thomas. The Old Man and his son were there, along with three other smugglers, distributors and dealers, two other kids, two unmarried mothers, and an escort turned girlfriend (because that's how dope dealers roll). Because he wasn't sure what pharmaceuticals were needed to fuel this exit to Eden, the Old Man packed everything he could sneak onto an Eastern Air Lines flight. Cocaine behind his belt buckle. Cocaine in film rolls. He brought a shaving satchel of rare herbs with heavy names like Oaxaca Red. He figured security wouldn't search a man traveling with his family, even if President Reagan had recently "run up the battle flag."

They sailed along, a dozen people partying on a boat designed to accommodate forty-nine. The parents drank Heinekens. The kids quaffed orange juice. Everyone ate lobster sandwiches and red snapper fillets. They napped on the white-pine deck and read Carl Hiaasen and Curious George in the cozy cabins below. The three kids—ranging from six to twelve years old—took turns steering the ship. And when they reached one of the area's lush, uninhabited cays, they slid off the stern and snorkeled right where they fell.

They swam to the shallows, where manta rays glided beneath them. And they nearly became fish food—or so they were thrilled to think— when a pair of plump, prehistoric-looking barracudas floated over for a look at their fathers' gold chains and shiny watches. When they went ashore, they fed hibiscus leaves and dahlias to wild iguanas and army-crawled beneath the decks of beachfront bars, where drunks and sun-stroked tourists dropped change between the floorboards.

Each day ended with the ocean smeared purple, the men holding their ladies close, and the kids clustered on the bow, dreaming of ship-wrecks, pirates, and buried treasures. The world around was fenceless and so was the future. But the Old Man was restless in this paradise.

He had broken a cardinal rule of dealing and become an addict himself. Coke and hookers, mostly. He left the party early in search of both.

I know all this because the Old Man was my old man and when I was six I watched him go.

My father and I are separated by only an adjective—Big Tony, Little Tony—and when I was truly little we toured Miami with our seamless tans, windblown blond hair, and Lacoste swimsuits. My father liked daiquiris, virgin for me and an extra shot of rum in the straw for him. He also liked girls, and he liked how approachable he was with a toddler staring awestruck from the next stool over. His first drink would disappear as fast as a cup of ice melt tossed into a breeze. But he sipped the second one, pushing aviator shades onto his head. His face got interesting then, his features adrift, and he would start talking to people. Dad liked hostesses in particular.

Hostess: "Would you like our special shrimp sampler?"

Dad: "I'd like to take a shower with you."

If you smoked Colombian weed in the 1970s and 1980s, I owe you a thank-you card. You paid for my swim lessons, bought me my first baseball glove, and kept me in the best private school in south Florida, alongside President George H. W. Bush's grandsons, at least for a little while. But the truth is, I never really knew my father, not as a man, not as a person distinct from the figure I idolized in the abstract. For the early years of my childhood, he was someone I adored. He taught me how to hit a baseball, read a newspaper, and shave (without the blade). By the time I was old enough to care about those things, he was long gone, leaving only stories behind.

At the Grand Canyon, he let me crawl to the edge for a better look. During a trip to New York in the dead of winter, he dared me, aged four, to lick a Central Park slide; my mother had to pour hot-dog-stand coffee on my tongue to get it unstuck. At Disney World he let me watch movies alone in the hotel room, where I fielded a call from my mother while he hit the bars. In Miami we sometimes played baseball using a big orange basketball, which sure was easy to hit but not so forgiving. The bat bounced hard off the ball, right into my mouth. It looked like Halloween when I flicked the light on in the bathroom.

As an older kid in Miami, if you asked me about my father, I would have told you he can't come to career day. He'll have to miss the father-son brunch. His work is in New England, where all the antique-furniture auctions are held, or he's in Vermont this month, where he develops property. I might have said he's in Key West, where he zips snowbirds into their wet suits or St. Thomas where he spits into their dive masks. If we were friends, I might have told you he was in rehab, and that would have been the truest possible answer.

I never knew the full truth. For most of my adult life, I had only scraps of information about my father. Some were fun, like streamers left behind after a party. Others were dark, like bats from the mouth of an unmapped cave. My mother almost never spoke of him, but I knew that he did drugs, sold weed, slept around, and bottomed out so completely that friends presumed him dead long before he was forty. My mother advised me to assume him dead as well. But I did the opposite.

As a teenager, I recoiled from this image of my father as a violent mess, and I began to build a better version in my own mind. A heartsick boy can compose a small, speculative history of manhood from a few black-and-white photographs and a knife left behind in a drawer. Such was the style of my own imaginings: I told people my father was a cross between Tony Montana and Willy Loman, a big-time drug dealer, licking his wounds somewhere in Colombia. I could accept this vision of him, and anyway, I needed it to survive. High school is hard enough without having to wonder about the blood you have, the brain you've inherited.

When I was twenty, I felt established enough to face the truth, so I called my father. He refused to see me. After a few letters, he changed his mind but I refused to see him. Each of us backed away reflexively, as though closing the door of an occupied bathroom.

I was almost thirty, and years into a journalism career, before I was ready to talk to my father again. Peering over a notebook this time, I saw him as a character in a larger story about outlaws. In a digital age, hackers and Internet pranksters are the mantle bearers, people whose work is massively influential but rarely romantic, almost never sexy. There are no grand vistas, no beer-commercial-grade photo ops, no tradition of carousing and womanizing, winning it all and losing it fast. There are no deathless pop songs about computer keystrokes.

And this criminal awe deficit, as I saw it, was the starkest in the weed business, where yachtsmen and beach bums like my father have been replaced by businessmen and botanists. Bronze skin and corn-colored hair have faded into cubicle complexions and cowlicks. Where there was once the thrill of foreign fields, leaky boats, and suburban stash houses there are now indoor "seas of green" and legal channels to market. I believe something was lost in this shift. Weed is undeniably better today—every bud is a green chandelier of head-ringing crystals—but it's infinitely less interesting.

Many of the old smuggler-dealers have come to the same realization. They see themselves as the last great outlaws, a people for whom pirates are idols and criminal vitality is the only worthwhile kind. They see themselves as heroes, in other words, righteous flouters of a silly prohibition. And they sure hope you will agree. My father and members of his ring are no different, which is why almost all of them were willing to talk with me. A sign of how little things change is that all but my father asked me to disguise them. I was happy to do so. These friends and family have given me a true story if not an honorable one. It's a public saga complete with a real pirate's booty: more than a million dollars lost, buried, or stolen. It's also a private pursuit that's more important to me with each day.

See, I recently became a father myself. We had a boy and it didn't take long before I saw what I was up against. On my very first Father's Day, in fact, my infant son came home from day care with a preprinted poem, a trifle called "Footprints." Millions of dads probably got the same lines, giving them no more than a sidelong glance before dinner. But the poem set off tiny sticks of dynamite behind my eyes. It contains every immutable truth our society pushes—and I fear—about fathers and sons mimicking each other through the generations. It ends with the most painful idea of all, a repetition of the lines "walk a little slower, Daddy, for I must follow you." I think it's the "must" that really stabbed my heart.

I, for the record, am not an Anthony, either on my birth certificate or so far in life. But my father still haunts me, making me terrified of the genes I carry and the man I may become. There must be a way out of this loop, I decided, so one day I set about finding it in the arc of my father's rise and fall. This is a personal story but also a story of generational change, of talents wasted and talents redeemed. It's specific to my father's experience but also representative of what I believe many children of the 1970s and '80s feel as descendants of the Great Stoned Age, the greatest explosion of illicit drug use ever recorded. I've tried to write a broad chronicle of marijuana-smoking, drug-taking America rather than a closed circle of family woe. Everybody knew a drug dealer back then. This is the life of one of them and, in a pharmacologic sense, the story of us all.

I

Inhale

1

The Jump

Miami, Florida, 1984
Milford, Connecticut, 1970–1975

My father sat in a quiet corner of the bar, holding a gin and tonic in one hand and a lighter in the other. His eyes crossed as he brought the flame to his cigarette, puffed once, and went back to staring. He had been staring all night, looking out through the feathery darkness beyond the bar where dozens of young women bounced and twirled, rallying to and fro in daubed-on clothes.

He could see the dance floor in the middle distance, slightly elevated toward an already low ceiling. The sounds of Shannon and Culture Club bounded and rebounded. Then "Girls Just Want to Have Fun" came on and the effect of the first note on the crowd was like spray from a hose. A friend of my father's, a coke wholesaler with a pencil-thin mustache, threw him an apologetic look and jumped into the fray.

Anthony Edward Dokoupil was known for his on-the-job sanity. If he was working, he was happy and healthy, drug-free, focused, flowing, time bouncing off him. He had enough hair on his chest to float a gold chain, his belly was trim, and when he walked he swung his legs in loose semicircles, exuding a practiced magnetism, a put-on air of immortality. Even sitting down he pumped out so much animal energy that my mother used to say he had shark's blood: immune to disease, fearsomely alive, buoyant so long as he kept moving.

It was the close of the 1984 pot season, the harshest of my father's long career. It was October and he was back in Miami, tired and disappointed, his body quiet, all his energies turned inward. He was angry at himself for letting some incipient late-night needs throw off his judgment; embarrassed about a botched stash house and a car crash; worried about security cameras that must have caught him running through the lobby of a hotel with a box of money. All eighteen thousand pounds of weed had been sold, nothing lost, no one arrested. But he had broken the pirate code, the bylaws of his life, nowhere written down but known by all, and he had three months to sit still and stew about it.

My father was also expected home. He had a work-life conflict, a problem so mundane that it was hardly a problem at all, and might even be a blessing. But it dragged my father into a state of furious resentment. He loved us, would die for us, but go home to us? Sometimes it was asking too much.

So he sat in a private club in Coconut Grove and continued to drink, reaching the snapped lime in the bottom of another gin and tonic, not even looking up when a familiar smell drifted into his range. When a joint burns it gives up the ghost of every day it grew in the equatorial sun, every bright and gorgeous ray of sun, every grain of soil. The smoke bounces off the back of the throat and envelops the nervous system, washing through the smoker like a warm tide.

From the mid-Atlantic states to Maine and as far west as Colorado, people at that very moment could smoke my father's weed and feel their socks loosen and their scalp tighten and all the stress of the day wash clear. Usually my father loved to picture the end consumer. The best man with the full coat pocket. The college kid with the stash in his glove compartment. Even the high schooler, yes, the kid on drugs, the mop-top with the Kinks on the stereo, a towel stuffed under the door, and a can of Glade in his hand.

Six million joints but no freedom for the man who sold them?

My father didn't think that was fair.

He thought of his partner Bobby, a Brooklyn garbageman who retired into marijuana sales, out making Manhattan his playground. He thought of Charlie and Willy, his contacts in the Caribbean, near the bottom of a Heineken, their hearts like steel drums, feet stomping seashells at some dockside bar. Finally, he thought of the everyday gawkers outside on South Bayshore Drive. People in rental cars nosing out of the lot at Dinner Key. Teenagers in Mohawk haircuts, kid siblings in Mickey Mouse ears. Moms and dads in pleated shorts, striped shirts, and leather sandals. People with such lives looked south on Bayshore and through tired eyes they saw it, rising brightly above a series of thatched outdoor bars and a glowing cobalt swimming pool: the Mutiny Hotel at Sailboat Bay, the scene of my father's sulk.

The Mutiny was the start of the American drug world, and though it was a generally safe place it swam with suspicion and sex and incipient violence, a palpable energy that attracted a romantic class of criminal. The most famous were South American cocaine dealers. They were unsmiling businessmen who slid into the banquet tables against the wall and hid a gun in the dinner rolls. My father's kind were rarer: the gringos, the grass dealers, the smugglers who tied off catamarans or cruising yachts, hair tussled, Top-Siders squeaking across the bow. America used to produce men like these, pool-hall handsome, caddish, light-minded men, the source of America's fun if not her pride.

My father was proud to be one of them, gathered into what looked like a four-star restaurant merged with a disco and crossed with a Hong Kong sex lair. He wore white linen pants and what has to be one of the only short-sleeve V-neck sweaters in existence. The carpet beneath his slip-ons was blue and shaggy. By the door to the pool, on the path to another bar, a single vulnerable orchid performed in a pin spot of light. For aristocrats there was a harpist in a G-string, replaced at midnight by roving jugglers and mimes, and finally topless dancers. What did it feel like to walk into such a world, a young father with an envelope of coke in his pants, a bag of cash at his service? The pull of other worlds weakened and then vanished, a feeling like flying, like staring out the oval window of an airplane the instant it leaves the land where you were born.

By 1:00 a.m. my father had forgotten his woes, swallowed his conflicts, and slid off his barstool. He was celebrating his six million joints. He couldn't tell anyone that's what he was doing, but it was easy to see whose load had come in, because they were handing out drugs like cigars when a baby is born. The night became a cocktail of jungle paintings, conga lines, pelican-faced crooners, and women with shimmery, minnow-shaped earrings.

Along about 3:00 a.m. was my father's pumpkin hour, when he rented a room upstairs. He invited what girls he could and hired those he couldn't. He heard the ding of the elevator, the click-clack of high heels on buffed marble. His room was as high as possible and facing the ocean, so no one could look in, and he and his friends could be naked for days.

Out on the balcony he let his senses fill with the creak of lazily swaying traffic lights, the smell of night-blooming jasmine. He watched the usual mayday flares streak skyward and, if he is anything like me, he followed a thought in his mind, the one we all have when it's late and the view is of everything, the one that's been reverberating in my brain ever since: How the hell did I get here?

Fourteen years earlier, in the winter of 1970, my father was staring out on a very different body of water. He was sleeping in an uninsulated cabin on Long Island Sound, waking only to watch the waves crisscross to nowhere and back again. Outside his door the euphoria of the Summer of Love had worn off. In the course of the past two years there had been well over a hundred politically inspired bombings, not including arson and vandalism.

The authorities responded with a violent spree of their own. They donned riot gear and whirled nightsticks. Bullets tore through clothes, pierced soft flesh, and exited slick into a sunny day. The first student died at the University of California, Berkeley, in 1969. Four more perished at Kent State a year later.

It was all too much for my father, a man who pukes when he sees puke and is so queasy around illness and human frailty that he would sooner leave the room than sign your cast. He resigned from Students for a Democratic Society, quit a graduate program at the University of Detroit, and came east to the Connecticut coast for a new adventure.

At first he shacked up with a couple of hard-drinking acquaintances, a dirty-haired married couple. They spent their hours moving full bottles of Jack Daniel's out of one case and slipping empties into another. It was factory-like alcoholism, orderly oblivion. In my father's considered opinion, it was uninspired behavior.

He had been an English major and a philosophy minor, and he was acutely aware of his own image, found romance in his own dissolution. He wasn't alone in this strange endeavor. As the decade progressed, thousands of middle-class white kids—spared the bread lines and tank brigades of earlier generations—swore allegiance to their own stories, trying to shape their lives into some sort of gorgeous experience. My father did this more self-consciously than most.

He read Norman Mailer on the "enormous present" in black America. He adored Jack Kerouac's alter ego in *On the Road*, a man who strolls through the magically lilac-scented slums of Denver, "feeling that the best the white world had offered was not enough ecstasy for me, not enough life, joy, kicks, darkness, music, not enough night." He read Allen Ginsberg and felt like *Howl* was about him and him alone, dragging himself through Harlem streets at dawn looking for "an angry fix."

My father had picked up a smack habit a few years earlier, memorizing the lyrics of "Heroin" by Lou Reed and the Velvet Underground. He was a contemporary of the New York author Jim Carroll, who was also a devout user in the late 1960s, and who described it as "just such a pleasure to tie up above that mainline with a woman's silk stocking and hit the mark and watch the blood rise into the dropper like a certain desert lily I remember . . . so red . . . yeah, I shoot desert lilies in my arm." My father began to call it "getting pinned." As in a thousand angels on the head.

He moved into the beach cabin to soothe mind and body alike. He hoped to beat the habit, which he had tried and failed to do a few times before. Drugs are known for their destructive potential, but in the dance of starting and stopping and starting again my father found a never-ending dream of renewal, the future full of possibility, potential, the pleasure of becoming. As the basis for a life, he thought, it was as good as any.

His cabin was actually a beach bungalow on the grounds of a summer resort. He had been hired as the off-season security guard, an inspired choice by the management. My father relished the way winter attacked a basic clapboard abode on the Connecticut coast. When he got cold, he sat in his used mint-green Dodge Dart and added songs to the sound track of his life. When he tired of watching the waves, he walked to the Beachcomber, local watering hole of the counterculture.

The walls were decorated with dusty nets and plastic aquatic life. The bar was unvarnished and uncomfortable with wobbly stools and no brass footrest. But the crowd's personal style ran toward a blend of Johnny Appleseed and Elvis. One of the regulars wore a brown coat with dangling leather fringe. My father sipped rum and coke and swayed to the Doors, scoping out the scene. Every song he heard, every conversation, seemed calibrated to give him the impression that the sadder he was, the smarter he was—but wipe away the generational honey-glaze, and really he had reasons to feel depressed. He had no friends, no future, and a frigid, withdrawal-wracked present without end. He started looking at every woman who walked in as though she might save him. Almost unbelievably, one did.

My mother, Ann, grew up in one of the wealthier suburbs of New York City. She was born in 1950, the first of five siblings in a home of smooth surfaces and a neighborhood of the same. Her father, Louis, was an abstemious, hardworking man who played minor-league baseball for the Brooklyn Dodgers in 1943, and then joined the army and saw a bit of war. He was part of a tank brigade for a while, and his experiences yielded one or two concerned postcards, according to family lore, but the defining experience was a good job on the base driving the commander around and playing Saturday baseball games in Texas.

Back home he took over a small family grocery and liquor store, and ran the shop with the care of a founder, not an inheritor. He worked long hours and never drank from the stock or borrowed from the till. He was such a clean whistle that he even loathed his Italian heritage because it inspired so many whispered connections to the Mob. He refused Italian food, forbid his kids from speaking the language, and showed his love in the unspoken style of so many mid-century fathers. For one thing, he taught them how to drive out of a skid.

There were a few ribs in this otherwise smooth existence, however, and these ribs would make all the difference for my lonely father, waiting for help in a seaside bar. Louis was a teetotaler, but his wife, Claudia, drank. Nobody knew it at first. She bought her booze at least one town away and hid the bottles in the closet of her youngest daughter's bedroom, the only closet no one would check. Mary had been born with a normal functioning mind, but her hips were askew and the doctors decided to operate when she was still an infant. One operation. Two operations. Each operation required an anesthetic, and the anesthetic may have curbed oxygen flow to the brain. By the time my mother was a teenager, Mary was in a wheelchair and in need of twenty-four-hour care.

When Claudia stopped vacuuming the house regularly and failed, on occasion, to fetch her children from school and activities, my mother didn't suspect alcohol at first. Claudia was masking clear liquors with Sprite and brown liquors with ginger ale. But one day my mother found the empty bottles in Mary's room, and she addressed the issue in the only way that made sense to her. She didn't stage an intervention. She staged a play. She pretended things were normal. Then she staged an insurrection. She *made* things normal. By the time she graduated from high school in 1968, caring for others came as instinctually as driving out of a skid.

In June of that year, after the ten thousandth airplane had disappeared over Vietnam and the nightly news had been hijacked by poorly groomed college students, my responsible mother got responsibly high on marijuana—a peaceful drug, a loving drug. She lit her first joint in her own driveway, on her last night under her father's roof. She shared it with two friends, and with just a few puffs everyone's head was a helium balloon. My mother loved the sensation—loved it so much she didn't hear the front door open or her father's footsteps on the grass. She loved it so much she got herself caught.

When Louis appeared around the edge of the garage, the two friends ran and my mother dropped the roach. But the air smelled like someone had run over a skunk and Louis wasn't an idiot. Marijuana use was rising sharply, moving from something associated with jazz clubs and migrant workers to what could plausibly be called a "youth craze." When my mother entered high school fewer than 5 percent of young Americans reported pot use—but that number would double and redouble in the next two years and then redouble again by the end of the decade.

Louis probably read about this incipient drug culture in *Life* magazine, the periodical of mainstream photography and hymns to the American way. He probably planted an elbow and spread the pages next to his register. Just the summer before the magazine had run four consecutive gatefolds under the headline MARIJUANA: MILLIONS OF TURNED-ON USERS, complete with half a dozen shots of bowl-headed kids smoking grass.

This was no hit piece. The magazine sought to correct "old fears" about marijuana, and it chose to do so in its Fourth of July edition. That meant ten million fathers, tired from working the grill and looking for a quiet moment before the sparklers started, could sit down to read about pot, "a mild euphoric drug known and used throughout the world for centuries." It "is not physically addictive, nor need it lead to crime, immorality or stronger drugs."

Yes, the article continued, we're living through "the greatest mass flouting of law since Prohibition." But the kids are all right! It's the laws that we should be most concerned about; the pot laws are "extremely severe," and it is this very severity that aids the counterculture, letting the kids turn the whole pot scene into a protest against the values and institutions of middle-class America. This, and not a little psychoactive chlorophyll, is what had ushered kids into a shadow world.

The magazine even tracked down Harry Anslinger, of all people. As the federal narcotics commissioner during the 1930s, Anslinger did more than anyone to move marijuana into the greenhouse of Hades, minting the phrase "assassin of youth" and promoting long terms in prison for simple possession. That same Anslinger told *Life* that, actually, on second thought, "when it's a simple case of a kid using the stuff . . . it should be turned over to health and school authorities."

The Fourth of July is a long weekend in the sun with children, so the magazine conveniently repeated all this in a question-and-answer section.

Is marijuana habit forming?
No.
Are current penalties too severe?
Yes.
Does it lead to narcotic addiction?
Most marijuana users do not go on to become junkies.

You can guess what Louis thought about drugs. He saw them as an obstacle to real life, not a back door to the truly good stuff. And yet he was smarter than the average American parent in 1968. Instead of debating the issue, instead of citing the law and lecturing my mother, he took the lessons of *Life* to heart and responded by making a simple bet.

He picked up the roach as a prop and proceeded with lawyerly precision: "If this is just a plant, as you say, and as a plant it's basically harmless, then it will soon be legal, right?"

My mother agreed. It will soon be legal.

"I'll bet you marijuana won't be legal in my lifetime," Louis said. He was in his mid-forties. After so much clean living, he looked like he was in his mid-thirties. They put five dollars on it, my mother beaming as they shook.

In the fall she moved toward my father, enrolling in a teaching program for special education. For that whole first year of college, she was her father's daughter, a good girl who wore natural fibers and rimless round glasses. She smoked some more weed, lighting up on her porch with two girlfriends and watching the screen door shimmy. But she dated thespians, not thugs or dealers, not even rebels. Getting really wild meant a long road trip, some magic mushrooms, sleeping in her car. The closest she came to the '60s was backing over it one night in Provincetown. A hippie had passed out behind her car. The '60s survived.

Everything changed for her the summer between sophomore and junior year. She visited her father's store just after closing time, when the cicadas were screaming. She knocked, and her father appeared, looking unrested. He had called her that week, arranging the visit. He wanted to tell her a story—just as soon as he was sure the bolt was safely locked.

To be inside the store after hours reminded my mother of all the work she had put in here, all the hours of stocking and restocking, the mop-bucket water and laborious change-making from a register with metal keys that bruised her fingers on busy days. She was happy to be rid of it and wondered if her father had other ideas.

"A few weeks ago a man robbed the store," he began, and my mother nodded, still not sure where he was going with this. The news itself wasn't so surprising. That day comes for almost every corner grocer. Louis knew that; he was prepared for it financially. But he didn't know how it would affect him, having a gun pointed at his chest, his head.

"It made me reconsider the way I'm using the years I have left," he continued, and it was already practically the longest conversation of their life together. Louis explained, in so many words, that he didn't want to be the abstemious one anymore. And when he finally came out with the point of this story, the words no longer needed to be said but he said them anyway: "I'm leaving your mother."

In the months to follow he moved in with a young blond woman, bought a cloth-topped red CJ-5 Jeep, then filled the center console with golf balls and covered the backseat with clubs. Some years later, he moved to New Mexico, where every turn off the highway is a driving range.

The funny thing is, my mother was not angry, not after the initial shock. Life is indeed short, she thought, and she did not want to be the responsible one anymore, either.

That fall of 1970, the same fall my father moved into the uninsulated beach house, my mother moved in down the street, pooling money with friends. She and three roommates hung bead curtains, organized parties on a rotating basis, and started selling pot and hash to fund the good times. One of my mother's housemates could get suitcases of dope smuggled up from Arizona. Her brother-in-law actually carried the stuff over the border, and her sister, his wife, trucked it north by Greyhound bus.

One cold Friday night, flush from a deal and tired of their own house, the girls walked toward the unrestful waters of the sound, through the front door of the Beachcomber, and right into my father, who liked the stool by the door. He noticed Ann immediately, a brunette in a floor-length red overcoat. He thought she looked like a Russian doll, albeit with a mood ring. And he liked his chances: She had three cute friends.

My father said hello. He said hello to everyone, in fact, including my mother's three roommates. Then he smiled and waited to see who returned it, like a man yelling into a series of canyons and hoping for an echo. The year after she met my father at the Beachcomber, a career-placement test noted my mother's "superior" judgment, an abundance of "common sense, foresight, and the ability to reach sound decisions." Yet of the women there that night, she was the one who smiled back at my father.

She liked the strange blue of his eyes, and his Kant-quoting ways, and the fact that he had been an SDS organizer in the Midwest. She liked that as war raged in Southeast Asia and protesters died right here at home, what Anthony Edward Dokoupil wanted most of all was to own a tree farm and learn to whittle. In fact, he already had the right acorns picked out, a special crossbreed he thought might catch on as an old-fashioned breakfast food. She liked the way he had "discovered" the earth, our fragile, interconnected home, and railed against "the plastic nightmare" of modern America.

It helped that he was good-looking, too, with a wide, eager face like a Labrador. In the months to come, she'd realize he also had a Lab's tendency to run off and return sparkly eyed and dirty, radiating love-me-anyway charm. But for now that quality was just background energy, a faint hum of electricity, which she found impossible to resist. She was a special-education teacher in training, after all, a person drawn to those whose best quality is a single magnificent sunflower set on the windowsill of a burning house.

Sometime after midnight, they left together, walking into the cold.

At her place, beneath an electric blanket, in a bed pushed against the radiator, they kept each other warm and talked about their strangely amazing lives. They made love and made love again and by dawn she felt needed while he felt cared for. On such a basis they stayed together for the next fifteen years, straight through the era ahead, an era remembered as the dawn of the Great Stoned Age.

Marijuana wasn't even illegal when Richard Nixon took office in January 1969. The problem of the "marijuana menace" in the 1930s, when pot was said to drive its users to violence and gymnastic orgies, resulted not in a prohibition but in a complicated middle position: a marijuana tax. Passed in 1937, it established federal control over its use by requiring people to pay a tax of $100 an ounce. Hardly anyone could afford that, so they would be busted for tax evasion.

President Nixon felt the drug was an attack on American values, however, and he was right. To smoke marijuana (no one yet called it cannabis) was to realize that the government had lied about the dangers of the demon narcotic and to wonder what else they were lying about today. "A new man was born smoking pot," Jerry Rubin wrote in his memoir of the '60s, "a longhaired, beaded, hairy, crazy motherfucker whose life is theater, every moment creating the new society as he destroys the old."

The battle between pot's motherfuckers and the White House began in September 1969, with the largest search-and-seizure operation ever undertaken by civil authorities, an effort to stop the flow of marijuana from Mexico. Federal agents subjected every northbound car, truck, trolley, or bicycle to a three-minute search and the line snarled for miles. Later they militarized the American side of the border, burying sensors in the desert to detect foot traffic, floating radar balloons to watch the skies, and putting drug-interdiction teams on twenty-four-hour alert from Brownsville, Texas, to San Diego, California.

Congress finally banned marijuana outright in 1970 when it passed the Controlled Substances Act, which gave the U.S. attorney general—

not health officials—the responsibility to classify drugs by their danger and potential for misuse. We all know how that ended. Marijuana was classified as "schedule I": a narcotic with no medical value and a high potential for abuse, just like heroin. This was significant because heroin use was an out-of-sight small problem (if you were not my mother), but marijuana use was big enough to justify an all-out offensive. It allowed President Nixon to treat innumerable middle-class concerns—among them race riots, braless women, dirty-haired kids, drum circles, and the extra-large foam middle finger extended from young America to old—as one single addressable issue: drug abuse. He called it "the modern curse of youth."

This wasn't even the War on Drugs yet. Nixon didn't unwrap that phrase until June 1971, by which point drugs and dealers were the cause of a stupendous panic that swept Congress, the Supreme Court, and a media happy to provide the words and pictures. The Senate Judiciary Committee investigated "the Marihuana-hashish epidemic and its impact on United States security." Supreme Court Justice Hugo Black argued that "traffic in deadly mind, soul, and body destroying drugs is beyond a doubt one of the greatest evils of our time." President Nixon himself set an emotional tone, calling drug dealers "literally the slave traders of our time" and framing the fight in terms of "our children's lives."

What could explain such a reaction? It was more than politics or culture, more than a fight over pleasure and probity. The War on Drugs was primarily a war on marijuana, which seemed to awaken an absolutely primal fear inside the establishment, turning one generation against the next in a fight over what was once unabashedly called "consciousness." The politicians never used the word, of course, but it played on the lips of marijuana users and their smiling wise-man suppliers, both of whom thought they had discovered the same fire that lit the universe.

They swung every joint like a torch in the dark, smoking to expand the borders of thought, to rise into the realm of the senses. By contrast the drug warriors fought to anchor consciousness to the here and now. They fought to defend the symbol world of old flags and new money.

And for millions of young Americans, my father and mother among them, the difference between these two perspectives was everything. It was the difference between life and death.

My father was drafted into the marijuana movement the same winter he met my mother, in the very same bar. He met a guy named Arthur, a former navy man who gave good eye contact and wouldn't buy you a drink without weighty cause. My father and Arthur hit it off immediately, and Arthur invited Tony to form T&A Roofing. It was an odd endeavor for two guys whose approach to construction involved showing up late and asking each other, "How's your hammer hanging?" My father ruined the roofs he didn't fall off of first. Arthur didn't seem to care. Weeks would go by between jobs. Arthur wouldn't work in light rain or medium cold. At night he would host poker games and lose big without flinching. He paid the tuition for his live-in girlfriend, bought a new Buick. He lived in a two-bedroom house with an attached garage. It didn't add up.

One afternoon Tony and Arthur were smoking a joint in Arthur's kitchen when the doorbell rang. It was a man from the phone company, there to shut off the phone. He was very sorry, he said, but the bill hadn't been paid in months and it was almost $100. Arthur's face was a mask of solemnity and respect. He said he understood completely. Then he went into his bedroom and came out with a hundred-dollar bill. The man from the phone company didn't whistle, but a hundred-dollar bill was rare enough in those parts that he could have whistled without ridicule. My father looked on, quietly astonished.

Spring gave way to summer, and Tony was over at Arthur's again, for another beer and another joint at the end of another long day of no work. Only this time when he walked in, he smelled something sharp and ripe on the edge of the house's usual odor. When he turned around, he saw that there was a little project on the living-room floor, a miniature Mayan ruin made entirely out of foot-long bricks wrapped in blue-gray crepe paper. A temple of marijuana.

Arthur smiled and sat cross-legged on the floor, which isn't easy in blue jeans too tight to mount a horse. He opened a package and plucked a few nuggets of *mota*, brownish-gold and free of sticks and seeds. They looked rare and exotic, precious enough to be pinned and labeled and viewed through a layer of museum glass. Arthur massaged a few grams into the folded hull of a piece of rolling paper, gave the outer edge an adhesive lick, and lit the joint for my father.

Dad recognized the taste. It was the same stuff he had been passed at parties, where a few hits made him feel like Mother Nature had just blown on his earlobe. He felt his skin tingle and the top of his head fly away. During the next few hours, my father's dope IQ skyrocketed. He learned the difference between shit and good shit; he learned about too much lumber (seeds, stems), bad nose (none of that good aroma), and dustiness (dried out, desiccated).

Arthur explained that this was a Mexican sativa, a good plant that grows tall and bushy in the hidden ravines of the country, where the dope waves green in the sunlight. The farmer harvests it and hands it off to the smugglers, he continued, ever so romantically, and the smugglers are mostly gringos for hire. They keep to trails where Comanche warriors once roamed and American train robbers took refuge, the *federales* one step behind.

Arthur showed my father how to process the load. He examined the quality of each brick, considering its smell, its feel, and the overall look, and that gave him a dollar value. Then he weighed the brick on a professional-grade scale, multiplied the two numbers, and tagged it with a strip of masking tape and a number in black marker. He threw the finished bricks into a nylon laundry bag.

And that was that.

In the space of an afternoon, my father, a man who would go on to sell tens of millions of joints, learned how to sell his first, and millions of lives were changed in the process. Maybe they changed only by a degree or two, but all the smoke that followed from that first fire put millions into an italicized state of mind, where they found a friend, discovered politics, made love. Certainly some people got busted but most just got high, joining the hundred million Americans who have done the same during the last forty years.

Recently, after a Gallup poll showed for the first time that most of the country supported legalizing marijuana, I got a note from Keith Stroup, the founder of the National Organization for the Reform of Marijuana Laws (NORML) and the grand old man of the movement. "Please tell your father," he began, "that I honor and respect those like him who risked their freedom to get good marijuana into the country before we had such a good domestic industry. I realized at some point in this struggle that if we had no marijuana to smoke, there would be no marijuana culture, and thus no legalization movement. So I am an honest fan."

When the processing work was done, Arthur asked my father if he could "move some weight." Getting weight, hiding weight, moving weight—that was the whole business, my father would soon learn. But he had no idea if he could move some weight, or how he'd even begin to find out if he could move some weight. So he looked at Arthur and put on a serious face and, not for the last time, he lied.

"Sure," he said. "I know some guys."

He said "sure" because he was seeking peril, adversity, a renunciation of normalcy; he was crazy for difficulty, for experience, for the kind of life he could only find if he lived in outermost beach houses in winter and shot heroin on condemned rooftops and dealt the drug his president hated to the friends who loved him for it. If he were completely honest with himself, he was also pursuing the feeling of being pursued. He desired a dream that journeyed toward nightmare, toward the ecstasy of demolition and the joy of doing wrong.

The best explanation I've found to describe my father's tendencies isn't even from a criminal or a junkie or a junkie criminal. It's from the Italian mountain climber Giusto Gervasutti. His notebooks were found in 1947 after he fell to his death in the French Alps. He was trying to explain why climbers risk their lives for simple altitude, but his words stand as the best explanation of the itch for extreme living of all kinds.

The itch "may take the form of a need to live heroically, or to rebel against restraint and limitation: an escape from the restricting circle of daily life, a protest against being submerged in universal drabness, an affirmation of the freedom of the spirit in dangerous and splendid adventure." It may take the form of "the search for an intense aesthetic experience, for exquisite sensations, or for man's never satisfied desire for unknown country to explore, new paths to make. Best of all, it should be all these things together."

Dealing gave my father all these things together.

Arthur fronted him five bricks, slang for kilos, a total of about twelve pounds of Mexican marijuana, for $1,250. My father drove it down to New Jersey, where he had spent much of his childhood. Happily, he found that his high-school friends had also quit heroin, gotten wise to politics, and were taking a turn as weed dealers almost as a democratic exercise. My father sold them ten pounds for $125 a pound, making about $120 in profit. That left half a brick—and he had plans for it.

He borrowed an ice-cream truck from a friend who worked for Good Humor and parked it in front of his parents' house with the jingle jangling. Kids ran up to him, and he had to shoo them away. He saw something out of the corner of his eye—the edge of a curtain lifting, a break in the blinds—but when he turned no one was there.

It was June 1971 and the brick was for his little sister, Carolyn, eighteen, who had just graduated high school. She was planning a cross-country trip with her boyfriend, and after a year of LSD in Greenwich Village she was strangely immune to the sound of an ice-cream truck on her street. My father laid on the horn a few times, just to call a bit more attention to himself. He wanted to show off a little, let the neighborhood know Anthony Dokoupil was the guy you needed if you wanted some weed.

Finally Carolyn came out of the house, squinting at the psychopath in the paper cap. As she approached she recognized the smile, wide as the teller window, white as the side of the truck. Carolyn hated my father, actually. He used to steal from her piggy bank, and when there was trouble at home, he'd skedaddle and leave her behind. But in that moment, none of it mattered.

The very process of securing a single joint in 1971 was a profound countercultural orgasm, a high before the high. The smoker had to know someone who knew someone who could score him a baggie, which he or she then hid from God, Country, and Family, and fired up only in private. People bought as much as they could afford, put it in a shoe box, and then watched the shoe box start to drain, hoping for the chance to score some more. It was exhilarating, that kind of sneaking around, and both my father and his sister felt the charge. They talked like coconspirators and then he gave her a coconut vanilla ice-cream bar, followed by a freezer-cold brick of weed, and as he passed her the package he could feel the power of the act. It glowed somewhere in his solar plexus, better than heroin, better than sex.

That summer Carolyn drove to San Francisco, selling those peace buds to pay her way.

From those first kilos of pot, my father would build his sales machine, selling enough smoke to hold Woodstock every day for a year. The journey accelerated quietly, taking shape while my mother was at class and my father sat on the porch of the beach house, dead sober beneath a wind chime. They had been together for more than a year, and he wanted to take care of her, the feeling uncoiling in some deep part of his brain and surprising even him.

He put on some records. The usual collection of drowsy, sorrowful road and drug songs that helped explain a generation to themselves. As a whole they shed advantages like neckties at a luau, and the music—from the chipper Beatles to the shrill sounds of Jefferson Airplane—made that act into myth. My father felt heady as Cat Stevens serenaded him, and he rooted through the board-game cabinet, looking for a pen and a scratch pad.

He made some calculations. Arthur sold him a kilo of Mexican dope for $250 or so. He could break it up into ounces and easily triple his money. But selling small meant dealing with a lot of potheads, which besides being a lot of work was a lot of exposure and not very glamorous. Wholesaling was safer, sexier. But street-level dealers needed another middleman like they needed another car on the road during rush hour.

The mark-up on marijuana was already crazy. My father could squeeze only dollars out of every deal, even before shelling out for gas, scales, baggies, pads, pen, tape, and the shrinkage and loss that comes in any business. To make this work, he needed either more customers or a much bigger margin. The only way to get both was to make a jump up the chain.

He wrote down JUMP. Circled it. Underlined it. He took a little walk around the room and returned to his pad, raised his pen as if to write, and came up with nothing. He needed to JUMP, but he had no idea how to actually do it.

To make matters worse, Arthur quit the roofing business to focus on dealing full time, so my father had to find other work. He started painting houses, complaining about the "poisonous" fumes. Then he reluctantly took full-time work in a concrete-step factory. He wore a plastic cap, poured water into concrete mix, and concrete into molds. The only good news he had was legal. Because of his on-again, off-again needle use, his draft status had been officially changed to 4-F, or "unfit for military service." A truer ruling has never been issued.

The man my father needed to meet was Eddie, a sinewy, sunken-cheeked, chain-smoking, thousand-yard starer of the dope-dealing variety. He ran a concert business, one that brought the biggest folk and rock stars of the era to the grand old Palace Theater in nearby Waterbury, Connecticut. Connecticut itself is a small town, so my father knew Eddie by reputation. He knew Eddie had a petite raven-haired girlfriend with an Ivy League education, and a nice house on a bluff overlooking a tidal stream. Dad had been present at parties when Eddie walked in—unmissable with his bald pate and rim of cascading black hair—and threw down some exotic strains of dope and an opium poppy. He'd then pierce the plump green seed, letting it ooze sticky brown serum. People sucked it, and then sat down and shivered like newborn mice.

My father had never actually met the guy, however, until one fine day in the spring of 1972 when he walked through Arthur's back door.

"Tony, Eddie. Eddie, Tony."

My father was still officially part of Arthur's distribution chain, so Eddie didn't flinch as he waited for Arthur to count out some money he owed. Remarkably, my father didn't flinch either. He started talking. He was a bullshitter before he was anything at all, a man who could twist words and bend situations. He read books like *Body Language* and *The Art of Reading People* and a slew of self-empowerment books, and he believed that he could talk his way into any heart, any mind. With the right combination of words, at the right time, he could cast a spell. It wasn't sorcery. It was just listening to people, to what they need to hear, and knowing how, when the pins tumbled into place, to pop the lock and push open the door, as he pushed it then.

He talked expansively about his market in New Jersey, and how he could grow it if he could get a better price. Eddie stitched an eyebrow at Arthur, who shrugged back to Eddie, and just like that a play was materializing. Who to work with: It's the most important decision a drug dealer makes, because your partners will either make you rich or put you in jail. There's not much in between. Eddie decided to work with my father. He offered him a much better buy-in price—$200 a kilo—and a bigger supply, a first order of fifteen kilos.

By convention in the dope world, wholesalers deliver product "on the arm," meaning the supplier fronts the goods at a radically reduced cost and the dealer pays the balance as he sells it. How much to front is another big decision in the business, akin to banks extending a line of credit. Eddie decided not to front my father the dope. He wanted 50 percent down, or $1,500, not an insignificant sum when the average wage earner was making only $7,500 annually. It was more than my father could handle.

"No problem," my father said. "I'll call you in a couple of days."

When my father entered the beach house, my mother was in the living room studying for finals, her last college exams before starting as a special-education teacher the following fall. She wore bell-bottoms and a knit top, and she looked up through the light pink lenses of oversize sunglasses, which she had taken to wearing day and night, indoors and out.

Loudly, my father let the outside screen door swing shut and kicked the front door tight with his heel. He began to pound around the room. With every footfall the plates in the kitchen bounced until he stopped suddenly and faced my mother. "I have the most amazing chance," he told her, and he unfolded the entire story of Arthur and Eddie and the market he thought he had in New Jersey.

My mother listened. She had a model for life as a drug dealer's girl. Her old roommate Connie was married to a man named Dale, a wiry guy of the sort who liked putting his face close to the fan blades. For their honeymoon Connie and Dale flew to Colombia, where Dale went off alone for a few days, scoring a kilo of cocaine, which his new wife smuggled home to their starter house on Long Island, where sixteen-foot pot plants reached for the sun.

So as my father spoke, my mother's smile widened and she started to nod her head, curls bobbing. She believed in weed and she believed in him, and she felt there was no question—none at all—that this was a great opportunity, certainly better than him working at that concrete-step factory, which she believed was the reason he had been flashing his temper recently. She even helped my father get the money he needed, calling her father, telling him that she and Tony wanted $2,000 to get their own place, to start to grow up. He sent the money the same day.

All Tony needed then were customers. He called an old junkie friend, Buddy Bone, who said he could sell ten bricks a month near the University of Hartford. Buddy introduced my father to Black Earl, aka Earl the Pearl, who bought a few bricks for the pot-hungry kids at Yale. Tony's New Jersey connections gobbled up another five or so bricks at his new low price of $120 a pound. In every case he ferried the dope in brown paper shopping bags: a bag of weed, a bag of love.

His customers became his friends, and his deals became a source of pride. It was a small-time trade, but it was his: his investment, his networking, his profits. For the first time in his life, my father made more money than he could fit in a wallet: $1,500 that month, $1,500 the next. In three months he'd made more than my mother made her whole first year teaching. Within six months he had quit his job at the factory. It was the last legit gig he would have for almost twenty years.

To understand how it could all go down so easily, you have to understand more about the kid-level response to Richard Nixon. The dawn of the War on Drugs, the moment when Nixon turned the federal arsenal against smugglers and dealers, was also the dawn of the century's greatest push for the acceptance of marijuana: the emergence of two Americas in mystified conflict with each other, a conflict that continues to this day.

In 1972 Nixon's own National Commission on Marihuana and Drug Abuse issued the results of a two-year study of the marijuana problem. Its conclusion: There is no problem. Pot should be "decriminalized," a move which would make its use legal or nearly legal in the land of amber waves of grain. More than thirty states did in fact reduce their penalties for pot possession. San Francisco became the first big city to outright decriminalize. The *National Review*, *The New York Times* editorial board, and the American Bar Association endorsed an end to all federal laws that considered marijuana use a crime.

Nixon was livid. He defended his ban on marijuana, saying that legalization "would simply encourage more and more of our young people down the long, dismal road that leads to hard drugs and eventually self-destruction." He redoubled the war on marijuana, aiming to pinch shut the borders and create a shortage, one that would push up prices and turn pot into an untouchable expense for the average user.

The effort worked all too well. Prices soon rose—but the result wasn't fewer smokers, it was more smugglers. Tens of thousands of young, white, college-bound or college-educated men "from higher social levels," as Interpol put it in a 1970 report to the international police community, started smuggling and dealing in quantity. Some nights every one of Nixon's sensors in the desert went off simultaneously. Radar picked up hundreds of planes—Cessnas and Beechnuts, behemoth DC-3s, Constellation airships—all of them delivering dope like U.S. aid packages.

Meanwhile, at Nixon's new border checkpoints smugglers got creative. Some went wide of the official crossing points, winding through canyons on foot, trudging across the muddy Rio Grande, or bringing the dope in on donkeys. Others hid it in shipments of vegetables, or furniture cushions, or in the paneling of a car, or the underside of a Winnebago, or beneath trunk loads of hockey sticks, soccer balls, manure. They used apples and oranges and cayenne pepper to hide the scent and beat the dogs. During droughts, it was common to smuggle plastic-wrapped dope inside water trucks, because not even the cops will want to be seen pouring water out on a hot day. Snake containers were another option; no one cares what's under a cobra's cage.

Demand was also rising, as it would throughout the 1970s: ten million smokers nationwide; fifteen million; twenty million; twenty-five million. Dope rings sprang up in every big border city: Tucson alone had eighteen, according to the authorities; San Diego had twenty. In New Mexico, a hundred pilots were said to be known drug runners. The coverage of these high jinks drew even more people to the industry. FLYING DRUG RUNNERS REAP BIG PROFITS, read one headline in *The New York Times*, sounding more like a special advertising section than traditional journalism. "You can make a lot of money," related the head of customs, as if to say: "Act now before supplies run out."

Before long a double standard developed. As was the case during Prohibition, when drinkers were overlooked while bootleggers were pursued with bullet-sweeping zeal, marijuana smokers were relatively safe while their suppliers were hunted like the last hogs on a desert island. The crucial difference between the two periods was in how marijuana smokers came to view their suppliers as extensions of their own compassionate community. In a twist on the Eugene Debs maxim "While there is a soul in prison, I am not free," the marijuana brotherhood believed that while there are suppliers in jail, no smoker is free.

From this line of thinking, smuggling and dealing gained a new and still more powerful attraction: not just money but fame, not just status but legend. The notion of dealers and smugglers as righteous heroes grew directly from the laws that supported use but banned sales. This all fits in neatly with the history of American crime. Briefly, it's the story of two kinds of lawbreakers: criminals, bad men who do bad things; and outlaws, "good" bad men who do "good" bad things.

The distinction developed slowly over time and across cultures, but by the twentieth century certain illegal exploits clearly took on a chivalric glow, the honeyed tones of epic. The outlaw became the darling of newspaper men who made him the darling of the American people, and in this way, the outlaw became a recognizable hero, updated for each generation.

For the Woodstock generation the update was the gentleman dealer and his accomplice, the gentleman smuggler. They challenged unjust laws and fueled the Great Stoned Age, supplying the sensual side of the antiwar movement, a symbol for all who wanted to flip off the hypocritical elite and dance around in the tall grass. They didn't invent the guitar, or the campfire, or sex in the mud. But they made those things better—and in doing so they made themselves divine.

In 1974 my mother was twenty-four and my father was twenty-eight. She was a teacher and he was officially unemployed. But with a household income of $16,000 they were earning as much as the average Manhattan professional in his fifties. They moved out of the beach house and into an old stone homestead attached to a three-hundred-year-old farm. The backyard was an estuary that ran for a quarter mile in both directions, ending where a new line of plummy beach houses began. To help them explore it, they bought a black Lab puppy, purebred, and they walked him daily, talking about their future together.

Around the same time my father secured his first cover profession, perhaps the coolest job in America besides marijuana dealer: ticket seller. I don't mean that he was the guy in the booth, flipping through alphabetized envelopes at show time. In a pre-digital world, you needed an advance man, someone to deliver paper tickets to all the places you could buy concert tickets in those days. That meant record stores, but also restaurants, bars, clothing stores. He left home each week with a satchel of tickets and returned with a satchel of cash.

Along the way he made marijuana drops, and at night the same weed would cloud the Palace Theater, as much a part of the show as the houselights and speakers.

The performers were singer-songwriter types, balladeers and acoustic acts, ideal to take in while high—ideal for a nation who, like my father, was looking for an emotional comedown, descending from the rage of the Rolling Stones' "Street Fighting Man" to the more subdued language of the Beatles' "Let It Be." There was no darting around the stage, no knee sliding, no windmill guitar playing. The acts simply appeared when the stage lights flicked on and spent the next few hours making soulful, toe-tapping noise. Along with my father's weed, the effect was like instant yoga, an evening in an ashram. Afterward the performers slumped backstage like beaten prisoners and smoked joint after joint of their own.

The Steve Miller Band, Steppenwolf, Blue Oyster Cult, Mothers of Invention, Lynyrd Skynyrd, the Eagles, Queen, Alabama, Hall and Oates, Dave Mason, Steely Dan, ZZ Top, Lou Reed. Eddie booked them all, and my father actually went to the concerts, freely moving between the floor and backstage, feeling like the ghost writer responsible for everyone's story, a thousand and one good times. My mother loved it as much as he did. She sat backstage with the acts, the green-room lit only by a candle stuffed in a wine bottle, my father off doing who knows what with God knows who, and she contemplating the same.

They both were "working on themselves" as devotees of the human potential movement, leach field for all that lost political energy. They bought tarot cards, paged through the *Tao Te Ching*, and actually read the *Whole Earth Catalog*. If the New Age ever came, they believed it would arrive one person at a time, starting with themselves.

My father used "the power of the ticket" and "the power of the plant," as he called them, not to mention the power of cocaine, a hot new drug universally adored and yet to be feared. In 1974, Dr. Peter G. Bourne, a drug expert who would later become Jimmy Carter's chief drug policy adviser, blessed cocaine as "probably the most benign of illicit drugs," a substance "not physically addicting, and acutely pleasurable." It gave my father a high that felt like a mother's love, a high that left him feeling warm and secure and utterly coddled.

But before long it was resulting in very little sleep, followed by terribly brittle recovery periods and another night out, where a new depth of craziness and paranoia would be reached and more drugs would be taken. One night, after snorting coke with the guys from the band Alabama, my father headed home with bloodhound eyes and skeletal cheeks. On the way he was cut off by a guy in a Corvette with a vanity license plate.

My father flipped the guy the bird and howled at him out the window. The Corvette let my father pass him again and then started to tail him, which only further infuriated my father. He flipped him off again and tapped the brakes and all but dared the man to pull up beside him. Then my father took a left where no left existed, and a wooden telephone pole stopped his car, and the windshield stopped his head. He opened the door and spilled out onto a quiet, rural street and the Corvette stopped behind him, popping and tinging in the night. All my father saw was a boot hit the pavement as the driver approached. If the stranger thought about helping it was only for a second, because by the time he reached my father the man's hand was already cocked, and he punched, kicked, and tore my dad for perhaps ten seconds. Then, as though on rewind, he walked backward, got into his car, and pulled away.

At the hospital later, my father was still raging. Eddie had to shush him, and comfort Ann who was blubbering. The wounds weren't life threatening: a dented head, a concussion, broken ribs. But the incident and all that it revealed—the loss of control, the crying girl, the risk to the business—hung in my father's memory like a rotting corpse. He could lose everything, he realized, it could all disappear.

My father returned to work with new discipline and his network only grew. Soon Buddy Bone and Earl the Pearl wanted almost twenty-five kilos a month for the New Haven area. The New Jersey market tripled.

Drugs made you friends, and my father was using that simple fact of the '70s to make new friends out of complete strangers. The best new friends were two guys in Dutchess County who could move twenty kilos a month.

Add it all up, subtract by the two or three slow months when the dope is being harvested in Mexico, and my father sold about a half ton of weed in 1975, earning $40,000 in the process. That was just a smidgen below the average salary of a major-league baseball player. Dope was "the only business in the world where a young adventurer can start out one day with a few thousand dollars and end up a couple of years later a millionaire," wrote *New York* magazine, in a cover story that August. My father was running hard in that direction.

My mother used the extra money to help educate the unwitting youth of the state. She bought bunting and corkboard for her classroom. She organized bigger holiday parties, deeper snack tables, fuller chip bowls. She liked the feeling of working without really needing to work. She liked having that hidden power. At the end of her first school year, an unsmiling boss came to see her about a report she had written.

"See this?" he said, pointing to the offensive document. "You've got a comma out of place here."

He wanted her to change it—to retype the whole damn thing. Summer bloomed out the window. This was the last week of the semester. She had new money, and love, and she wanted out. But her administrator droned on.

"Our standards are our kids' standards . . . If we don't do it, they won't do it . . . We simply have to do better."

"I agree," my mother said, cutting him off. The room filled with a silence like what rushes in when a lawn mower goes quiet.

"I think that comma is where it needs to be," she said.

"Fix it," he replied in a hard voice.

"It doesn't need to be fixed."

"Fix it," he said again, "or you're not getting your check."

My mother had graduated from New Haven, as they say, but it wasn't Yale: She merely acted like it was. She spun on the heel of a sensible shoe and made for the door. She heard him say that leaving was a fireable offense but he was willing to give her one last chance.

"Fix the comma," he called. "Fix it or you're fired."

"You fix it," she said.

My father held off on any big gestures until he hit a particular personal milestone. By late summer, he was almost at his goal: selling a ton of weed. Put another way, he was now a Class I violator of federal law, a fact he relished like the Eagle Scout ranking he never quite reached. When he dropped the last hundred pounds at Buddy's, he tore his shirt off and put it in a plastic bag, like it was going into the trophy case at the front of his old high school. He gave it to my mother, who was not even close to being my mother yet, and told her to save it for "our son." The truly crazy part is, she did. When I went away to college, she gave me a bandanna-tight Rolling Stones "Tour of the Americas 75" shirt, baby blue. Under the Stones logo is an image of a bald eagle.

My father's celebration continued into September. He bought a new canoe, new hiking shoes, new fishing rod, new backpack and tent. He also bought a very fine wooden-handled folding blade. A whittler's knife. Then he drove and hiked and drove again through rural Maine to Quebec and back. Some way through, in the lake-dotted forests near the roof of America, less than ten miles from the Canadian border, he saw a sign on a hundred-acre wood. He bought it.

That extended his Walden-like journey. He doubled back to visit one of his new customers, a Connecticut boy who'd moved to a cabin near the Sugarloaf ski resort. Together they got high and used words like *communion* and *breathe*. For the next few days, he set off into the woods. On the first night four white-tailed deer visited his tent, and my father took out a notebook, a rainproof, acid-free, thick-stock journal. He recorded the deer, "beautifully content and well fed in the rain." The next day he killed a sucker fish to protect the larvae of the lake and apologized to a bass who swallowed his hook. At nightfall, he collected driftwood and whittled it, poorly, but without drawing blood, which has to be considered a success. And on his last morning, he paddled his canoe out to the middle of a lake clean enough to drink from and clear enough to catch fish by hand. He considered grabbing dinner from a shaft of sunlight. Then he saw it. A bald eagle, careening through the cold, crisp air.

"I am free now," he thought.

2

Dealer McDope and the Golden Age of Marijuana

South Florida and New England, 1976–1978

Anthony Edward Dokoupil—veteran needle user, graduate-school dropout, drifter-laborer of the driving-nails and pouring-concrete variety, a sometime painter and onetime security guard—was, by his thirtieth birthday, making more money than 98 percent of American men. It was 1976 and the golden hour of the golden age of marijuana love was approaching.

After Watergate and Tricky Dick's resignation and the fall of Saigon, marijuana was more than a protest drug; it was a victory drug. Bongs lined mantels like championship trophies. By decade's end all but two states (Arizona and Texas) would go on to reduce the holding of small amounts of marijuana from a felony offense to a misdemeanor, and in eleven states—containing more than thirty million people—pot use would be outright "decriminalized": reduced to a finable transgression, no more unseemly, legally speaking, than speeding or crossing the street against the light.

The speed of this shift was breathtaking to behold even at the time. In 1970 President Nixon closed America against the "enemy force" of pot smugglers, who along with other drug dealers were "public enemy number one." Six years later, half of all Americans between the ages of eighteen and twenty-five had tried the product my father was selling. A third of all high-school kids had done the same. And the country swelled with more pot smokers than there had been Truman voters a generation earlier. Inhale in America in 1976, and someone was liable to yell, "Hey! Smoke this! It's better!"

On their land in Maine, my parents spent the summer of marijuana's rise in a state of peaceful repose. They were acting out the lessons of the *Whole Earth Catalog*, eating vegetarian hot dogs off a tree-stump dinner table and ruminating on the fragility of the known world. Every day they hiked and camped. When it was dusk, and the fireflies glowed, they collapsed in the uncut grass of a vast waving field.

In the mornings, when it was too chilly for sex, too bright for wine, they drove to town for coffee and doughnuts. They picked up the newspaper, awash in retrograde bicentennial patriotism, and discovered that both presidential candidates had come out in favor of more progressive laws on marijuana. Jimmy Carter, whose three sons had tried marijuana, endorsed decriminalization, and Gerald Ford at least agreed that smokers shouldn't be going to jail.

"Did you see this?" took on a note of ritual as my father smashed pastries into the slot beneath his mustache and my mother read out the news from Portland and beyond.

Sometime that summer my father realized what in retrospect was an odd fact: He feared congressmen more than cops. The latter could lock you up for a while. The former could put you out of business forever with the pull of a lever: a vote for legalization. He imagined the Marlboro company flipping a switch to produce Marlboro Greens, the first mass-market marijuana cigarette, and it occurred to him that there weren't many people making money off moonshine these days.

When the fall came, my mother went back to teaching at her old school—the drama of comma-gate having subsided—and my father went back to dealing. He was desperate to expand his business, so he hired a couple of new dealers as well as an apprentice who he came to love like an heir. It was my mother's younger brother, Dougie, a community-college kid with a patchy beard and the lingering soft edges of youth. Dougie liked New Riders of the Purple Sage, a country-rock group with a hit called "Panama Red" and an album featuring a sketch of a mustachioed gringo of the same name, obviously a marijuana maven, who Dougie thought looked a hell of a lot like his sister's boyfriend.

It was more than the sunken cheeks and the furry curled finger of a mustache that made Dougie decide to wholesale for my father. It was the clowning physicality of the weed business. It was the hugs. My father was always embracing his crew, theatrically kissing their cheeks and pumping their hands, giving the room his biggest goomba-goomba smile as he joked that so-and-so was a narc or a woman or a fag. It was pretty crude stuff, to be sure, but by the old codes of masculinity the change was profound. My father told Dougie he loved him, which to a boy raised by a taciturn, standoffish World War II vet felt uncommonly warm.

My father looked at Dougie and saw all the makings of a huge earner, which is why he bought the kid an old car to help him get started with deliveries. It was a sign of Dougie's talent that he soon had his own ride. He partnered with a rich kid from school, the heir to a small fortune who owned a fresh red BMW. Together they plumbed the pot markets of half a dozen major universities. They drove bags of dope down from Boston to New York to D.C., and returned with bags of cash.

Everything worked smoothly until one night that fall, when the boys felt their car shudder and stall on its way across the George Washington Bridge, which enters Manhattan at 178th Street, then one of the worst areas in the city. They coasted the rest of the bridge and then restarted the vehicle on the shoulder only to cough and sputter to a halt again, this time at the bottom of an off-ramp in a rancid, broken-down stretch of dead row houses. They were out of gas.

A kid emerged and then another and another. The kids, Dominican kids, started hollering, asking if they could be of service and the question reeked of violence and sent shivers up Dougie's spine.

Today it would be obvious that dope is the one true Esperanto, but it wasn't at all obvious to Dougie. He opened the trunk, pulled the last of his weed out, and offered it to the boys, the largest of which he half expected to backhand the package to the ground before pounding Dougie's pasty white form into the pavement. Instead the boy started to laugh, and then everybody was laughing and the contents of the package were vigorously consumed. When Dougie told the story to Big Tony, the boss man wasn't angry or full of advice. He gave his young deputy a hug.

In November, Carter was elected on a platform that included decriminalizing marijuana. The nation's potheads rejoiced. Keith Stroup and the staff of the National Organization for the Reform of Marijuana Laws (NORML) fired flares from the window of a New York hotel and bounced around on some mattresses with the fine young ladies of COYOTE (Cast Off Your Old Tired Ethics), the sex-workers lobby, whose support was enthusiastically welcomed.

The host of this pot-world bacchanal was Thomas King Forcade, a self-proclaimed hippie Robin Hood who used smuggling money to help fund NORML and launch *High Times*—the *Playboy* of pot, the naked ladies of the centerfold replaced by hi-res shots of marijuana buds. "Dope was no longer a fad or a problem," one of the magazine's early editors later wrote. "Dope was a world." And *High Times* covered it, "a vast underground society that had its own myths and folklore and social etiquette and pecking order, songs and language, heroes and humor."

The magazine claimed four million readers a month, few of them subscribers for the same reason you wouldn't want a magazine called *Piracy and Plunder* sent to your door two centuries earlier. The ads ran to bongs, rolling papers, and counterintelligence equipment. The "Highwitness" news pages covered busts, scams, and new legal openings. The features were a mixture of service journalism—"How to Smuggle Like a Pro"—and epic tales from the underground.

High Times exalted men like my father, the brave men who provide "a metaphor for civil liberties" and "a gateway to outlaw consciousness." It talked in terms of the "contrabandist executive elite" and "aces of the dope air force." But perhaps the coolest ego trip was the board games advertised in the back pages. One was called SCAM: The International Game of Dope Smuggling, but the better seller seemed to be Dealer McDope, which was based on an underground comic character by Gilbert Shelton.

"We've all had fantasies of making the million dollar deal," as the introduction to the rule book put it, with "tons of contraband and that enormous bank roll in our pocket. Lots of folks are coming out these days telling us what dealing big time was all about, but we know one thing for sure. McDope went to all those places, played and panicked, scored and whored, and now that he is 'legit' he wanted to pass along to you the way it was really done. So sit back and cop to some fantastic entertainment."

My father was living his life as a game of Dealer McDope. He began in Doobietown, U.S.A., aka Milford, Connecticut, and grew quickly into a player there, rolling the dice and drawing a winning combination of Deal, Bust, and Karmic cards. For the last few years he'd had the real-life version of "Perfect Karma," which sent cash his way and allowed him to "ascend to Nirvana immediately," aka the woods in Maine where the deer are unafraid and eagles fly.

But there's a lot of game left to play, a lot of cards left in the deck.

"Smak City!"

"Schizoid Informer!"

"Screwed by the Karmic Kock!"

Eventually everyone draws the equivalent of "Watch Your Ass! It's a Karmic Fuck!"

My father drew it near the end of 1976.

His business tanked.

He got the news in the form of a phone call from his Dutchess County customers. He had given them a few dozen bricks of Mexican, and two weeks later they wanted to give them back. This had never happened before. It was good weed, this Mexican stuff. It was grown in the mountains between Puerto Vallarta and Guadalajara, and the high was formfitting to your mood. It could make you feel like a coyote howling atop a pyramid at sunset or a snugly bear donning a nightcap and blissfully turning over on the couch. The problem wasn't the weed. It was the market. Everyone with a Mexico connection was getting a Karmic comeuppance.

In 1976, so many people were smuggling and dealing professionally—and so many people were smoking—that quality mattered more than ever. Just as *Rolling Stone* made everyone a rock critic, *High Times* coached smokers upscale, publishing an annual Top 40 guide to "the most potent, precious and prettiest crops," and seeding the magazine with lines like "a fine strain of marijuana, like a fine wine or cigar, has its own characteristic flavor, appearance, and aroma; it is as unlike any other plant as two snowflakes. Learn to distinguish the vulgar or presumptuous, domestic window-box hybrid from the truly amusing little-imported thoroughbred."

Plenty of Mexican farms were ahead of this shift, including the number-one selection of the *High Times* Top 40 of 1977, a strain of Oaxacan Red that when harvested and sent to the streets looked like something scraped off the undercarriage of a lawn mower on a wet morning. This was typical of old-school American pot, which was grown outdoors, smuggled by boat or plane, doused in ocean spray, soaked in fuel, infested with spiders, and never less gnarly and natural and unpredictably weird than nature itself. Every item on the Top 40 looked like a piece of animal scat or something half chewed and spit into a napkin.

But while Mexican could still be great, most Mexican was bad and getting worse relative to the market. Mexican farmers were stuck in a past when American gringos smoked whatever shriveled plant could be grown out of mule piss with minimal effort. They didn't display a sense of basic pot science, which demands an understanding that good pot is a matter of resinous buds. The female plants produce resin to trap pollen from the male plants, so it's best to cull the male plants entirely and let the lonely girls pump out resin in vain. This is something the Mexicans didn't always bother to do. Less forgivably, they clung to the metric system. Those were strikes one and two against them.

Strike three was more interesting, and ultimately it's what doomed my father's booming trade. Aside from quality, smokers in the mid-1970s began to think more about story as well. Where was the dope sourced? How did it get here? You can see the roots of half a dozen future food trends in this impulse. To sex up their brands, some Mexican dealers started dropping beads into their loads, telling people to spread the word: This stuff came from the Indians themselves. A thousand years of history.

It didn't work.

Mexico has Indians, ruins, lush forests, unfamiliar seas, and lost worlds, as the Department of Tourism will happily confirm. But every issue of *High Times* had a price list, a kind of S&P of weed, a Dow Jones for marijuana. It was called the Trans-High Market Quotient, and it used reader reports and the well-earned phlegm of experience to distill supply and demand into a specific price for almost every kind of dope on the market. Like any market it was prone to wild, irrational shifts, and arguably this was one of them. But at the end of the day, the message was clear.

The people didn't want Mexican reefer, which until that year had been supplying 90 percent of the market. They wanted the intrigue of Caribbean dynasties, Far East war zones, Arab kingdoms, and South American jungles, which translated into basically four countries of origin: Jamaica, Thailand, Afghanistan, and the big winner of it all—comprising eighteen spots on the Top 40, and retailing for up to $750 a pound—Colombian Gold and Colombian Red, the best-selling strains of the 1970s.

My father's wholesalers sent a small baggie of what was selling well in the city: some leafy, golden stuff that looked like wild sunflowers passed through the insides of a bear. It was Colombian Gold. They also sent along the unwanted Mexican kilos, which my father sold to a low-grade dealer in Philly.

A couple of years earlier, at my mother's urging, my father had gotten a teaching certificate from the University of Connecticut, New Haven, a piece of paper that said he could educate the youth of the state. He had applied to seven or eight schools, with no luck. But he might have gone back to that path, perhaps beginning as a substitute English teacher. He might have dropped out of the drug trade entirely in 1976, but who could think about going straight with the Carter administration in office?

He had to get some Colombian. He tried a local connection, a friend of a friend in Bridgeport who gave him about eight bales, or three hundred pounds of dope. (Yes: Colombia tossed out the metric system and dealt in pounds, not kilos.) It was terrible stuff. Young, seedy, dry. You would have to smoke the whole three hundred pounds to catch a buzz, and my father called his contact to say so. He was certain the code of the brotherhood of the righteous weed dealers would ensure a full refund. Not this time. This was Mob weed, Mob rules. You bagged it, you bought it.

"You owe us fifteen K," said his contact.

"Fuck you," my father replied. "You gave me shit."

The guy countered that he could send over a killing crew. My father paid.

But what could Dealer McDope do now?

After she drove to San Francisco selling Anthony's weed, Carolyn Dokoupil, my father's sister, moved to Miami to go to paramedic school. It was 1973 and before long she was dating a man a lot like her brother. It was not what she set out to do. Her boyfriend had been a smiley-eyed mechanic in coveralls the day she met him. After they started dating, however, Billy buttonholed his way into the pot business, promising a friend of a friend that he could sell a bale of Colombian marijuana that he had no lines on selling and could not even transport, since his only vehicle was a motorcycle. Billy sold that bale and then another. As his confidence grew, so did his connections and, ultimately, his paydays until one night he was ready to kiss the straight world goodbye for good.

When the change took hold Carolyn was working her shift at Sambo's, an all-night diner yet to be picketed for its racist name. One of her customers was eyeing her like something on his fork. The manager called Billy to pick her up and get her home safely, which he did after a fashion. He arrived in a cherry-red Porsche he hadn't owned as of that morning. When Carolyn climbed into it wondering what fun was in store, Billy told her to take off her apron.

"You quit," he explained.

He was wholesaling tens of thousands of pounds of Colombian

reefer a year, serving as a middleman between Cuban gangsters and wholesalers in Texas, Louisiana, and the Carolinas. He bought a house in Florida and a vacation home in Hawaii, and the money came in so fast that Carolyn's fingers turned greenish-gray from counting it until Billy started weighing it instead.

Like my father, Billy was desperate to expand his business ahead of decriminalization, which Keith Stroup of NORML predicted would happen as early as 1978 and "certainly" by 1980. A new Gallup poll showed a clear majority of Americans agreed that pot should be decriminalized, and that fact alone helped remake the world of smokable pleasure, narrowing the distance between tobacco companies, which created model pot programs, and legions of hey-man hippie dealers, some of whom turned into rapacious capitalists.

One of Billy's associates was beaten with a sack of healing crystals and robbed of weed by the owner of a head shop. Not long afterward, Carolyn got into bed and Billy told her that she had a new Colt Python under her pillow. Then he opened the bedside table, where a second pistol rested atop the clutter. That was just about all Carolyn could handle.

She was twenty-three. Her entire wardrobe was tie-dye, denim, and swimwear. She wasn't ready to shoot someone or be shot. She wasn't ready to go to prison, either, and she knew—since she wasn't cursed with a coke addiction and didn't have a gringo strain of machismo in her petite paramedic body—that while smokers were safe, dealers were still subject to long, hateful prison terms: as much as a year per pound of contraband. By the scale of Billy's operation, a year per pound would put them behind bars until sometime shortly before the sun exploded.

A few months later Carolyn was washing dishes and looking out the window onto their quiet dead-end street when a blue van barreled into view, swerved, shimmied down the paved straightaway where neighborhood kids rode bikes, and came to a halt in her driveway. The door of the van opened and out spilled one of Billy's drivers, along with a shower of pills. The guy ran into the house as though pursued by bees.

He found Carolyn in the kitchen and said, "Oh man, oh man, oh man. I just hit some telephone stuff!"

"You mean a telephone pole?" Carolyn asked.

"No, a Bell South guy. You know. In one of those cherry pickers."

A phalanx of police cars appeared and hurtled toward the house as though pulled by a tide. Billy shot out of bed at the sound of their sirens, and when he saw the lights, his pose was that of a man watching a building collapse. He had coke in the house. He had guns in the house. Because of some sort of problem with a hand-off, he had a quarter ton of Colombian Gold in the house, which on sight of the cops suddenly seemed very, very fragrant.

If the cops came in, they were all screwed. Carolyn was screwed. Billy was screwed. The driver was screwed. Billy told the driver to get out front and face the consequences, which to his credit he did. That gave Carolyn time to put fresh coffee beans in the grinder and throw onions into a frying pan with a topping of eggs.

Outside a young cop already had the cuffs out and a couple of Dade County deputies were heading into the house. They sat in the kitchen and started asking some questions. Time passed. They sipped coffee and listened to Billy and Carolyn explain about their poor, poor friend, and the dark hole he had fallen into. Eventually the cops left.

Carolyn resolved she would leave too. She'd had enough of feeling like she needed a joint just to process the fact that her life revolved around selling joints. Before she could go, however, my father showed up.

The sun was blazing. It exploded off the hood of Billy's cherry-red Porsche and skated across the driveway. Everywhere my father looked, the light was hard and cut into his eyes like glass. He cussed his forgotten shades and slapped at the bugs dive-bombing the back of his neck, which felt cooked even in the shade of the veranda. This was Indian summer in Miami, and even in one of his almost translucent concert T-shirts, my father sweated like a man wearing a rubber diving suit.

Desperate to get his hands on some Colombian reefer, he had called Carolyn, which he rarely did unless he wanted something. She wasn't happy to get the call and could tell he was fishing. What's your boyfriend do? Is he a big distributor? Can I get a piece of the action? My father could talk, he could charm, but he couldn't bullshit family.

"Don't come down here," Carolyn had said. "It's not a good time."

My father came anyway. Carolyn had been casual enough to put her address on a letter. My father had stake money and, on the power of his sibling connection and sheer charisma, he planned to show up and beg to be let into the operation.

He knocked three times, hard.

He was standing outside the door to a stranger's house. He held a duffel bag, letting it slip to his last knuckle, feeling its heft, counting the seconds, which stretched into minutes. What was taking so long? He let his mind wander, a trick he used to settle his nerves. That was always his greatest gift and maybe his biggest weakness: the ability to go blank in such moments and let the brain bubble up what it likes, a phrase maybe, something off topic, the title of a book he'd just read, *Ninety-two in the Shade*, which led him to think of its author, Thomas McGuane, a Catholic like him, which led to his own thoughts of being a writer someday, his idea for a pirate story, for a children's book. Two hours could go by without my father even noticing.

When the door finally opened, Billy was standing there wearing nothing but jean shorts and a mustache. Down a hallway and around a corner, members of his crew were watching a movie.

"Hi," my father said. "I'm Tony."

My father was the opposite of most men in awkward situations. Instead of going shy he could seem almost pert. His voice would get this vibration, like he was about to tell the raunchiest locker-room story you ever heard if you'd just sit a while. Anyway, it was a voice you usually heard out. But it was a scenario you shut the door on.

"Oh, you must be speechless," my father continued. "I'm looking to buy some Colombian reefer and sell it up north."

Billy slammed the door and found Carolyn on the couch.

"Do you have a brother named Tony?"

She nodded.

"Get rid of him."

When the door opened again, Carolyn put a hand over her brother's mouth and carefully shut the door behind her before batting at him like some sort of overzealous lover.

"What. Are. You. Doing. Here." She paused to wait for an answer. "I. Told. You. Not. To. Come."

"What do you mean?" my father said. "I called ahead."

Carolyn took a break from beating her brother and walked back inside. My father noticed that she was wearing a bathing suit. It might have been Tuesday. It might have been Sunday. Every day was the same. The place reeked of human excess, and he got a whiff of it as the door shut. It was especially heavy with what my father would later recognize as the scent of money, the kind that fills coolers and dirties hands.

Billy came back outside, wearing a polo shirt. "What are you doing here? No one told you to come here," Billy said.

"I'm not leaving until you give me some pot to take back north," my father said, flashing that fist-size smile of his.

And so my father stood there, and Billy stood there, and little worms of anxiety spread in their chests, albeit for different reasons. At some point, Billy figured it was crazier to leave him out there than to bring him in. The two men played pool in Billy's game room, smoked a few joints, drank a few beers, and then Billy declined to sell my father the hundred pounds he requested. His minimum was three hundred pounds.

Late that night, he took my father's $25,000, threw it in a bedroom, and told my father to go home, call in a couple of days. He'd sell him the load for 90K, including more than $60,000 on the arm. My father had his Colombian. He didn't know it yet, but he also had a mentor.

It was exciting to drive that three hundred pounds north in a rented Lincoln Continental. My father got into the car feeling as though somewhere deep in his brain the Doors had just appeared onstage in a tiny, floodlit stadium. He got out twenty-four hours later feeling like Jim Morrison deep in the ground. Not even making his drops managed to raise his pulse. It was routine without ever being new: Two bales to Buddy Bone in New Haven. Two bales to Arthur near Hartford. Two bales to Poughkeepsie. Two more to Dutchess County. Less than two weeks later the cash washed in. My father had $59,000 for Billy and a tidy $12,000 profit for himself. Not bad for a few days' work. But that drive.

Under Billy's tutelage, my father decided to reinvent his business, becoming a manager, a person who delegates and philosophizes. He bumped up his Poughkeepsie people to a trunk load of their own and paid someone $5,000 to drive it. He used the same sum to recruit one of my mother's former roommates and her good guy friend J.B., who also served as staff mechanic to Dealer McDope's new garage. My father bought two one-ton Chevy pickup trucks with hard tops and arranged for his original connection, Arthur, and another guy, a friend of Arthur's, to jockey them north.

He also hired gophers to do chores for his growing empire. It was good money for friends and insulation from the front lines for my father. The lowest notch on the totem pole was Fred, a golden retriever of a man with kind eyes and a simple mind. He drew a salary for odd jobs, like buying new scales in Brooklyn or watching my father's dog, Captain. Another guy bought my father a rotating fleet of used cars and scouted out viable stash houses, posing as a photographer with a need for privacy and very little light.

Soon this merry band was moving some serious weight: at least a ton a month, sometimes three tons, and my father had his first $100,000 payday. In a single month, he made ten times what the average American made in a year, double what big-city lawyers, doctors, engineers were making annually.

He also started acting more like the man in charge. He made Arthur move into a new house, something with a more private driveway. He made Buddy Bone use the storage space in his mother's house to stash long-term product. Additional orders and customers came on board. Earl the Pearl got several extra bales a month. A man in Vermont named Smiley got a few bales a month. A friend in Maine got a few bales.

Meanwhile the movement continued to spread. The legislatures of

New York, North Carolina, and Mississippi lifted all criminal penalties associated with a person's individual taste for weed, and marijuana was knocking on the door of Congress. Peter Bourne, the president's chief drug policy officer, told the House Select Committee on Narcotics about the success of the state laws. He reiterated the administration's support for a clear-eyed, humanistic approach to drug abuse, one that included the repeal of all federal laws against pot use. And he was joined by a big tent of political stars: Midwestern mayors, members of the black caucus, conservative columnists who foreswore pot but rhapsodized about personal freedom and states' rights.

At last President Carter himself took the floor of Congress on August 2, 1977: "Penalties against drug use should not be more damaging to an individual than the use of the drug itself, and where they are, they should be changed. Nowhere is this more clear than in the laws against the possession of marijuana in private for personal use." Therefore, he continued, "I support legislation amending Federal law to eliminate all Federal criminal penalties for the possession of up to one ounce of marijuana . . ."

He went on to stress that this was "decriminalization not legalization," and that he was concerned about teen pot use, and that traffickers would still be vigorously pursued, mercilessly incarcerated, public enemies of promise. None of it mattered.

In the American pot world the president's words were taken in and experienced like a pardon for all crimes past and future. *The New York Times* announced the news on its front page: CARTER SEEKS TO END MARIJUANA PENALTY FOR SMALL AMOUNTS. What followed was pot's proudest moment, the actual golden hour of the golden age, a summer of rejoicing and celebration, when smokers seemed to twirl around every lamppost and smile from the crook of every tree, at least for a little while.

As summer gave way to fall, Billy bought Carolyn a house beside a national park near Denver, Colorado. It was a ski chalet with windows so high you'd have to swing a tall pine tree to dust them. She stopped eating meat, started meditating, and became a volunteer for the forest service. She was through with Billy—but Billy was scalawagging around with a new Dokoupil.

He deputized my father, bringing him down to Miami to help expand the operation and position the business for the possibility of legalization. They figured their sales machine had to be among the most reliable, so they focused on growing the product side, which was limited only by the amount of dope the team could smuggle out of the Florida Keys.

The Keys are the southernmost part of the United States, closer to Colombia than to Chicago, a coral archipelago that starts at the marshy southern tip of the Everglades and curls a hundred miles southwest toward Havana and Cancún. Billy's connection would pull a marijuana-laden shrimp boat up to a special deep-water dock and pile the product in an old fishing shed, the contents of which Billy was responsible for smuggling north and sending to market. He used mobile homes with special shocks; put the equivalent of War Admiral and Seabiscuit into one of Billy's vehicles, flip a switch, and the pounds vanished.

It was a good scam with a major flaw: It was everyone's scam. The Keys, the Glades, and the Ten Thousand Islands region on the Gulf of Mexico side—the whole southern tip of Florida—had become the entry point for almost all the marijuana in America. The feds knew it and treated Florida as though it were a six-hundred-mile bong through which pot was pulled into the lungs of the country.

There's only one road out of the Keys: Route 1, which was a private railroad until 1935 when a hurricane knocked much of it into the sea and left the state of Florida with the job of lashing and suturing the land back together again. The road was always choked with cops and tourists, but the only way for Billy to get more dope into America was to drive more of it out of the Keys. So he asked for volunteers. Who would be willing to make the drive two or three times a day for $25,000 a trip? Anyone? The only guy dumb or crazy or self-destructive enough to say yes was my father, of course. He didn't need the money. He needed the feeling.

He picked up the Winnebago from the Dadeland Mall, Miami's largest, and drove south, passing through swamp followed by sea and salty little towns and more of the same. A straight flat bridge was built every two miles or so, and where there was no bridge, the waves were liable to lap over the road, which made the journey feel as much like boating as driving. The turnoff for the shed was marked by a painted rock, and the gate, which looked locked, came open after two tugs on the bolt.

The fishing shed looked more like a New England barn with a dock behind it. Cubans materialized out of the afternoon sunlight and some of them carried MAC-10 machine guns. One of the unarmed guys approached and smiled at his gringo driver with the brass balls. My father swelled with a pride he didn't show. Then he got back in the mobile home, turned it so that the vehicle's door was toward the door of the barn, and put down the little stepladder.

The crew started to work. A bucket brigade of men handed bales to my father, who stacked them everywhere there was open space, from the bathroom to the back bed to inside the stove. He counted about two hundred bales in all. Finally, he flipped the switch for hydraulics, and as wordlessly as he arrived he left, hearing only the roar of his own neurons.

As he drove he felt the sun, a full ten degrees warmer than on the mainland. Through the window he watched the water change color, passing from blue to green to black to milky white, all of it hiding the same peril that sank Spanish galleons and made these islands a pirate hideaway. Four hours passed like a song on the radio.

My father met Billy back at the mall, in the food court. Someone else picked up the truck and set up a mobile dealing station—like a food truck for pot—or delivered the load to a stash house. After an hour, my father got up to leave again. Another Winnebago would be waiting outside, ready for another trip.

"Fucking nut," Billy said, as my father walked away.

But my father just spread his arms and smiled.

Throughout the fall, his dope IQ continued to grow along with his business. Billy taught him how to be a criminal, a professional one who writes phone numbers down in code and always pre-books his plane tickets under a false name, so the cops can never check ahead. He stressed one point above all: Don't travel with a lot of cash. If you must take money, always put it in a series of official-looking manila folders—and if asked always say the folders hold personal papers. Never forget to smile.

My father took all this in and added his own insights into the trade. His conversations began to sound like snippets from a night course on entrepreneurialism.

Anthony Dokoupil on personnel: "Don't have people working for a shirttail. The service they do is what keeps you in business."

Anthony Dokoupil on infractions: "If you're high, bye-bye. If you're wired, you're fired."

Anthony Dokoupil on networking: "The best thing to say is nothing, and the best thing to do is work alone."

Anthony Dokoupil on ethics: "Never short-stack. Pay by the laws of the multiplication tables."

He started calling his team of wheelmen and the route they took north the Reefer Express. He called his product Dade County Pine, in semiconscious homage to the long-dead forest that once stretched from the Everglades to the Atlantic. Because it had the aroma of a grassy knoll, very clean and sweet, like the air after a thunderstorm, he joked about attaching a tag to this new dope, explaining how the product was sourced and transported as though it were not dope at all but an imported rug. My father's tag would have read:

This resinous Colombian bud incorporates every imaginable color and shape into a kaleidoscope of exotic beauty. Sticky, seedless, and sold by the ton, it is imported by strong men with brush mustaches and wiry chest hair, men who have braved hustlers, honchos, honkies, *federales mucho*, and informers galore. Their prize, your glory, has long hairs turned red by Mother Nature and leaves of heavy resin that ball like glue between the thumb and forefinger. Never again will you wonder, Do I feel anything? The answer is: Yes. You do. For connoisseurs only. Medical note: This is a great choice for sensitive lungs. The strong chlorophyll content will cool the body like a summer monsoon.

The country was in a recession, but Billy and my father never once worried about money except for how to transport it. Most of the millions of dollars my father sent to Billy went via Eastern Air Lines. In those days my father could buy a ticket, check his suitcase of money, and never get on the flight. Billy walked right into baggage claim at Miami International Airport and took his money off the conveyor belt. This went on even after somebody else's suitcase was abandoned and recovered by Peter Bensinger, the head of the DEA, who opened the prop at a Senate hearing on drug money, laying $3 million on the witness table.

A referral brought my father to the door of a criminal lawyer (heavy emphasis on the criminal) who knew the ins and outs of money laundering and who helped my father incorporate two front operations: a rare-furniture concern that my mother used as a hobby machine and a custom-home company that my father managed.

He opened a business banking account with a string of drug-backed cashier's checks, bought land in Vermont, and retained a full-time building staff: three carpenters, a crew of woodworking specialists, the best in the area. The houses they built were opulent faux-rustic mansions of the sort that one imagines trees themselves would build if they ever needed to show off their use and beauty. The first sold to a Timex Corporation executive for $200,000 (more than $750,000 in today's money). From then on, everything was legit as far as Uncle Sam knew.

In the weeks and months that followed, my father went on a spree. He bought a good smuggler's house in Middlebury, Connecticut: dead-end street, concealed garage, stream, woods. He hired a mason to build a barbecue that aliens might mistake for Stonehenge east. Another crew built a secret compartment underneath the kitchen sink, a false-walled cabinet where he could stash money, drugs, contraband. The place itself was chockablock with antiques—oak rolltop desks, marble-topped side tables, a mahogany dinner table.

My mother spent her weekends waving a number on the New England auction scene. She also joined the Middlebury Racquet Club and sweated it up with the professors' wives and IBM widows. At home she ordered Château Margaux and Château Lafite Rothschild by the crate, and chopped farmer's market broccoli to the sounds of Steely Dan on new McIntosh speakers.

My father junked the Dodge Dart and bought his first Mercedes, a four-door "executive line" with a fat-rimmed steering wheel and glistening dash. He decided to buy a tie and a blue blazer with gold buttons and a pair of classic gray trousers with a sharp crease.

Together my parents sampled the best restaurants in New Haven and New York City, where it wasn't unusual to spend $1,000 on dinner, a show, and a weekend in a fancy hotel. They followed their whims, forgetting their anti-consumerist roots and spending cash with abandon. One of their favorite new places was Le Château, a French wonder in South Salem, New York, about forty minutes west as the Mercedes flies. It was a stone-and-timber Tudor-style mansion built in 1907 by J. P. Morgan as a gift to Reverend William S. Rainsford, who lived there until his death and the home's eventual resurrection. It was a place where kids are meant to stare silently at their soup or stay home entirely.

Initially my parents felt uncomfortable in such splendiferous surroundings, which stirred up feelings of fakery and shame, and made my father walk so self-consciously that anyone looking on would assume he had a severe sunburn. The diners struck him as old and staid, like guests of the original tenant, and when he looked down at his new tie it seemed suddenly alive and warm-blooded, less a garment than a predator, a nuclear mutation that had sprung out of a puddle and gone for the throat.

My mother never felt more like a grocer's daughter. The menu was in French, a language neither of my parents spoke, yet one they did not want to appear to be unable to speak. If you had asked them that night about Honeygrass Farms, their land in Maine, their idyll for all-time, they wouldn't have known what to say. It was as forgotten as a children's toy. The canoe had rotted and then been stolen, the camping gear slowly mulched into nothing, lashed by the weather.

They bridged the manners gap by politely snorting a little cocaine in the bathroom (my father) and politely pointing to the items on the menu they most hoped to enjoy (my mother). It worked like a dream and they ended the night by politely feeding each other strawberries drizzled with chocolate and glazed in Grand Marnier. They were themselves again, a bomb of a man and his sparkling fuse.

This golden age of marijuana came to an appropriately golden close in 1977, at the hippest Christmas party in Washington, D.C. No one was prepared for tragedy, because the party itself seemed proof of untouchable triumph. It was NORML's holiday bash. Four hundred guests were expected, so Keith Stroup secured a cream-colored town house on S Street, one so big that he worried about filling it.

The house was open plan. From the first to the fourth floor there was no ceiling, the roof floating somewhere over the staircase, the dance floor as exposed as a stage. People streamed in, shucking coats and emitting unconscious burbles of excitement. The lights went low and the music went up. A psychedelic juggler tossed glowing orbs until the sea of people coming through the door swallowed him up.

There was no real food, but waiters moved through the crowd with silver trays of caviar and hand-rolled joints of weed grown in Kentucky, a sample of what was possible in the domestic market to come. There was also a lot of loose cocaine, and the party would have been legendary even without its unusual guest list.

There were badge-holders from the Food and Drug Administration, the Council on Drug Abuse, and the National Institute on Drug Abuse; people from every echelon of the anti-drug establishment and their counterparts at NORML, *High Times*, and the great outlaw underground of pot.

Everyone assumed the War on Drugs was over. The White House's midterm drug-control policy was the treaty. "Drugs cannot be forced out of existence," it said. "They will be with us as long as people find in them the relief or satisfaction they desire." And so the forces of good and evil were allowed to mingle like never before, sending up smoky wreaths and radiating an unprecedented glow of fellow feeling.

There was the millionaire founder of a rolling-papers conglomerate; the scion of CBS founder William Paley; the daughter of *Playboy* founder Hugh Hefner; eight or ten members of the Carter White House; front-page writers for *The Washington Post* and *The New York Times*; and overseeing it all Mr. Marijuana, the Prime Minister of Pot, that man from NORML, the great Keith Stroup and his not-so-silent backer Thomas Forcade, the smuggler-dealer who founded *High Times*.

At about 11:00 p.m., there was a commotion at the door, followed by whispers, elbows, and exclamations. No one could quite believe that Peter Bourne had just walked in, the self-described "first drug czar," the first person to be given authority over both the treatment and law enforcement sides of federal policy, the person who most held the dreams of marijuana in his hands. Bourne was the only senior drug-policy official ever to back decriminalization, which had just been endorsed by the Senate Judiciary Committee.

Here was America's top drug warrior and yet some of his views aligned with America's top drug lobby. Some of his tastes did as well. The word spread that Bourne was here for more than a hello. "Peter's here," a friend told Stroup. "He wants to get high."

At the top of the house, in a room guarded by an ex–secret service agent, Bourne joined a stunned circle of partygoers and stayed in the circle as a small, bullet-shaped container of cocaine—a contraption with a twist top that loaded a hit with each turn—made the rounds. There were at least five journalists in the room, including *High Times* staffers, an editor and reporter for *The Washington Post*, and the poet laureate of the drug scene, Hunter S. Thompson. When the bullet came to Bourne, he coolly loaded the tip, hit, reloaded, and hit again—a one-and-one. As Bourne finished, Thompson threw his arm around a writer for *High Times*, sighed loudly, and declared, "My God, man, we'll all be indicted."

He was wrong.

What happened was worse than an indictment. The forces of change had come together—only to vanish up someone's nose.

One year rolled into the next and it seemed like the marijuana movement would continue unchanged. Nebraska became the eleventh state to set free the pot smoker, removing all criminal penalties for personal use. Almost one in five people used the drug at least once during the course of the year, and my father continued to contribute mightily to that unending market.

He transformed himself into the kind of kingpin he used to adore from a distance. He got the opportunity because Mexican authorities began to spray pot fields with paraquat, a deadly herbicide that ruined the last dealers of Mexican reefer, including none other than Eddie, my father's old wholesaler. Eddie had lost the concert business by the time my father found him in that suddenly shabby-looking house overlooking the tidal stream.

"Eddie, Tony. Tony, Eddie."

A play was developing, just like it had five or six years earlier, and by the end of the conversation, my father had jumped again. He was Eddie's supplier. He was Eddie's guy. Actually, he was more than just Eddie's guy. He was the guy in his corner of New England. And the realization of that fact seemed to rewire my father's brain a little.

He began to host parties, where he rolled joints from dope soft as overcooked pasta, oily enough to stain clothes, nearly resinous enough to hold fingerprints. From behind the false wall in a cabinet in the kitchen, he produced opium, hash, and so much coke he put it in a sugar bowl on the counter. These weren't beer-and-nut parties, the men in packs, fingers slung over bottles of beer, women wondering why nothing has changed since high school.

These were more like kids' birthday parties that happen to be for adults: there was running and screaming and carrying on. My father was the host, the self-styled Great American Outlaw who curled his way from toke circle to toke circle, talking rhyming nonsense. "Tony's my name, smoke's my game." And again two minutes later. "Tony's my name, smoke's my game."

My mother had also allowed the business to do a number on her synapses. For years she had been merely an observer, but in late 1977 and early 1978 she started running the switchboard for some jobs. She relayed information about where to "pick up the pizza." At times she was also my father's bookkeeper. She hid money in our front hall closet when the space under the kitchen cabinet overflowed. She was a first-issue subscriber to *High Lady*, the magazine of empowered women. For Christmas, the master carpenter at Fox Run made her a nutcracker with the head of a penis. "To my favorite ball buster," the card read. "From Santa."

But perhaps her most triumphant moment came one cold winter morning in 1978, when she stepped in to get Billy a crucial infusion of cash. She woke before dawn, dressed for her teaching job, and drove to the Tweed New Haven Airport, where she carried a satchel of blank lesson plans to work on during the flight. At her feet: a suitcase heavy with hundreds of thousands of dollars.

As the sun bounced up from behind the rim of the earth, she was sitting in a Lear jet, taxiing down the runway, two attendants and a pilot catering to only her needs. From the air, she called in sick to work, her stomach flipping with excitement, and by the first bell she was looking at the curve of the world and thinking how fine it was to be this clever, this sneaky. Was there a finer feeling in all the world?

In July 1978 my mother and father and the rest of America learned that Peter Bourne had resigned from the White House. His one-and-one had held for six months and it might have held forever, but Bourne, a psychiatrist, came under scrutiny for writing a comely female assistant a quaalude prescription under a false name. There was an honest explanation, but 'ludes were popularly known as an aid to languid, tantric sex and the press went for the twofer.

To confirm the cocaine story, a reporter called the last people you would expect to tell on another drug user: two staffers from *High Times*, who have never been identified, and Stroup, who was out of his gourd on cocaine and furious with Bourne for his support of Mexico's paraquat spraying. Stroup and company confirmed the story: "Drug Czar Does Cocaine at Pot Party." It broke on *Good Morning America*.

Bourne has always denied having anything more than "good old

American whiskey" at the party, but it didn't matter. He had been there and that was enough. He resigned within thirty-six hours, and the incident killed drug reform for Carter, who dry swallowed his previous policies on marijuana and flipped a mental switch in the White House and American newsrooms.

The White House announced a new "war on marijuana." It expanded the size of the DEA, preached the need to snuff out smugglers and wholesalers. *Time* covered marijuana's possible role in killing chromosomes and causing "psychotic reactions, personality change, impaired learning ability and development of a chronic lethargy." *New York* magazine ran an essay called "Thirty-six Hours of Insanity: A Marijuana Nightmare." It ran another warning that "what whiskey did to the Indian, marijuana may do to white middle-class America." *Reader's Digest, Ladies' Home Journal, The Saturday Evening Post* all ran half a dozen articles on marijuana's links to cancer, heart attacks, sterility, loose sex, male breasts.

Suddenly men like my father were slave traders again. More, they were militant slave traders. "The romance is gone," as one federal agent put it. *The New York Times* magazine ran a ten-thousand-word piece about "the dark and violent world of the Mexican connection." *Time* revealed "the Colombian connection," which "owns an armada of ships and planes" and has "an army of bush pilots, seamen, electronics experts, roustabouts and cutthroats."

High Times declared "Dope War II," which meant that the heroic men of marijuana were once again enlarged and rewritten in the public mind. They were transformed from pied pipers to horned toads, from good-bad men to bad-bad men. In the process, the size, scale, and nature of marijuana rings was wildly exaggerated. It had to be in order to justify a drug war with real bullets.

But no matter how sophisticated they seemed on the evening news, even the biggest, most famous cases were on closer inspection skunky with incompetence, failure, family tragedy, heinous narcissism, grandiloquence, and the stupid pursuit of some long-ago childhood adventure that can't ever be found. At least they were consistent. There was really only one kind of big-time marijuana dealer and smuggler, and my father was it.

When he learned of Carter's reversal, he didn't consider curtailing his trade and my mother didn't consider asking him to stop. On the contrary they sent a deputy to Chicago to scout the market and inaugurated a monthly tradition: Saturdays at Scribner's, a modest post-and-beam building with knotty-pine tables, wainscoting, and the best seafood on the Connecticut coast. To accommodate the gang, the owner wheeled in a big circular table, where members of the Reefer Express drank and smoked and shook the ceiling beams until the small hours.

Dealer McDope had arrived.

3

The Old Man

Among the people who mattered, my father was known as God's pocket with reefer and cash. In more than eight years he'd never lost a load to the cops or missed a payoff to his partners. He had never cheated or cried. And he could turn over tons of dope in days, send a wave of money washing across time zones, across a team of wheelmen and sailors and endless gophers, all the way back to the dirt, to the farmer working the end of a hoe in the equatorial sun.

When a customer's men flaked, he dispatched members of his own team. When a bale fell into the sea, he dealt from his personal reserves. Sure, it helped him to help his customers, but it was also a criminal promise, a handshake and a hug into the all-enclosing fraternity of the Great American Outlaw.

People called him the Old Man because he could get a bit melancholy about his life, a bit bored with the work of getting and selling drugs. Breaking the law is like anything else. It can become a job, a grind, so routine that you sell the equivalent of enough marijuana for another Woodstock and feel like you haven't accomplished a thing. Such was the state of my father's criminal soul. He would tell friends, "I'm not made for this world," and they would laugh. "The Old Man!"

But he was serious. His only solace, as befit a man of his times, was cocaine. The drug still had the Big Weekend approval of mainstream America. It also had a high that felt like all life's advantages, an ingestible form of great parenting, a proud lineage, and everyday purpose. Each hit made my father a new man and each new man wanted another hit, another bubbling behind the breastplate like the perfect locker-room speech—which happened to be exactly what my father needed to go on. His future was waiting for him offstage, in a prison cell, on charges of smuggling marijuana. And when the future got out, it brought off what has to be one of the greatest one-shot smuggles ever attempted—and created the biggest East Coast dope ring of the Reagan years.

The story begins in 1944, the year that Charlie Montfort and William F. Terry III—my father's future partners, and in Charlie's case, my future stepfather—were born, and their lives began to arc toward each other and the rest of pot-smoking America. Charlie was a sickly kid. In high school, however, he became a scholastic wrestler, a champion of the ninety-eight-pound weaklings. By graduation he claimed victory over both the navy champion and the army champion, and accepted a scholarship from the University of Maine, where he claims to have trained for the 1964 Olympics. During the trials, an opponent—let's just call him a bully—made a St. Louis arch with Charlie's body, breaking vertebrae in his back and ending his athletic career.

But Charlie had other talents. He excelled at math and logic. As a senior he aced IBM's test for programmers, landing a job with Mutual Life Insurance in Portland, which ran IBM mainframes. But soon Charlie found himself torn between the starched satisfactions of traditional power and the feel-good hazards of protesting the establishment. For a while he balanced one against the other. He wore a suit to work but spent his lunch hour out near the highway, waving a cardboard sign and hollering, his voice coming and going in gusts.

"End the war!" *Zoom.* "Give peace a chance!" *Zoom.*

In 1968, after his bosses complained, he quit and moved to San Francisco, where he swam in the counterculture by night and tuned computers for Macy's by day. But his two lives still didn't mix well. He got up to five vodka martinis a day at lunch. He was waiting for an excuse, a reason to break free, and he got it one morning in January 1971 when two oil tankers collided under the Golden Gate Bridge. The prow of the *Arizona* sliced forty feet into the *Oregon*, which gurgled out more than a million gallons of black fuel. By sunrise the poison had reached the far corners of the bay. It lapped the shores of Alcatraz and Angel islands, licked the pilings at Fisherman's Wharf, and blanketed the moneyed coast of Marin County. Dead marine life washed in with every wave.

Charlie skipped work and joined a rescue crew, furry freaks wiping down wildlife until their own hair and clothes were shiny and smeared. The president of Standard Oil tried to calm everyone down. He assured the public that his firm would buy *new* animals to replace the dead ones, importing them, if necessary, a promise that only further goaded the volunteers.

Charlie didn't return to Macy's until the following week, and his boss called him in immediately.

"Where the hell have you been?" he said.

Charlie hadn't bothered to call in sick.

"Helping with the cleanup," Charlie said.

"That's the hippies' business," his boss said.

Charlie thought about that for a moment. In those days the view from the executive suite in the Macy's building near Union Square was unimpeded for hundreds of miles, a view like secular stained glass, and Charlie felt the presence.

"I guess I'm with the hippies," he said.

"Excuse me?"

"I quit, sir."

"You can't quit, you're in the middle of a project."

"That's your business."

Charlie went into the Macy's computer room, cleared out his stuff, and sat down to write one more code before security could show him the door. He arranged the punch cards to celebrate his birthday. The following year, if Charlie's defiance went unnoticed, everyone in the department would get a bonus—a double-large check courtesy of the hippies but straight from the man.

The next summer Charlie ran out of cash, so he returned home to Maine with a pound of Oaxaca-grown Mexican weed in his duffel bag. He sold it on the beach in Ogunquit, a fishing town between Kennebunkport and Portsmouth, and he amassed a little nest egg, building it a joint or two at a time. In the fall he moved into a cabin in Wells, a one-man hippie commune with beams so crude they still had bark on them. There he founded Slam Bang Construction and entertained a new friend, a man named Willy Terry.

In his lifetime, Willy was a musician, a pilot, a father, and many other things besides, but most crucially, he was the biggest marijuana smuggler in America, the quintessential "good" bad man of the era. He looked a bit like Robert Redford circa 1975, with feathered blond hair, a long, lean body, and the bounce step of the high-school track star he had once been. He could trace his line back to the *Mayflower* and the man who built the oldest surviving wood-frame house in America.

He also happened to be Jimmy Buffett's next-door neighbor, my father's partner, my stepfather's best friend, and eventually a rat so big he gave the feds more cases than they could possibly pursue. He was the only son of a flawless American clubman: a sportsman and mechanic, president of his local men's club, golfer, Boy Scouts volunteer. But what Willy most wanted to do was play the guitar and sing.

Charlie met him in Maine and helped him manage his performances, driving him to Boston and Providence and points in between. Willy made his first marijuana run to Mexico sometime in the late 1960s. Back then kids could drive a van across the border at Laredo or El Paso and start looking for a supplier, who would also be looking for them. There was no trick to finding a dealer: put the word out with taxi drivers and bartenders, then drink in plain view of the door for as long as it takes for someone to come get you.

The safest smuggling route, if you didn't mind smallish loads, was to carry your product across the Rio Grande and into the United States, dropping it off wherever you could reliably hide it. That's what Willy would do. He picked Texas, near El Paso, and after the drop he'd walk back into Mexico, find his car, and drive back into America the same way he'd left. Sometime later, maybe a couple of days, he'd retrieve his dope from the underbrush and there'd be joy—and a 100 percent markup—on the coast of Maine.

In the summer of 1974 Willy tried for his first two-hundred-pound load. He put it on a raft and walked it across the drought-shallowed Rio Grande. Then he sank the raft under some rocks and a few days later, he went for the pickup but he wasn't alone. A team of customs agents had been tailing him since the checkpoint at El Paso.

They had noticed his muddy shoes. In the dry season in Mexico, there's only one place your shoes might get muddy on such a short trip: the Rio Grande. On that alone customs followed him, and Willy led them right to the dope.

He got a year in prison and served less than six months in Danbury, Connecticut, close to his parents. It's a correctional facility instead of a penitentiary, and a plaque outside the counseling center read: "You are the designer of your life. If you want something, you can plan and work for it. Nothing is easy, but nothing is impossible either."

Charlie visited Willy in prison, and Willy always looked bright as ever behind wire-rim glasses. They had read enough penny novels to know that prison was like graduate school for the criminally ambitious. And that plaque outside the counseling center was right on.

"I'm learning a lot," Willy told Charlie.

"Anything interesting?" Charlie said.

"Yeah."

"What's that?"

"Fuck Mexico."

In early 1975 Charlie flew to St. Barts to meet with Willy's contact from prison, a revered older smuggler who had made a name for himself with solo guerrilla tactics. When strong winds snapped the mast of his schooner off the coast of South Carolina, he lashed it together with rope and limped back to St. Barts, waving off help from the Coast Guard and concerned sailors. Charlie found him sitting in a room with five other people. The furniture was wicker, the tables were glass. On the beach, the waves broke languorously along the shore. A just-arrived three-day-old Sunday edition of *The New York Times* was doing nothing on a side table. No one was talking.

Charlie picked up the paper and started to read. On page 40 there was a small article about a tall-ship festival to mark America's bicentennial: dozens of vessels, an international naval review, the whole harbor crawling with the Coast Guard and private yachts. It was called Operation Sail.

"Can we use this in a scam?" he asked, and everyone smiled.

Operation Sail was the brainchild of sixty-year-old Frank Braynard, the founder of New York's outdoor mall, South Street Seaport, and previously the Shipping News reporter at the old *New York Herald Tribune*. His team worked out of an office at One World Trade Center, and he too was using the bicentennial as a diversion—"a delicious excuse," he said—to bring together the biggest collection of windjammers and warships since the war for Greek independence in 1827.

In the summer of 1976, the stage was set for both events, the smuggle and the celebration. Braynard called his festival a seagoing salute to America's birthday. Charlie saw his work in a similar light. He and Willy were sons of the revolution, fighting for freedom: the freedom to get stoned, the freedom for adults to control their own lives, expand their own minds.

Operation Sail grew and grew until more than a dozen tall ships were scheduled to make a majestic Fourth of July journey from the lower bay, past Brooklyn and Governor's Island, past the Statue of Liberty, past the canyons of Wall Street, and up the Hudson to the far tip of the island. In their wake would come an armada of schooners and yawls, cutters and catboats, ketches, sloops, brigantines, barques, barquentines, eighty or more international military vessels, frigates and destroyers, submarines, amphibious trucks. And less classifiable fare: a Chinese junk, a Spanish galleon, a "history barge."

More than five million people were expected to watch live, either from the shore or from the deck of twenty thousand private vessels. And at the symbolic center of it all, the USS *Forrestal*, an eighty-thousand-ton aircraft carrier that would host President Ford and Vice President Rockefeller: the boys of honor, overlooking their bathtub of toys.

Willy went to the Sierra Madre mountain range in Colombia, the highest in South America. Charlie secured two piers in the lower bay, near Sandy Hook, New Jersey, where the tallest of tall ships—the ones that couldn't clear the 127-foot Brooklyn Bridge—would be based before and after the parade. These piers were right out in the open. But that was the point.

Two theories of crime dominate the underworld. According to the first, crime is best carried out in secret, where no one can see and thus no one will know. That's true, but according to the second theory, the best way to keep something secret is to do it out in the open, to act like it's the most natural thing in the world. In other words, never whisper, always yell. That way no one will listen to you.

At dawn on June 25, 1976, six marijuana-laden sailboats appeared off the East Coast, tacking north. By Friday, July 2, the sailboats were anchored at the mouth of the Hudson. By July 3 they were just another group of toys in the tub. The Coast Guard was busy with inexperienced boaters, drunks falling overboard, idiots capsizing because of an ill-placed keg. There was so much work that they told people who broke down or ran out of gas to just drop anchor and someone would get them in the morning. No one bothered the gaggle of longhairs with bales and a fleet of U-Haul trucks.

At full dark, a firework show began. As a helicopter dragged a hundred-foot electric American flag above the Statue of Liberty, the masses sang "The Star-Spangled Banner." Meanwhile, eight tons of Colombian was on its way to the streets.

In the years following the bicentennial, Charlie and Willy grew rich together, selling an annual load, sometimes two, with eight or nine tons of Colombian marijuana apiece. Willy cleaned it of seeds and stems and most of the leaves, so there was no wasted weight, no wasted labor.

With the proceeds Charlie moved from Maine to a bungalow on St. Thomas with views of Magens Bay, a white sand beach that's among the most popular in the world. He founded Salty Dog Enterprises, a bullshit American postcard and beer jacket purveyor. Willy moved to St. Barts, where he bought a small house on a hill and then a big house on a higher hill.

Jimmy Buffett lived next door, and Willy and Jimmy played the same stage at Le Select, Buffett's Coral Reefer Band headlining over Willy's band, which was called Will He Make It in the Contraband. (As a matter of fact: Yes, he will.) After shows the party was either at Buffett's Autour du Rocher, a disco attached to a five-room hotel and an all-night jewelry shop, or at Willy's house, where the cherub statues never stopped tinkling chlorine and the pool stayed warm all night long.

In 1979 Buffett was arrested after he told *Rolling Stone* that he moved some marijuana through the islands, an admission since repeated hundreds of times from the stage. He later denied actually handling drugs but admitted that some of his best friends were dealers. He scattered one smuggler's ashes off the coast of Provincetown, dipping the wing of his seaplane in tribute. With his songs of island high jinks, Buffett added still more enchantment to the whole marijuana-running world, providing propaganda for the lifestyle in the late 1970s when lots of dealers were dropping out or switching to cocaine.

Charlie and Willy never wavered in their commitment to reefer. They discovered that their stateside partner was diversifying. He was a Boston guy, and he ran a combination of cocaine and weed, accepting shipments of both drugs in endless varieties, like a café collecting bags of coffee, breakfast buns, and cage-free eggs. It was bad news being tied to that kind of organization. If one of their far-flung smugglers fell, you can bet they'd try to take the whole ring down. So Charlie and Willy started asking around for a new contact, and they kept hearing the same name: the Old Man.

The trio met in the open air, cross-legged on a blanket my mother shook out. She arranged cheeses and breads, kneeling on the hem of her white skirt. My father leaned back on his hands and listened to the starlings call. He was barefoot with jeans rolled above the ankle, summer flannel cuffed to the elbow, unbuttoned to mid-chest. As the light faded he heard the first notes from the stage.

This was the Tanglewood Music Festival, a rolling series of concerts held every summer on a serene estate in western Massachusetts. My father and mother pointed themselves toward the Shed, the steel pavilion where Jimmy Buffett was due to perform that night, August 14, 1979. And what a picture they must have made: young lovers, nestled and comfortable, his body and hers in a pose they had taken years to perfect.

After Buffett took the stage Charlie and Willy arrived from the direction of the music, not the parking lot. Decades later, my father would remember that he hated them both on sight, but that's almost certainly a false memory, a mirage. In the pencil-sketch light of early evening my father would smile at the devil himself.

He shook their hands and showed his teeth, and then Charlie started shaking his head and wincing, as if each note from the stage were a tiny gleaming knife in his eardrum. "This son of a bitch can't play," he howled to my father's delight. "I told Jimmy, you need to hit a C there and you're hitting a D, but listen to this shit. He just can't do it." Willy unzipped a guitar and strummed it in time with his friend onstage, his eyes closed, the lyrics of "Treat Her Like a Lady" or "Come Monday" on his lips.

Charlie had once dated one of my father's drivers, who put the parties in contact. By coincidence they were all going to be in Maine in another week, so the flirtation could continue. My mother and father had rented a century-old cabin near the beach in Kennebunkport.

In the mornings Anthony went into town for coffee, where he lingered over his mug, sitting in an old diner booth, reading the paper and listening to the hypnotic sound of rubber tires rolling over gravel and then stopping. Charlie appeared and slid onto the bench across from him. He said, in so many words, "I know you know and we certainly know, so how about it?" He said, "Can you move product by the ton?"

For the first time in his career my father had no reason to lie. He felt like breaking into a countertop musical number to explain as much. But instead he just nodded and sipped coffee and waited for the next prickly soft echo of pressurized rubber on gravel.

"I'll have to talk to my crew," he said finally.

"Of course," Charlie said, and my father nodded again.

He was trying not to smile.

The secret to my father's bottomless potential was a man named Bobby, a connected Brooklyn kid, former navy man, and a city employee, a guy who lived beneath the lid of a Yankees cap, shoulders round and muscled, perpetually hunched, as if someone were trying to peer at his cards. He seemed to know everyone in the tristate area. If you needed a forklift by 3:00 p.m., Bobby knew who to call. He knew how to make it legit, too, with registration numbers, permits.

Bobby had a New York market, a network he'd cobbled together from his old neighborhood, where his father had pushed a fruit cart outside the factories and his mother had sewed name tags into uniforms. He joined the navy in 1971, worked the pantry on an aircraft carrier, stocking toilet paper, toothpaste, the basics. It turned him into an organized man. The ports of the Middle East and Asia turned him into a wise one.

He returned to Brooklyn, married young, and joined the Sanitation Department. "I'm a garbageman," he'd say brightly, because he never saw himself as a garbageman for life. The collection hours were 6:00 a.m. to 2:00 p.m., perfect for a fledgling pot dealer who could use the afternoon to make sales. He made his first big jump in the dope world in 1977, when he ran into one of my father's wholesalers at a Christmas party. This particular wholesaler, Nicky, was a friend of my father's from high school, a braggart who paraded around promising big loads from the Old Man, his bottomless connection. Bobby got an earful before midnight, secured a deal by dawn, and picked up the product a couple of weeks later.

Nicky met his customers at the northern end of the New Jersey turnpike at a rest stop: two trucks parked in opposite directions, windows rolled down. "From the Old Man," he would say, jerking his thumb toward the covered bed of his pickup. Bobby opened the tailgate and took his first whiff of the weed, which was spongy and yellow-green.

"Shit," he said, "how many can I have?"

All through 1978 Nicky added bales to Bobby's orders and Bobby sold them. But Nicky's big mouth became a problem. It was inevitable. He bragged to the wrong guy, who asked for a meeting, where Nicky brought his pickup loaded with reefer and his curious consumer brought a gun. It was a heist, and it meant the loss of a couple of hundred pounds of weed, maybe $100,000 worth.

In response my father cut Nicky from the deliveries list and handed all the business to Bobby, the only downstream dealer who could sell big enough to fill the role. Bobby was also the ideal behind-the-scenes complement to my father, who could be recklessly confident.

My father and Bobby met in a bar in Brooklyn to discuss Charlie's offer. It was typical for a gang to consider a new partnership. Everybody in the big-time dope world was incomplete: They had a source but no market, or a market but no source. Dope circles were always forming and reforming on this basis, molding into more interlocking configurations than the Olympic rings. Billy in Miami wouldn't mind what my father and Bobby got into as long as Billy still had a market.

But Bobby started shaking his head. "No," he said. "No, no, no."

They already had a second supplier. His name was John, a slaphappy bald man whom Bobby and my father adored, unspooling the hours inside the best bars in New York City, the three of them in love with one another like British boys between the wars. Howl, splutter, guffaw, repeat.

John was the son of a big New York State funeral-home family, and as a teenager, he'd distributed calendars with the home's name above every month, so you always know where to call for coffins. He went to college but fell in love with boats and crime stories, and in the late 1970s an older cousin showed him how to satisfy both loves at once. On an early smuggle, he spent a night at the Seamen's Club in St. Martin, slept with a Colombian hooker, hitched a first-dawn ride on a church bus, and still connected with a trawler full of the finest Colombian Gold. He could get all he wanted. He just needed a man like my father to sell it.

All of which is to say that Bobby was right: They didn't need Charlie and Willy.

They also didn't need any more trouble. The bigger my father got, the more people came crying for jobs, crying for extra bales, crying about seeds or stems or low-quality dope, crying about price. It was typical bullshit, which is why my father's reputation survived, but bullshit could still be dangerous. If a buyer was angry enough, he could rat you out or rob you or kill you. If he was reckless enough, he could invite violent crime or federal custody.

The very fact that Bobby and my father were partners was proof of the danger all around. Looking back Bobby viewed the robbery as a reason to stay low, limit the number of trucks on the road. My father viewed it as something in the rearview mirror. He viewed it as a reason to push down the pedal.

Next he brought Charlie's proposal to Ann, who agreed with Bobby. She had learned enough to distrust my father's crinkled smile. His mouth was always the most expressive part of his body. It was closed and bolted against distraction when he was thinking, and dropped into a little *u* when it was late and he was stewed. In the late 1970s, as his business grew, he used every version of that face every day, until the spectrum narrowed and narrowed into just dashes and angles and he toppled over, passed out on the floor.

For him the years were remarkable from a business perspective. For her, quite naturally, the years linger in memory as the period when they decided to start a family. It was something that bubbled out of my father one morning in bed. They lay body to body. A silver sky bled orange just over the tree line. I wish I could be more specific about what they were thinking. A teacher and her bleary-eyed boyfriend with the hefty business in contraband: The ideal parents? They had never been married, in part because they didn't want to mingle their finances. But they played their first round of high-stakes cosmic ring toss that very morning, hoping for the stuffed bear.

In retrospect my mother explains the decision as part of a grander plan, a fond hope that a child might subdue my father, who she worried about more than herself. Even when he was happy he was a man with a temper, a rage he could summon using the most basic raw materials: a sponge left in the sink, a dog leash gone missing. He peed on things: a balky radio, a smoking outboard motor. When his Mercedes broke down, he walked around to the hood, calm and spookily vague about what his plan was right up to the moment he squared his shoulders and unzipped. Which makes it sound kind of funny, but Ann heard reports of far worse than a golden shower.

My father owed Billy about $100,000, for the product that was taken at gunpoint, and to square the debt he agreed to deliver some furniture to Carolyn in Colorado. Billy still felt partly responsible for Carolyn's well-being, and Tony had the ledger at his antique business.

"Call it a sale," Billy said, and my father agreed.

He rented a U-Haul truck and headed west. But it vexed him to seem weak in front of his sister, and to fight his feelings he did lines of cocaine from Davenport to Des Moines. When he got to Colorado, where Carolyn was feeling really good for the first time in years, he went grinding up the mountain to Carolyn's house, accelerating through a little hollow—where he flipped the truck.

Carolyn ran out to see if her brother was okay, but when she saw him she went back inside and locked the door. After so much cocaine, it was as though he had turned to concrete inside, and so the flow of his normal emotions was faster, like a river pushed through a small corrugated tube and turned into a gusher. It was rage, and Carolyn knew it because she had seen it before in their father.

"It's astounding," she later told Ann. "The person he hated most was our father and there he goes and repeats all the sins. Like father, like son. It happens in societies all over the world—it's one of those wonderments."

By the fall of 1979, my father had decided to visit St. Thomas, where Charlie and Willy waited to talk about the next season of business. Bobby still thought the trip was crazy. He saw it in terms of exposure and evidence, as though he had access to the mind of a DEA agent. He could see the agent taking notes, talking into a two-way radio, asking for a detail on this Anthony Dokoupil. He could see the prosecutor pacing the courtroom, underscoring the extreme strangeness of Tony's sudden wealth and the coincidence that he hangs out with known drug dealers.

My father cornered Bobby before leaving. He wanted an assurance that Bobby could sell tons at a time if my father secured it. Bobby said he could, but he continued to press my father for a reason.

"Just promise me you'll sell it," my father said.

"Just tell me why," Bobby countered.

Lives turn forever on the power of small incidents, tiny bumps against the wheel of progress, making people hold on tighter and tighter, confident that when the wheel turns over again they will rise to the top of the arc. My father had such an incident in the weeks before his trip. He was in Miami with Billy, who had a few thousand pounds of weed in a stash house on Star Island between Miami Beach and the mainland. My father was due with his little convoy. But before he arrived, the police did. A nosy neighbor had dialed the force, who flushed Billy out back, where he threw his datebook into the bushes and rolled up his pants legs. He walked the shoreline to the bridge, climbed it, and stood with the fishermen. He rolled his pants legs back down. A patrol car picked him up anyway, perhaps because of the seawater pouring from his sneakers. The neighbor couldn't identify him, so he was cut loose.

It was simple luck that my father hadn't been parked in the driveway, simple luck that Billy hadn't been identified, a bang-bang moment of fortune and misfortune, as though both men had fallen out a window only to bounce off an awning, crumple into the shrubbery, and walk away with little more than torn coats.

Many men would have had a contemplative smoke, considered their loved ones, and either quit the business altogether or at least stuck with the safest possible partner and only one possible partner besides. But not the Old Man. For him a near miss had become part of the fun.

He boarded an island-bound flight in November 1979, the very same month that Ronald Reagan announced his candidacy for president, framing it in the language of sobering up and buckling down, of purging "past excesses" rather than reelecting Carter and seeing "this great country destroy itself." Although Reagan would later be called opportunistic and cynical, especially on drug policy, his disgust for marijuana was not a new or subtle accessory.

The country had changed enormously in the eighteen months since Peter Bourne had resigned in disgrace, tarnishing the pot movement in the process. As political reversals go, this one was unmistakable: as big and bizarre a reversal as War is Peace, Freedom is Slavery, Strength is Ignorance—Pot is Poison?

When Reagan declared himself, he was fresh from a major radio address on marijuana, mocking the way potheads wheeze on about the plant's harmless charms, "exhaling smoke on every line." He seemed to know that attacking marijuana would tap into a growing displeasure with wayward teens, slack productivity, and a society of apathetic Carter voters, seemingly content to sit out life in a duct-taped beanbag chair. He revealed what "science now knows," including the dubious "scientific facts" that smoking dope leads to cancer, sterility, and "adverse and irreversible effects on the mental processes."

My father alternately relished and ignored the new tenor from Washington, as did Charlie and Willy, who greeted my father inside Ferrari's Ristorante, a mid-scale Italian joint that Charlie owned. It was on the crown of the island, where the roads were etched into the mountain and a mistake meant a half-mile roll in the bush. Three men. Three Heinekens. Three mustaches. One career path. The buzz of the jungle outside beggared the electricity.

Willy told Buffett stories and generally clowned around like some general's kid or the heir to a public fortune. My father felt confirmed in his opinion of Willy as a pain in the ass, ostentatious and self-amused, like a jock reciting lines in a high-school play. Later that night when a woman asked him what he did for a living, Willy looked her straight in the eye, as though to say, You seriously want to know? He told her, "Terry cloth. I invented it."

My father heard Bobby's voice in his head: *Why do we need this idiot? He's a risk, a loudmouth. He's probably being watched by the feds already.*

The next day the trio ran out of cocaine, so my father called his gopher in Connecticut, who flew down a few more ounces of fun. Marijuana smuggling, like almost all major nonviolent crimes, is never really about the money. There has to be chemistry, and so far there wasn't.

The summit returned to Charlie's house, with its many hammocks and views of the faint white waves of Magens Bay, a thousand feet below. My father invited a couple of girls back from the bar, but they declined and it threw him into a funk, one that deepened when Willy excused himself to play a gig on St. Barts and Charlie's girlfriend came over.

Dad found his bed and slipped into it alone, feeling like a fool. He was ashamed of himself. What was he thinking coming down here, playing the big shot, defying his wife and his best friend and probably getting himself pinched at the same time?

He had the uneasy feeling of being in another person's thoughts, and just as he began to tell himself that it was the drugs talking, he heard a sound like footsteps on the path between Charlie's room and his own. He knew immediately that it was over. He was busted.

There was no use running. He got up and walked to the balcony, stared at the night sky, soaked in the profound sadness of the moment. He would never be a father. The footsteps grew louder, more distinct, unmistakable and numerous. He deserved what he got, but that didn't stop him from fearing it.

When the door opened, he had his back to it and it felt like his entire sensory system was located in between his bare shoulder blades. That's where the eyes of the law would first fall.

"Tony Dokoupil?"

He turned slowly, not wanting to get shot, too consumed by emotion to realize that the voices were female. He turned expecting grim, doughy-faced white men. Instead he saw two splendid women in white T-shirts and flimsily knotted white skirts, a brunette and a blonde. The women from the bar, he realized, and in that instant my father's mood moved from one pole to the other. Oh the shock. But oh the excitement, too, the knowledge that he was using the full register of experience rather than just a few clicks off the mean.

My father leaned down and kissed his new companions on the cheek, sweetly, then swung an arm around the brunette's hips and lassoed her to his side. He kissed her hard on the mouth, smashed his face against hers. She let him slide his tongue between her neat white teeth and into her mouth. The blonde took his hand and the hand of her workmate and dragged both bodies toward the bed, where she swung her own weight in a semicircle and pushed her colleague and her mark down. She tore her skirt off with the flourish of a magician, laughing, self-conscious, and the brunette did the same as best she could from the bed. Before my father fully knew what was happening, they were on him and it was over in more ways than one.

He and Charlie settled their business in the morning and my father went home content. He was moving out of frame again, his life off center, skewed, a series of glances at the mainstream, none more defining than the one he took with him into 1980, the rise of Reagan and the prospect of fatherhood. The high-toned responsibility of having a child did not subdue him, it enticed him. He loved the shadow of catastrophe, how it erased the elevator stillness of the everyday, the emptiness that made him quake with anxiety. A child gave my father a life, a reason to live, and thus something to lose—without which he might as well be betting with play money.

It also made him ashamed, or one has to assume, because he returned from St. Thomas with a tolerance for risk that seemed as much about fun as it was about self-erasure. He flew to Miami for a "breather," a few days of fun with Billy. No work, no stress. He threw $40,000 into a manila envelope and made his way to airport security. No one smuggles drugs into Miami, but they sure as hell buy them there, so for any flights from New England to Miami, you can expect the gate agents to be looking for stake money. That's why Billy had told him years ago that it's best not to fly with cash at all, or to check the bag and pick it up on the other end.

My father's bag went through the machine and was yanked off for searching. The agent went right for it and even Tony was shocked to see the envelope in the light of the airport. It didn't look official. It didn't even look like an envelope. It looked like a rectangle trying to be a cube.

"What's this?" the agent asked.

"Just my papers," Anthony said. "My business papers."

The agent turned the cube over in his hands.

My father's heart pounded and his head swam and he was hit with the realization that he was happy to have been caught, found, stopped before he could go on with his plans to bring new life into the world. He wanted to kiss this fat, beef-faced agent with the barely closed uniform and mace on his hip. He wanted to thank him, but some instinct made him protest.

"So what!" he broke in. "So I got a bunch of money. It's mine. It doesn't belong to anyone but me. I didn't break any laws. I can have money. I didn't steal it."

"How much money?"

Somewhere in my father's head he knew that $10,000 was a cut-off point for legal travel.

"About $9,000," he lied.

The guy shrugged and released my father back onto the path of destruction. His "breather" ended up being a two- or three-day binge at Billy's house. Women were called, professionals who brought with them professional tolerances. On the first night some sort of baby-oil orgy ruined the mattress in Billy's master bedroom, so he suggested a change of venue: the Sonesta Beach Hotel, one of the swankier resorts on Key Biscayne, a breakwater island between Miami and the coast of Africa. The chickadee huts by the shore shaded conventioneers and wedding parties. ABC booked the beach for skin-flick television specials. And the ocean was always there for those in need of a briny rebirth.

Billy doesn't much remember the party, but he does remember the moment the party stopped and his friend Anthony seized up on the couch, choking and sputtering, utterly unreal, as though his body were yellow rubber and his insides a cocktail of special effects cooked up for the big screen. Billy had to go knuckle deep into this strangeness and pull out my father's tongue. My father woke up like that—like a snake eating a man.

"What happened?" he asked, after Billy had withdrawn his paw.

"I was gonna ask you the same thing, asshole."

Afterward my father returned to the usual work of making a baby. He even gave Ann a gift to ignite the fires of procreation, a negligee from Lisa's in Coconut Grove. She opened it and smiled and took the piece into the bathroom, whereupon she noticed something wrong with it. Was it *used*?

She called her friend Connie, who was by then divorced from her own Anthony-like first husband and the proud owner of a Porsche Carrera RS. "Honey," she said. "Are we done yet?"

We were not.

My mother was feeling guilty. She had her own fling. He was older, powerful, crooked in a way that struck my mother as new and exciting. She met him as the buyer for the antique business. He was an auction-eer. After she bought a few of his pieces, they started working a little scam together. She went to all his sales and waved her number like a fan, bidding up the prices and batting her eyelashes.

A few months later Tony took his Miami act north, stowed away with a girl in a hotel off I-84 in Waterbury, Connecticut, and after spotting him at a party with this lady—who was pretty and clean but clearly not in it for love—Ann felt a bit differently about the whole relationship. She had an unfamiliar feeling of anger, which blossomed into fury, and she decided to confront my father. She found his room and knocked, and when he came to the door, a fight ensued. There were tears from him and pleas from her, and then a shift in the mood, a pebble-size change in the flow of the conversation.

Anthony became the agitated one. His whole existence narrowed to a single goal: to stop the yelling. He disappeared into the room and picked up his whittler's knife, the one he used to slice the twine on a bale of marijuana, the one I would find sitting innocuously in a drawer in Miami years later. With the three-inch blade extended, he threw it at Ann. If you want to be lawyerly about it, he tried to kill her, except he missed.

Ann called Connie again.

"Honey," she said. "Can we move on?"

We could not.

In love, more than any other human affair, you don't know what you're doing. You act and react. You run off in the direction of yes, flee in the direction of no, and sometime later you explain the decision in whatever way feels right. In the end the only thing for sure is what happened. And what happened was my mother stayed. She worked up the gumption to leave, but then she felt she couldn't do it because, finally, she was pregnant.

The month when it happened my father had been around more because he had been arrested. He had gone to Texas to help Billy and stayed to party with the buyer. The police found him spinning the wheels of a rental car outside a roadside bar, an open container of vodka sloshing around on the seat next to him.

My father was scared of being a father. He was so scared he tried to destroy himself, and when that didn't work he tried to destroy my mother. But when he could avoid it no more, he finally embraced it. He attended Lamaze classes and devoured the new books on children and parenting. One day he came home with bags and bags of almonds, unsalted, plain, whole almonds. He'd read that they were "brain food" for babies, so he sliced and crushed them onto three meals a day for Ann. Then he read to the bump and played classical music for the bump. Eight days before I was born, he wrote the bump a letter:

My Dear Baby,

I've been meaning to write you a few lines now for a couple weeks but have not had the time. Since the doctor gave mommy a due date of December 15th, you could be here any day now. We're both very happy and anxious to see you so we can show you our love and care. We have a nice maple crib for you with warm blankets and covers. Your room is yellow and has a bassinet in it from your Uncle Joseph and Aunt Ruth. There is also a nice antique dresser with a big beveled mirror for your little things. We haven't picked out a rug or curtains yet because we don't know if you'll be a boy or a girl. We could have learned your sex by using a sonar sound machine at the hospital that gives an outline of your fetal shape (and thus your sex) in mommy's uterus where you are, but it's based on x-ray radiation and mankind has not learned enough about it to satisfy Mommy and me that it wouldn't cause you or mommy any harm. We read about armed services veterans who have been exposed to various kinds of radiation during government tests of bombs (yes, my baby, Man builds bombs to kill other men), who have since developed cancer. So we can wait to see your sex at birth, rather than risk your health, so essential to happiness and success.

Love,

Dad

That Christmas eve this man who cared for his unborn child so much he would not risk sonar was in the delivery room as his part-ner gave birth. It was the coldest December on record in Connecticut, more than a dozen notches below zero, the snow measurable in feet, heaped in gray piles that lined the roads like dirty institutional laundry. My father was as calm as an anonymous Good Samaritan on the drive to Farmington Medical Center, where he was to coach my mother through the labor and then cut the umbilical cord.

A decade later my father wrote me a letter recounting what hap-pened that night at the hospital. I was turning ten, so of course "the story of the beauty of the miracle of your birth" was not exactly the first item on my wish list. In fact I have no memory of ever receiving the letter, so either my mother screened it, and then out of some muscle-memory reflex kept it, or I read it and part of my brain jumped on a live grenade to protect the rest of it.

It's a breathtaking document. My father is the same straight-backed Good Samaritan, although a little more cheerful and sparkly eyed. "Mommy and I were in the hospital waiting happily for you," he begins, "with mommy pushing and pushing and me next to her holding her hand and wiping perspiration from her face."

After three or four hours "you crowned," a term helpfully defined for me, a fourth grader, using the phrases "silver dollar sized patch" and "mommy's vagina." That set Dad up for his big conclusion: "So after a little while of waiting like this, the doctor decided to give mommy an episiotomy, that is, he cut her with a knife to make the birth canal bigger so you could come out. As soon as he did this, sure enough, there you were!"

My father almost passed out at the sight of me. An invisible hand smothered his face and crushed his chest. His vision went fuzzy, the world went gray, and his brain cried out for oxygen. The nurse held me by the foot, blood-specked and fish-belly white. She was yelling, "It's a boy, it's a boy," and waiting for my father to make his legs and arms work so he could cut the umbilical cord and wash me off in a tub of warm water. He tried to speak, to explain himself, but words turned to gum in his throat.

He ran into the bathroom and shut the door. He felt almost dead at the sight of new life, almost suicidal at the thought of how that life needed him. He patted his pockets, located a flip-lighter and a pinkie-size bone of his own imported Colombian reefer. He considered it medicine, a way to slow his breathing so he could think for a second.

One hit, two hits.

He was starting to feel better when the nurse banged on the door. Her voice was a serrated blade through his lungs. He cussed and put out the joint. How much time had passed? He had no idea. Smoke was everywhere. When the door opened the cloud ducked out and up and danced along the ceiling, looking for a way out. I was wrapped in a blanket, perched on my mother's chest.

"I have to take the baby," the nurse said.

"No!" my mother cried.

She looked at my father and waited for the nurse to do the same: "Take *him*!"

"I'm sorry, miss. I understand, but I have to take the baby."

It was only for the night, not forever, and by New Year's my father was holding his child, whispering hopes and dreams into my ear in a house full of love and friendship. These early moments, minus the dope scare, ended up in "Grandma's Brag Book," a little photo catalogue with, of all characters, Peter Rabbit on the cover.

What a heavy choice for a mass-market photo album. I happen to know the story of Peter Rabbit because I read it to my own son. It's about a little bunny whose father went into Mr. McGregor's garden and ended up dead and eaten, "put into a pie."

"Don't go into Mr. McGregor's garden," Mrs. Rabbit warns her only son. "Your father had an accident there." But the little bunny doesn't listen to his mother. He follows something else, something deeper and unexplainable. He follows in his father's footsteps, to see and feel what Dad saw, and he nearly dies in the process.

Mother was never one for deep readings, but she knew enough to silently resolve to "break the chain," to end the cycle of sons following fathers down through the generations to their doom. I discovered one of the reasons when my own son was an infant, and I called my mother late at night, telling her that the baby had croup, a barking cough that makes it hard to breathe.

She gasped, not because the baby was sick, but because she slid down the sound of my voice and into her past, to when I was an infant and had croup. She'd put me in a steam bath to clear my lungs, and she went to call the doctor, leaving Big Tony holding me in the shower mist. He put me down and shot up instead. He plunged the needle in where the forearm becomes bicep, where the veins crest for an instant, blue like a hidden river, and he sluiced in the heroin. It's a pretty part of the body, delicate and vulnerable. And yet mainliners call it "the pit," as in "Hit me in my pit," and when the needle gets done with it, it's not so pretty anymore. By some cosmic joke, I was born with a birthmark in my pit, a little chocolate splotch that I've decided is either a magic shield or a sign of the devil.

My father recovered himself and resolved something else entirely. His realization came while smoking another joint on his back porch in Connecticut in the spring of 1981, a few acres of woods and a stream spread before him, a handful of springy green buds on a black rolling tray in front of him. As he got high, he got reflective, and he picked up his product. He bounced it in his hand. He crushed it, breathing in the tang, feeling the sticky resin between his fingers. He put it back on the tray and just stared.

Two months before I was born Reagan was elected president, crushing Carter by nearly ten points. As a candidate, he'd branded marijuana "probably the most dangerous drug in America," an explanation for everything. Why is your teenager refusing to cut the lawn? Marijuana. Why is your industry falling behind Japan's? Marijuana. Why do you have to lock your door at night? Hard drugs—which start with marijuana.

Did this mean Anthony Edward Dokoupil was probably the most dangerous man in America? Was he the new public enemy? It was ridiculous. And yet even my father had to admit that he had become a massive drug dealer. Besides his work with Billy, he was selling through Willy, and as he thought about his new multiton scores, a still-grander image of himself formed like a beast in a forest clearing. He would be a smuggler extraordinaire, the Greatest of Great American Outlaws, a pirate of pot. If you were going to be such a figure in the '80s there was really only one city for you.

"Miami," my mother told friends. "It's a really healthy atmosphere."

4

The Pirate Code

My father was greeted like an arriving duke, which would not have pleased him so much if he'd known the reason. It was not an instinct about his character or even his money. It was the fact that he was there at all, in downtown Miami, sitting in a tulip chair at Flagler Federal Savings and Loan.

This was the spring of 1981, a third of the way through the most violent year since Miami incorporated in 1906. Rapes and muggings had doubled. Murders reached a national high. The death toll was so intense, the bodies such an unexpected flood, that the Dade County medical examiner expanded his morgue space, leasing a refrigerated meat truck from Burger King.

The city had been hit by a trifecta of big, ugly national stories, starting in 1979, when gunfire interrupted a weekday afternoon at the Dadeland Mall, one of the largest shopping centers in America. A white van with "Happy Time Complete Party Supply" stenciled on the side dropped off two men with MAC-10 machine guns. They walked into a store near the entrance to JC Penney, shot one man in the face, and sprayed another man with so many bullets that the coroner later gave up counting the holes. So started the Cocaine Wars, an ongoing bloodbath orchestrated by the cartels of South America as they wrestled for territory.

The following year brought one of the goriest race riots in modern American history. It began on a Friday evening, after an all-white jury acquitted four white police officers in the beating death of a young black insurance agent, a former marine with four children. By Saturday a young white man, not unlike my father, took a wrong turn on his way home from the beach. He was dragged from his car, hit with a block of concrete, stabbed with a screwdriver, bludgeoned with a metal newspaper box, run over by a car, and left with one ear lopped off and his tongue cut out, facedown on the tarmac. When authorities rolled him over, they found a red rose in his mouth.

That same year Fidel Castro decided, "I'll flush my toilets." He opened up prisons and insane asylums, and put their occupants onto rust-blotched freighters and listing fishing trawlers so full they carried people in their nets. Many of the 120,000 Cubans who made the trip were law-abiding or merely criminals by Castro's puritan definition. But thousands were indeed hard-core thugs, people whose creative business style inspired the chain-saw-to-brain scene that would appear in *Scarface* a couple of years later.

Put it all together and by 1981 Miami was "a boiling pot, not a melting pot," in the measured words of the mayor. The Miami Beach commissioner warned of "absolute war in our streets," and a member of Miami's Special Homicide Investigation Team (yes, the SHIT squad) called the city "the most dangerous place on earth." As though confiding in my father personally, the governor of Florida added, "If you want sustained stability, don't come to Miami."

My father came to Miami. He was an oddity, in other words, a statistical anomaly, the only lonely white person heading to Miami for every ninety who fled the city, according to canceled voter registration cards. That's why his handler at Flagler dispatched a beautiful young broker whose cheeks glowed like crushed flowers. She met my father in a new Cadillac, and they eased into traffic on Biscayne Boulevard, the most notorious city in America opening before them.

For Cubans and Haitians and thousands of other immigrants, Miami was a place to be different, a land with the same air and sun but none of the limiting physics of their homeland. For men like my father, Miami was a place to be more intensely the same, to join a hundred thousand other members of the drug world in the tropical sun.

Besides, Miami had charm. Every T-shirt in south Florida seemed pushed to its structural limits. Sleeves torn off, great vents slashed into the fabric, revealing rib cages and lower backs. Some of the more casual tops only looked like T-shirts but were in fact simple beach towels, modified by a hole cut in the middle, then thrown on like a Caribbean riding coat. Young women, as my father could not fail to notice, walked dogs and smoked cigarettes in bikinis no larger than the remnants of a burst balloon.

Just off MacArthur Causeway, half a dozen cruise ships glistened at the docks, a skyline set afloat and lying on its side. Behind them the real downtown loomed soft-edged in the heat, shuddering as though still rising from the swamp. Even at two in the afternoon everything pulsed sorbet shades of mint and fuchsia.

My father and his escort floated through Coral Gables, spun around the traffic circle at Cocoplum Plaza, and merged onto Old Cutler Road. Right there, just south of Coconut Grove, through a tunnel of banyan trees and belly palms, he found a nice three-bedroom in the biggest planned community in southern Florida. Across the street there was a park and a lagoon. On the ceiling of the master bedroom was a mirror. My father was home.

For most of the next three years my family sat level on life's great seesaw. My mother left her teaching job in Connecticut and became a full-time homemaker, aided by a cleaning lady, pool guy, and lawn team that attacked the property on a weekly basis. I took my first steps in the neighborhood park, my hair a lopsided puff of white cotton candy.

Business boomed. Dad sold more than twenty thousand pounds of Colombian Gold in 1980. He did it again in 1981 and again in 1982. Each scam was cautious, clean-minded, and disciplined. It worked like this: Charlie and Willy got an old tanker or tugboat of weed from Colombia to the Caribbean islands. From there the load was parceled out to private sailboats, some of which belonged to unwitting East Coasters who paid to have their yachts moved north for the season. Timed to blend in with regatta traffic, the sailboats headed for summer spots: Chesapeake Bay, Cape Cod, the Hamptons, and other points as far north as Maine. Charlie kept the vessels outside American waters until they sailed north past Nova Scotia, where they turned and hugged the coast, heading south and therefore attracting less interest as potential drug boats.

My father and Bobby met the bales wherever they made shore. They bought a seventeen-foot refrigerated rig with MARIO'S FISH painted on the side and a twenty-six-foot vehicle marked GLOBAL MOVING. They secured a warehouse in a rancid, tumble-down section of Brooklyn, way out near the Atlantic. And they took every precaution. They rotated stash houses, fired workers who showed up high or drunk. Although they felt like heroes—like four-star generals in the dope brigade—they acted like nobodies. They were shiny stressed-out faces in traffic, the embodiment of nothing to see.

In the Reagan years many dope rings switched to cocaine, which was an easier smuggle and a more profitable sale. To gross the same million dollars, a cocaine dealer needed to sell a mere thirty pounds of an odorless product small enough to fit in a backpack, while my father moved more than a ton of bulky, pungent plant matter you'd be lucky to fit in a pickup truck. Cocaine was Tinker Bell. Marijuana was the Big Green Elephant.

My father and his friends looked down on the cocaine dealers, the more famous of Miami's outlaws. Cocaine struck them as a lower-class criminal enterprise, the domain of a different kind of outlaw, who would make poor company for gringos with college degrees and vegetarian tendencies.

The cocaine cowboys were sports cars, speedboats, discos, machine guns, and cleanly shaven faces. The marijuana dealers were pickup trucks, sailboats, acoustic guitars, baseball bats, and Pancho Villa mustaches. As a public nuisance they were the buzz-muffle of an airplane over your house at midnight, the glow of brake lights on the highway. The cocaine cowboys murdered cops and bribed judges while marijuana dealers tipped their caps at the law and wished their competitors a happy chase. The marijuana dealers were in some ways never more than kids in paper pirate hats, playing in the yard, burying tinfoil-wrapped chocolate doubloons.

They were not killers. At least not to themselves.

Reagan took a different view. He announced a War on Drugs, which was foremost a war on marijuana, and he made the metaphor real. For the first time since prohibition the Coast Guard fired on American ships suspected of smuggling. For the first time since the Civil War the military pursued domestic criminals. For the first time ever the FBI and CIA joined the hunt for narcotics. And in the process the hey-man hippie merchants of marijuana were redefined as true enemies of the state, pursued like terrorists, prosecuted like armed combatants, vilified like pirates.

It's hard to believe it all really happened. A ragtag army of Vietnam-era castoffs, cokeheads, and beach-bum marijuana dealers squaring off against all the toys of the Cold War. It sounds like a bad movie, something on the same shelf as kid ninjas save the universe, and yet . . .

Navy pilots really did buzz the coast in hot pursuit of smugglers. Massive four-prop air force radar planes really did circle the Caribbean, spying on foreign ports and looking for the beep-beep of a mother ship. Between the first joint my father ever sold in 1972 and the ten tons or so he sold in 1982, the federal budget for drug enforcement rose twentyfold, from $43 million to nearly a billion dollars.

To justify that kind of war chest, the Reagan administration resurrected old ideas about marijuana's virulence and added a few new ones, spread with the help of a war-joyous press corps. *Family Circle* ran a story about marijuana's "slow erosion of life"; *Reader's Digest* covered pot's "devastation of personality"; *Science News* unveiled a landmark study "proving" that marijuana is "a cause of heroin use," a line picked up by the new parent activists, who began talking about all those pot-smoking teens as "pre-addicted" junkies.

The government won over parents by making sure the pot problem felt ubiquitous. The telltale signs of teen marijuana included "keeping late hours," "schoolwork suddenly gone bad," and being "furtive about phone calls," according to *Parents, Peers and Pot*, the most requested U.S. government publication of all time. Some versions added "not doing chores," "forgetful of family occasions (birthdays, etc.)," and "not cutting grass." The First Lady echoed these risk factors in an interview with *U.S. News & World Report*: "Children [who smoke pot] get very laid back and cool," she advised. "They undergo a personality change, become combative, secretive, unable to get along with the family."

Clearly, something had to be done.

In June 1982, Reagan appeared in the White House garden to officially declare his intentions. "We're taking down the surrender flag that has flown over so many drug efforts; we're running up a battle flag. We can fight the drug problem, and we can win. And that is exactly what we intend to do." Marijuana was the only drug to merit specific mention.

The hysteria continued in a wave so big that it swallowed all boundaries, made it impossible to go too far. Dealers were compared to vampires, murderers, and traitors. And before long the War on Drugs began to sound like a comic-book battle between good and evil, which is why the absolute best gauge of the times is when the War on Drugs actually became a comic-book battle between good and evil.

In 1983 DC Comics, the publisher of *Superman* and *Batman*, produced a special issue of its New Teen Titans series, a superhero story aimed at elementary-school readers. The Titans battled a "Plague!" of drug pushers "who couldn't care less if kids died using their garbage."

Foom! Klang! Krak!

The gang clobbered the skulls of a remorseless drug ring. But they were too late! Three kids overdosed and died before the Titans could save them. In every death pot was a gateway to the underworld. Speedy, the battling bowman, was himself once a pot-smoking teen; he's wiser today. "They said pot had no bad side effects. That was before they did further research."

On the back page of the comic Ernest J. Keebler, the noted Dutch American political scientist, cookie maker, and magical elf, made a patriotic case for drug-free living. "When the Founding Fathers wrote the Declaration of Independence in 1776, they were announcing to the world that America would be free from the control of another nation," Dr. Keebler wrote. "When we make a declaration to stay away from drugs, we are saying to others and to ourselves, that we are in control of our own lives." But it was Nancy Reagan who set the tone. "Picture yourself in a battle," she wrote in a letter on White House stationery, on the inside front cover of the comic book. "In fact, it is one of the most important battles our nation has ever fought."

My father gathered the daily grenades against his profession and tossed them back at his attackers. This was hard for politicians and parents to understand, but all high-level drug dealers and most low-level dealers felt superior to politicians and parents. It didn't matter that Reagan and his cronies called them beasts because in some grander sense they thought of themselves as beauties, their works not vile breaches of the social code but good and proper extensions of it.

Reagan could call drug abuse "a repudiation of everything America is," but the drug dealers went on feeling like the bedrock of the nation. They were self-made, self-directed, self-styled. They broke laws but they obeyed the natural commandments. They were good talkers, fine dressers, friends to women and children. As far as my father was concerned, he and his friends were American in the extreme.

The outlaw is "our fighting vicar against aristocracy, against power, against law, against the upstart, the pretender, the smugly virtuous, and the pompously successful person or corporation whom we envy," in the words of Emmett Dalton, an early twentieth-century bank robber who became a professional scriptwriter after prison. The outlaw, Dalton concluded, "is our hero of democracy."

Every morning my personal hero woke at about nine, taking a habitual line of coke off of the antique dresser next to his bed. The table bloomed with loose cash and a glistening gold Rolex, a gift from good old Billy after one of my father's daredevil smuggles out of the Keys. Through the window he could see a tinkling blue pool and tiled patio, framed on three sides by a small but glorious lawn. Each blade of grass was as green as a basic green crayon, as thick as a butter knife, and always wet with warm dew or rain—an instant foot treatment for whoever walked to the plantain tree for cereal toppings.

In the kitchen he drank orange juice, still shirtless, rubbing his belly, massaging his chest, imagining the juice as it filled the dark places inside him. He swallowed a multivitamin, which he swore he could feel healing his broken chromosomes. When he was done, he looked at two-year-old me in my Jet Set jean shorts and striped Ocean Pacific polo shirt, and he did something twitchy with his mustache—my cue to run and hide, beginning the daily drama of hot pursuit, a game he loved as much I did.

Before the sun got too high we changed into our bathing suits and headed for the beach. My mother was always in a one-piece, even before she had me, but this wasn't a mommy suit. It was cut high around the thighs, low around the top, and it stretched drum-tight around the mid-section. The belly was a work of art—a great Warholian screen print—and she looked like some kind of novelty drink, the sort of beverage a cartoon alcoholic dreams up on a dry island. My father lifted her upward for a kiss as though the tilt might spill something cold and boozy and absolutely delicious.

We headed to the Sonesta Beach Hotel, which did double-duty as one of my father's favorite hangouts for partying and parenting alike. The poolside bartender Geno made a name for himself by pouring sweet rum into the straws of his piña coladas and daiquiris, and my father went to see him or a deputy right away. He downed the first drink, sipped the second, and started walking toward the water.

As my mother anchored an umbrella and unfurled towels at a safe distance, my father pointed his chest toward the midmorning sun, took off his shirt and sandals, listened for a moment to the roll of the waves and the hiss of the tide, and returned to us ready for his nip of fatherhood.

Anyone walking by would have seen a loving dad, a pillar of his community, the perfect family man. He smashed his mustache into the top of my head, smelling me in that deep, needful way parents have with their kids. We played Wiffle ball in matching Speedos, and that night he and my mother took showers and put on clean clothes and forgot they were parents and drug dealers.

On such nights my father looked at Ann and remembered their first drive together in his dented green Dodge Dart, her body sunk down into the seat, a flowery skirt over her perfect knees. She'd rolled down her window and put her brown toes on the dash and smiled that boozy smile.

Over the years they slurped cream of escargot soup, used those tiny silver spoons for salmon mousse and Grand Marnier soufflé, downed oysters at the Miami River Raw Bar. They drank Margaux and Lafite and perfect simulacrums of a Havana daiquiri. My mother's evening wear was rayon Peruvian island knit. My father did all his shopping at Neiman Marcus and Saks Fifth Avenue, depending on which was closer to his parking spot.

One night at the Hotel St. Michel in Coral Gables, they drank too much wine, did too much coke, and were gently tossed out, the check appearing at my father's elbow, the waiter whispering something deferential but clear. Outside my father dropped $20s and $50s at the feet of street performers, and folded the same into the change cups of the homeless and hungry. That was Anthony Edward Dokoupil at thirty-six: high and wild, generous and kind.

Before Thanksgiving 1982, he appeared in the palm-fringed lobby of the Miami Herald Building on Biscayne Bay, where he donated $10,000 to the annual food drive. That same year his sidekick, Dougie, my mother's younger brother, was diagnosed with cancer. My father gave him painkilling strains of weed throughout the chemotherapy process. He also helped pay for many of his procedures, including the cost of freezing his sperm. A decade later Dougie became a dad.

Our daytime family default was one of the jungles, Parrot or Monkey, both of which offered regal creatures riding bicycles and buttoning their own Oxford shirts. At the planetarium, we ran our hands over a piece of glacier and grinned inside a pair of diving bells. At the Seaquarium, my father disappeared altogether, leaving my mother in the awkward position of explaining to me what that long purple thing was and why the whale was rubbing it against our side of the ring. Dad's timing was always good that way.

They pushed my stroller through the Coconut Grove Arts Festival, the Key West Arts Explosion, and Art in the Heart of Miami Beach, walking around like albino elephants sniffing the shooters on a hunting preserve. They bought things in pairs and triplicate. It was all a good deal, all certain to appreciate in value. There were the three banana portraits, including "skid row banana" and "junior never learned to look both ways." The dramatic chair sculpted out of a single hunk of wood, which mostly went on to future service collecting wet towels. The American flag wristband with attached eagle sculpture.

Every few weeks we took a family outing to Vizcaya, a Gatsby-esque villa built for the millionaire cofounder of International Harvester. The mansion is a dream of antique grandeur with ten acres of gardens, fountains, statues, and reflecting pools. As I ran around on lawns thick enough to stumble on without injury, Mom and Dad sat on white wrought-iron benches, fingers interlocked, their perfect lives in fullest bloom.

"Shall we buy it?" my father said, and he felt as though he really could.

Mom said, "Definitely," and felt like she already owned it.

Part of the fun of being a criminal is the crisp satisfaction of living by the criminal's code. Forget the U.S. justice system, the pope, your parents, God, the devil: The criminals themselves decided criminal conduct, like ten-year-olds in a tree house. All in favor? Yea. Now pull up the rope ladder and let's write some bylaws for the life.

First of all, no guns.

Second, a handshake is binding; your word is your signature.

Third, everyone shares equally in success, suffers equally in failure. It doesn't matter who's at fault. Legal fees come out of everyone's take.

Fourth, keep your mouth shut. No rats.

Fifth, and this is nonnegotiable, no drugs during a job.

The motto: "I'm okay, you're okay."

These were the real rules of my father's trade, bylaws of the brotherhood, a code nowhere written down but known by all, breathed in like a mist and spread through the gang and beyond, permeating the pot underworld. There was honor among the scammers and it was talked about to the point of cottonmouth.

An extended declaration of the smuggler's code would include a ban on selling cocaine, a prohibition on partnering with the American Mafia, and a moratorium on physical violence. It would end with a pious declaration, a finger pointed at the real enemy, the unjust War on Drugs, and the real criminals, Ronald Reagan and all who support him.

My father's criminal code was mostly an homage to another group of men, a clan all marijuana smugglers seem to have been sweet on: the pirates of the Caribbean, the real ones, who had a real golden age from about 1715 to 1725.

In many ways, the era of piracy and the era of pot are an uncanny match. Both the pirates and the marijuana smugglers cursed and cussed, sang bawdy songs, gambled, whored, profaned the holy days, gave in to lust, reveled in uncleanliness, and were greedy for life, liberty, and merriment, which they gulped down to the last.

They shared the same latitudes and the same appetite for intoxication, the pirates indulging in hogsheads of claret and brandy, the marijuana merchants indulging in everything invented since. "Sobriety," wrote one eighteenth-century pirate scribe, "brought a man under subject of being in a plot." He need not update the line for marijuana smugglers.

They also shared florid personal styles and working titles, from Calico Jack to Bubba Capo, as inspired as their facial hair. Edward Teach, aka Blackbeard, had "a Large Quantity of Hair, which, like a frightful Meteor, covered his whole Face, and frightened America more than any Comet," in the words of one of his biographers. My father walked into a room mustache first, jawline obscured by fuzz, hair to his collar.

But there are even deeper parallels. The pirates were angry about being "pressed" into the Royal Navy; the smugglers fumed about Vietnam. The pirates protested the lightless horizons belowdecks on the world's biggest ships; the smugglers rejected the air-conditioned anthill of their parents' America.

Both groups of men also stepped onto a stage prepared by forerunners going back thousands of years to the first pirates, the oldest spiritual guerrillas. Both were called Robin Hoods, the pirates because they stole from the rich, the smugglers because they defied the powerful to give pleasure to the poor, or at least an intellectual underclass that didn't trust money or power. Both operated in bands, clasped into a brotherhood, a confederacy of overlapping, interlocking, endlessly splintering and cohering groups.

And for both sets of men money was never the point. The pirates lived for plenty, satiety, pleasure, and ease, punctuated by the wild drama of adventure. "A merry life and a short one" was the motto of Bartholomew "Black Bart" Roberts, reportedly the most prolific pirate of the golden age. The smugglers of course would heartily agree. As Jimmy Buffett sang at the time, "I made enough money to buy Miami, but I pissed it away so fast. Never meant to last."

The arc of their lives matched as well. In the beginning both groups had an abiding sense of social mission. The pirates, as one captain put it, wanted "to revenge themselves on base Merchants, and cruel Commanders." The marijuana smugglers wanted the personal liberty to toke up. The pirates saw themselves as relatively harmless, secure, in the words of one eighteenth-century journalist, that "Whatever Robberies they had committed, they might be pretty sure they were not the greatest Villains then living in the World." The marijuana smugglers would drink to that.

And the very reason pirates still glow in our imagination is largely a matter of the pirate's code, which was a real document, a way to behave in the midst of epic misbehavior. The pirates conformed to a pattern of nonconformity just as the smugglers acted rationally in the service of irrational excess. The articles of agreement, as they were known, restricted pirates from drinking on the job, required clean weapons, and specified an orderly way to divide a bounty, including arranged compensation for the injured. Protests were put to a vote, amendments added, disagreements settled more or less peaceably.

The historian Marcus Rediker thinks that pirates, through their example of a democratic, fair, and tolerant society, "built a better world." If one believes that marijuana is good for mankind—that it's a powerful medicine, a door to meditation and knowledge; that it makes people more peaceful and fills them with love for all living things; that if it were consumed more there would be less war, conquest, avarice, and suffering—then my father and his brothers in the business succeeded as pirates did. They "built a better world" through weed.

Unfortunately they also suffered as pirates did. Both groups inspired new laws, treaties, and task forces, and over time both groups let their mission drift, their discipline waver. They grew drunker on the job, more daring in their exploits, less interested in a grand social cause than in sex, drugs, and survival itself.

The number of pirates slipped from the thousands in 1715 to the hundreds a decade later. Scores were arrested, hanged, and then displayed as a warning to all who might turn toward the life. Many were honorably antiestablishment until the end. But the vast majority ended up beggarly, disabled, or jailed, and many suffered all three before sleeping in a pauper's coffin. Pirates sailed under the black flag and died under it. Marijuana smugglers worked in the service of freedom and lost their own in the process.

This last fact lit a slow fuse in my father's brain. Even as he enjoyed a marooning life of movies at noon and fatherhood by the heart-swelling hour, he boiled with forbidden euphoria. It's the kind of kick that changes a person.

My mother picked up the call in the kitchen.

It was Billy's wife, the mother of his two little girls, and she had bad news: Billy had been busted. It was the summer of 1981, my first summer of life. With Miami in turmoil, and my father on a kind of paternity leave, Billy had taken a job in South Carolina, a break from the normal routine of Key West drops and long, dangerous drives north.

The job had gotten off to an auspicious start. Billy met a girl at a bar the first night he was in South Carolina. As a rule, smugglers believe that trucks with innocent pretty women in them are less suspicious than trucks with guilty mustachioed men. So he invited the girl along for his job, explaining the whole plan and enjoying the way she seemed to hang on his every word. Such was the ego of the true American outlaw that Billy and my father assumed—I mean really believed—that every girl wanted to sleep with them.

The next day Billy left the stash house with more than a ton of Colombian dope in the back of his pickup truck, the girl riding along beside him. He stopped at a four-way intersection feeling fine. He noticed some workers were laying pipe or cable along the road to one side. One of them, a ham-and-egger in a hard hat, jeans, and an orange vest, walked over slowly as if he were about to let Billy know about a cement truck pulling in.

At the door he pulled a gun from beneath his vest and with that the whole job site sprang to life. "DOWN ON THE GROUND! DOWN ON THE GROUND!" For an instant Billy thought to run, and he turned to his companion—this poor girl—but she too had produced a badge and a gun and had Billy against the door of the cab, and then out of it, and as he laid down on the pavement he saw a cop pull a shotgun out of a parking cone.

Billy pled guilty to possession with intent to distribute more than two thousand pounds of marijuana. One of his men fled to Tahiti and never returned; he could have stuck around. Billy was a good pirate, a stand-up guy, as they say. He didn't tell on people; it was a state charge, anyway. He was sentenced to two years of mechanic work on a farm in central Florida, where he turned bolts and met his children at wooden picnic tables.

When my mother first heard that Billy had been busted, she was consumed by fear, a great tide of emotion she had been swallowing for years, tamping it down with all the good in her life. She was not exactly like other mothers, however; she was a little more of a gambler. Rather than thinking about her exit strategy ahead of a similar disaster, my mother began to think about how she might mitigate the losses, maximize the gains.

She wanted to break the chain, but she calculated that if Big Tony were busted, she would have no choice but to become an overworked single mother with a kid in a crowded public school. She saw no point accelerating such a change, so she committed herself to staying with him, saving money for the one thing the government could never seize: an education for me.

It wasn't easy. She sometimes ran into old friends and it would occur to her that they were not raising a drug dealer's child; they were not defying their president and risking their freedom. She began to have bad dreams, visions of the jackboots in her flower bed, the battering ram at her door. But she had a plan and she stuck to it.

Not that it was easy for my father, either. He liked to talk about skill, but as law enforcement personnel at all levels jockeyed for victory, the dope business became almost a pure gamble. Customs agents ran patrols called "goat gropes" along the waterfront roads and marshes of the East Coast. The Coast Guard applied "random boarding" at port. The DEA stopped people at airports for "walking slowly, walking quickly, being very tense," or "appearing cool," according to a published report. Even cases that resulted more from classic police work often began with a tip from some idle person, happy for the chance to display their smarts.

Hardly a week went by without a perp walk, drug-on-the-table press conference, or raw video footage from the latest raid. In Florida the DEA confiscated so much weed, it borrowed a circus tent from Ringling Brothers in order to store it all. (The feds couldn't just burn marijuana like lawn clippings. When Kentucky state troopers had tried that, they complained of "light-headedness" near the bonfire.)

The acid drip of this kind of anxiety began to eat at my father by 1983, shortly after Reagan declared "all-out war on big-time organized crime and the drug racketeers who are poisoning our young people." He asked Congress to fund 1,200 new investigators, 200 new prosecutors, and a dozen regional task forces. The New England office of the Organized Crime Drug Enforcement Task Force in Boston opened a file, which would grow to contain my father's life and the lives of his friends.

In St. Thomas, Charlie sat at a bar called Horsefeathers, a burger-and-beer joint built into a grounded schooner, spitting distance to the water. In St. Barts, Willy hung around Le Select, a whitewashed open-air café where he and Buffett played and locals danced on crushed shells. Undercover agents, out-of-place men dropping conversational hooks and snares, cased both joints.

And in Miami my father felt the appraising eye of the city's new super-narcs: righteous DEA jocks with lats that jumped from shoulder to ear, wiry FBI agents with mother-of-pearl snaps on their gun holsters. Every day his nervous system dealt with the fact that the vice president, the First Lady, the commander in chief, every functionary and official beneath them, the might of the American military, all the law enforcement in the land, and a thousand parent groups had pledged to hang him. Mix in a new baby and enough white powder to substitute for flour in the world's largest cake, and it's no wonder my father began to make some unusual business choices. If you were to graph his net worth and his brain-cell count, the lines would make a perfect X, with his money piling up as his mind boiled away.

At around the $500,000 point, criminal proceeds become a significant headache until they're stored properly. In the best-case scenario, drug money is washed through a legitimate business. But that became harder to do under Reagan. The IRS had gotten aggressive in its pursuit of all financial irregularities.

My father kept $100,000 to $200,000 in a Miami safe-deposit box, inside a small mirrored building of safe-deposit boxes. He was a philosophy minor in college, so he chose "Plato" as his access password. But he didn't trust safe-deposit boxes. To put money in a box in broad daylight rather than an FDIC-backed savings account always struck him as more or less an admission of criminal behavior. So in 1983 he started creating his own safe-deposit boxes. All it took was an Igloo cooler, sandwich baggies, rubber bands, a caulk gun, and a shovel.

No one knows how many money wells my father made, least of all him, but Connie's shed on Long Island barely shut with all my father's shovels inside. He definitely put $100,000 in her garden and $200,000 in the soft ground near her woodpile. There exists a picture of my father and me standing in front of that woodpile, sometime around Thanksgiving judging by the weight of our coats. I'm about five, holding a football and smiling. My father has his hands on his knees, and he's smiling too, like he's very proud of my college fund underfoot.

Burying money, of course, was even more incriminating than a safe-deposit box. The DEA tested money for mildew, moisture, and other signs of "unconventional storage." Faded, mummified money was automatically suspicious. But in my father's ever more cloudy state of mind, this seemed like the best possible path to go down, and he went down it again and again. Then he got a brighter idea.

In June 1983 my mother took me to her family's cottage on Cape Cod, the same cottage she had visited as a child. It's a modest rectangle, but the road to the front door is soft sand and the bay is visible from the porch. It's also the only red house on the block, in addition to being ours, and we loved it. I spent the first six summers of my life there, and parts of many of those that followed.

My father sometimes found time to fly into Hyannis or drive the arm of the Cape and stay for a couple of weeks. Simple summer fun, it would seem, but life with my father in 1983 had become a splotchier experience. Richard, a ruddy Boston lawyer who is widely remembered as "Always a Dick to me!" and his partner, a young stockbroker, joined us for some knock-around fun.

On the Fourth of July they packed an arsenal of illegal explosives into fat polyurethane pipes, causing everyone else on the beach to huddle together in the background, watching through splayed fingers. But the purpose of the visit was more business than pleasure. These guys specialized in investing dirty money in legitimate ventures, and the venture they were pushing that summer was Carolin Mines—a Canadian company forecast to become the biggest gold producer in North America.

With the dollar unsteady, gold prices were soaring, Dick explained to my father, and the world's other big-producing countries had baggage that turned off gold buyers. Daddies want to give their little girls a pendant, not fund an evil empire. Canada was clean by comparison, and Disney might as well have invented Carolin Mines for the movies. The mother lode was known as the Idaho. The closest town was called Hope. It was all located in remote British Columbia, shouting distance to Alaska and the famous Yukon, and for confirmation, my father didn't need to hire a dog sled. He could read about it in *Barron's* and *The Wall Street Journal*.

Granted, the mine hadn't actually begun producing yet. There had been some construction delays, funding problems, a cyanide spill, two environmental shutdowns, a weak dam, thousands of dead salmon, and hundreds of very angry townspeople downstream. There was also some market volatility. Shares of Carolin were trading for 20 cents in 1980, and peaked near $60 in 1982. In 1983 they were somewhere in between those numbers. But after a "tuning up process," as the company called it, the mine was primed to reach its potential.

Not everyone knows that, Dick said. The time is now.

My father took long walks on the beach to think about it. His long walks were always with our dog, Captain, the purebred black Lab that my father bought precisely for moments like this, when he saw himself as though from the porch of a house along his route, a woman in a sundress tracking him with binoculars, his every movement heavy with significance.

"Darling," he could almost hear the binocular woman say, calling her husband down from his stepladder, where he was hanging an American flag. "Who is that beautiful man with the beautiful dog?"

"Why, it's Anthony Dokoupil, dear. I have seen him around, and made a point about finding out more. I hear he's some sort of drug dealer."

"Well, my heavens. I only know him for his fireworks."

The only hitch in this reverie was the dog. My father refused to neuter him, never trained him, could not control him. The dog humped anything that moved, pissed on everything that didn't.

"I'm going to kill that dog," my father roared when he came back inside.

"What happened?" my mother asked, knowing she could probably guess.

"He pissed on some lady," my father said.

My mother laughed.

He may have hit her right then, just as her face broke, when the lip was taut. Or he may have stored the anger away and pounded her the next day or the day after that. The lip was split just the same, and the emergency room doctors heard about a balky cabinet or slippery floor at that red house on the sandy lane.

Ann told Connie and Connie was once again ready to help her run, taking me along. But this was my father's worst transgression in years. He apologized profusely for it. Anyway it was just a slap. Not a punch or a knife. Not worth uprooting plans. Because how else would my mother pay for private school?

Later that year, my father gave Dick and his partner the first installment of what would become a $660,000 off-the-books investment in Carolin Mines. He told my mother that this was their nest egg, and she believed him.

He was the same kid he was at the Beachcomber, talking about books he wanted to read, one he wanted to write, his hair vibrating as he spoke. Life was hard, scary, but that summer he was sure the wheel of progress was pulling him skyward, never doubting his direction until it was too late to change it.

In the fall of 1983, after the marijuana season was over, my father had his first grand mal seizure, a total convulsion of body and mind, akin to what doctors induce through shock therapy, only without the benefit of a soft bed, a body strap, and a rubber mouth guard. When the musician Eric Clapton had one in 1978, it was enough to scare him sober. He woke up in a hospital bed, declared rock bottom, and founded a rehab center with all the money he saved not doing drugs. My father did not.

At least five more times that fall my father lost consciousness. He heard voices and woke up with empty pockets. What he could not have known, and no one ever told him about, was what his face looked like, vacant as a corpse, and what his body did when his brain flicked back on and his muscles twitched with the roar and crackle of life. Some people call it the funky chicken dance, which makes it sound kind of fun. My father nearly died, but he kept on working.

Late in the summer of 1984, he and Willy agreed on their biggest load yet, an eighteen-thousand-pounder into New York City. Told to secure space, one of my father's gophers rented a warehouse on Hunts Point in the Bronx. My father signed off on the selection, and even delivered one of the two truckloads of dope, sticking around long enough to process it for Bobby's buyers.

He was high, however, and the skull-and-crossbones code of honor got its first hole. Because he was high, he never realized that his stash house was across the street from a juvenile detention center. Because he was high, his gopher felt okay being high, too. And so they both elected to commit a crime in full view of guard stations and police cars.

When my father walked off to God knows where, for God knows what, Bobby arrived and took one look at the guard stations across the street and went into full damage-control mode. He ordered everything thrown back into the trucks—scales, bales, twine, knives, brooms, and boxes—and left without sweeping the floor.

He drove the lead truck toward the highway, hired help following in the second truck, and both accompanied by a third vehicle, a beat-up sedan known as the chase car. The War on Drugs, much like the War on Terror two decades later, called on average citizens to spot evildoers, and sometimes those citizens felt compelled to do more than just call the 1-800 number.

As the trucks searched for a way onto I-278, the Bruckner Expressway, the chase car noticed that someone in an unmarked car stayed with them, following them through side streets, alongside a rail yard, and all the way to an entrance ramp some miles down the road. It seemed like too many turns to be a coincidence. So when traffic accordioned near the on-ramp, the chase car did its job—crashing into the curious citizen watchdog. That ended the chase, but it drew a lot of attention, more than any gang can comfortably afford.

A couple of weeks later my father, Bobby, and Bobby's best friend had collected the last $500,000 owed for the job. It sat in a medium-size moving box inside a hotel near LaGuardia Airport. Bobby called Charlie who would bring the box of money to the Caribbean, starting the wash of cash that marked the end of the season. As they waited for the little guy, who was by then nicknamed the Shrimp, my father did some more coke—to hell with the pirate's code—and his mind began to wander toward his own personal after-party.

Everyone in the drug business back then seemed to believe in a certain mystical class of women. They had classics degrees from Sarah Lawrence and bodies so fine and light they could traverse a lawn party without bending a single blade of grass. Like criminals with a code, these were call girls with class, the fairy tale of the realm, and in this way the sad plain reality of sex with hookers became like pirates bedding princesses.

In the middle of this daydream in the airport hotel, Bobby's friend went downstairs for more cigarettes. Minutes later he burst back into the room like he had discovered a carpet fire. "It stinks down there," he said. "There are all kinds of suits and guys standing around without luggage or apparently anywhere to be."

My father was too high to safely operate a juicer, but he took control of the stage, volunteering to go down for a second look. He too noticed men standing around without luggage, not even glancing at him, like they were pretending they didn't notice him when in fact his presence set off pinball madness in their brains.

My father tucked into the bar for a drink, something brown and fiery. He wanted to clear his head. Like golfers, drug dealers learn to account for the elements: I'm high, my father thought. It's just the drugs talking. When the suits were still standing there a couple of rounds later, however, he hustled upstairs.

"It definitely stinks down there," he said, and the sentence went off like a gun. Everyone stood up and danced in place. All of humanity, the totality of life, narrowed to a single question: What the hell were they going to do? They could leave the money in the room and walk out different exits. But couldn't the agents just open the room and trace the money to them? What were those guys waiting for anyway?

My father decided that the best move would be whatever was least expected. If the feds expected them to sit up here and wait for the boom, they would launch a surprise counterattack. They would pack their bags and pick up the box. They would get it into the elevator, and when the elevator door opened they would crab-leg it for the front door, hoping to look like three men late for a flight who for some reason were also carrying a moving box.

It was a terrible idea. The year before, in one of the big Fifth Avenue hotels in New York, John and my father walked into the lobby with an even bigger box of money, a million dollars or more. It was hardly hot weather, and yet they were carrying money in an old air-conditioner container. They felt the box breathe slightly before it caved completely in the middle of the marble lobby. They buckled with it, so none of the money fell out on the floor. Then they dragged it back to the elevator. The moral of the story was simple: Use a luggage cart. Apparently my father had forgotten.

The elevator ride felt like a journey down in a Huey helicopter in Vietnam, the descent punctuated by an open bay door and furious combat. The men burst into the lobby, feet working, brains screaming, eyes boiling. They slowed only for the magic eye of the automatic sliding door to the outside world, which closed behind them and didn't open again until they were inside a car driving toward their warehouse in Brooklyn.

A few hours later all was quiet and Charlie arrived wearing a new suit from Sears, which on a man just over five feet tall put one in mind of a decorated wooden figurine. He backed into an old firehouse driveway my father and Bobby used for drops, and they put the last of $6 million in his trunk.

"Am I sagging?" Charlie asked.

He was sagging.

"Shipshape," my father said, giving Charlie the A-OK sign. As Charlie edged into traffic, my father and Bobby broke to pieces. If they were about to be busted, they figured, Charlie could get busted, too, pulled over for smuggling cash. They said their solemn goodbyes. No talking during the off-season. That was one of their rules.

My father called a livery cab for a ride to the Gramercy Park Hotel in lower Manhattan. It was his come-down room, the place where he felt safe and protected. He'd stayed there about fifty times, often in the worst room in the building, on a middle floor with a view of an airshaft instead of the picturesque park, the last large private green space in Manhattan. It calmed him to get the oldest, shittiest room because it made him feel invisible, and that's how he wanted to feel. On the seat next to him, he had a gadabout bag filled with $250,000.

But his mind had yet to fully quiet down and he began to notice things. The car behind him on the bridge had a suction-cup antenna on the hood. The one in front of the hotel had two guys inside sipping coffee.

In his room he chained the door and pulled the blinds. He slipped his bag under the bed and turned on the TV. He did cocaine for the whole first night, waiting for the fateful knock. At some point he passed out and when he awoke he noticed that his shoes had been moved and the TV now made a funny sound, a tiny whine, like the casing had been opened and loosely closed. He placed the television in the hallway like the remains of a room-service hamburger.

Then he called my mother and begged for help, which she denied. He wanted to bury the money at Connie's again, but Connie refused and my mother wouldn't budge, either. He swallowed a handful of Valium and sat on his bed until the whole room filled with water and he swayed like sea grass. Surfacing, he called the front desk, ordered up eight manila envelopes and a bag of rubber bands. He stuffed each envelope with six rubber-banded stacks of money, two rows of three, $30,000 per envelope, the quarter million in loose bills transformed into boring-looking business papers.

He showered and found his way to Kennedy Airport, the Eastern Air Lines terminal. Inside his mood lifted for the first time in seventy-two hours. Here was the Grand Central of terminals, four acres of marble and wood, encased in aqua-colored glass. Eastern was the airline of the '70s and '80s just as surely as Pan Am was the airline of the '60s.

Its pilots freelanced as flying aces in the dope air force. Its ground crews moved bricks and kilos. My father himself sold a ton of airline dope that fall, the contents of a dining truck driven right off the runway. The hard part was stifling the urge to wink at every uniformed worker. Then he was past bag check, beyond the reach of the suits, flying home, just not home to me.

In recent years I've looked for a moment that defined my dad and I return to this one again and again, largely because of its purity. After he landed at Miami International Airport he had a simple choice, a literal fork in the road in Coconut Grove. He could go straight and find his family, or he could turn left and face trouble. My father always turned.

The Mutiny was in full fury when he arrived with his friend, the coke dealer with the pencil-thin mustache. Valets and bellhops scanned the balconies, poised to dodge a falling body or lick a shimmering cloud of falling cocaine. For about $100 a year people got gold membership cards, each one numbered and emblazoned with a pirate head. The real pirates just slipped in through the pool entrance.

As my father found his barstool, my mother was probably still wondering if he would make it home for *Saturday Night Live*. By the time he slid off the stool, he had forgotten the feds and the fuckups and was thinking only about his successful sale, his six million joints.

Every room at the Mutiny had a Jacuzzi and a balcony view of Sailboat Bay, a corner of Biscayne that bristled with beautiful boats. My father rented the highest room possible, ocean-facing so no one could look in, and called his friends at the escort service, placing his order with the precision of a chef's grocery list. Out on the balcony he watched the sun bounce up behind the horizon and he followed a thought in his mind, the one we all have when it's late and the view is of everything.

Then he stopped thinking entirely.

Later that winter, after my father's long, slow descent had begun but before he knew it, he took me to Disney World, where we celebrated my fourth birthday and generally went bonkers all over the park. The most memorable part of the trip wasn't a ride or a character, however; it was the hotel room. My father left me in it. He did it one night, two nights. His plan was working fine—father by day, barhopper in Orlando by night—until my mother called, patched through by an operator directly to her son.

It reminds me that there are really two versions of my family's story, as there are two versions of every family story. There's the good one—dopey, smiley, basically a lark—and there's the bad one, which is everything that happened in between the good times, filling the gaps and threatening to transform our irregular but essentially happy lives into a tearjerker in the tropics. My father was funny and charming but also frightening and self-destructive. It's impossible to pinpoint exactly when his personality flipped, but it did, and it flipped the story of my family with it.

II

Exhale

5

Three Little Blond Boys

My father was born in New York City in 1946, the second of four siblings. One day, many years later, when my father was all grown up, he began a journal and recalled his childhood this way: "I was traumatized many times over . . . I can almost feel the dozens of times that I was brought to crying . . . I felt no love or nurturing or happiness or joy . . . I lived in a grossly abnormal and dysfunctional home. 'Home' is not even an accurate term for the apartment we lived in . . . I never had a chance."

These aren't even his memories.

In his journal, it's all labeled "pre-memory"—as in before the age of five. And yet there were other working-class Catholic boys with circumstances like his who didn't become schedule I narcotics dealers. His two brothers, for example. David, the eldest, went on to an aeronautical engineering degree at Berkeley, a long marriage, two children, and a fine career with a leading maker of archival equipment for libraries. Joseph, who came after Anthony, humped it as a foot soldier in Vietnam, came home, married his high-school sweetheart, had kids, and kept on humping it as a mail carrier for the U.S. Postal Service.

To make sense of Anthony—to understand how he came to the low life and came to love it, along with many other seemingly blessed young men of his era—it's necessary to go back a ways, to reconstruct what he insists is "the pattern of our life." My father was one of three little blond boys. His father, Henry, was one of three little blond boys. His father's father, Paul, was one of three little blond boys, the first of our line of Dokoupils to come to America from what was a

Czech-speaking part of Austria. My father says every generation had a demonic Dokoupil patriarch, a man who withheld love and affection and warped his children's lives. Ergo, Great-grandpa Paul "never had a chance," and Grandpa Henry "never had a chance," and Anthony himself "never had a chance," which of course means I "never had a chance" and neither will my son, little blond boys both.

My father was still a stranger to me when he explained this family pattern, but I felt the pull of his logic immediately. We tell children they can be anything they set their minds to, pretending it does not matter where those minds came from. But there's no escaping the calculus of family. The math has to work and that's what scares me.

The first Dokoupil to come to New York City was John Joseph Dokoupil, a Czech laborer who arrived in the late 1890s with his wife, Rosa. Both were in their early twenties. They settled on East Fourth Street in what's now Alphabet City, and John got a job at the Power-House, an electric generator about ten blocks north on the East River. Three boys followed in quick succession: Anthony in 1896, James in 1897, and Paul in 1898.

My father remembers his great-uncle Anthony—his namesake and by extension my own—as a charming, blue-eyed man with a firm dislike for traditional work. According to legend, his father, John, got this first American Anthony Dokoupil a job at the PowerHouse, which he quietly resold to another man, who worked the job as Anthony but earned only a fraction of the wages. Anthony pocketed the difference, and this allowed him to work as a gambler and bookie and eventually as an illegal gin maker and runner of Canadian whiskey during Prohibition. Or maybe he worked as a loan shark. No one seems to know for sure. My great-aunt Jean, who married Henry's brother Jack and is the oldest living relative I have, talks about this ancestral Anthony as a "muckety-muck, a big shot, a wheeler-dealer, a gambler. He always had bucks. He was really good."

"But what did he do?" I asked.

"He was a shrewdy," Jean said. "I don't know."

Whatever it was, it made him rich. It got him out of the city and into an estate in Westchester. The shrewdy's younger brother, Charles, is said to have died of an opium overdose in his twenties and left not a trace, not even a memory of a memory in the minds of those living today. All of which leaves Paul, my great-grandfather: the youngest brother of a criminal and a drug addict. You might think he could do no worse, but he did; he became an unmarried teenage father. According to the Catholic Church, which confirmed the birth with an elaborate placard, a boy named Henry was born on Christmas eve in 1915, which, as spooky, unsubtle fate would have it, is the same day I was born sixty-five years later. His parents, Paul and Geraldine, were seventeen years old. According to the City of New York, they were married when they were eighteen years old.

And what followed is an old story of dashed dreams, soured lives, and the unwanted son who rages forward into a new generation. Paul got a service job at another power plant in the East Seventies and moved his young family to the neighborhood, renting a second-floor railroad apartment with a potbellied stove he liked to lean against in the winter, a cup of Fleischmann's rye whiskey in his hand. In the summers, it was beer and a breeze by the street-side windows.

In every season, it was common for him to get knee-walking drunk, and for Geraldine, a riotous Italian girl, to call him a drunken bastard. The only thing these third-generation Americans could say in Czech was "beer" and "money for beer." Paul kept a keg next to the kitchen sink, when he could afford it. The Paul Dokoupil household did have a dog. Its name was Combat. Its purpose was to help Paul home from the bar.

Two more boys followed Henry in quick succession. Jack was the favorite son and James was the mama's boy. Henry was sort of the whipping boy. He took the blame for things to protect his siblings, but he also caught fury simply for being alive. It was Henry, after all, who had gotten Paul into this mess of domesticity and for that Paul whipped him badly with a belt buckle, flecking off patches of skin. Decades later, people said Henry's back looked like a moonscape.

When the Depression hit, Paul made his great mistake of a son quit school—where the boy was apparently an honor student—and get a job. Henry consented and by 1935 he was working at a box factory while his two younger brothers were high-school graduates. He worked two years at Densen and Banner Corrugated Box Company, answering phones and filling orders, then climbed into a sales job with

Acme Box of New York City, where he managed old accounts and brought in new ones, previewing the basic nature of his offspring's knack for the pot business.

Then the war came. James, the middle child, joined the marines, took German machine-gun fire during the Battle of the Bulge, and came home to become an accountant and commander of his local VFW. Jack joined the army, defended the Pacific Islands, and remained in the service for another three decades. Both men married and are remembered by their children as quiet, loving fathers. They drove the station wagon, worked the grill.

Henry also joined the armed forces. He enlisted in the Army Air Corps in 1939, when he was twenty-one years old and still unbreakable. He was good-looking. People used to say he was built like Aldo Ray, the tough-guy star of *What Did You Do in the War, Daddy?* and *The Naked and the Dead*. Even my father was impressed, once telling me, "He was an Adonis, Tony, an absolute Adonis." And actually, he rather was. Pictures of my grandfather confirm an Easter Island–like gravitas, a face that is all shadows and planes until it's lit by the kind of smile that helped him sell commercial paper products by the ton.

In May 1941, in a falling-down church on East Seventy-ninth Street, where the convent hadn't been painted in twenty-five years, Henry married Phyllis, a pretty Italian girl he had known since childhood. Phyllis dreamed of being a designer and was known to work magic with a sewing machine. If you needed a hat for an important occasion, Phyllis was your gal.

But just weeks after their wedding, Phyllis was pregnant and Henry was gone, transferred to a new Army Air Corps base at Manchester Air Field in New Hampshire. The first squadron of A-20 attack aircraft arrived on Saturday, December 6, of that year, during a family-friendly weekend that also brought Phyllis up for a visit. The following morning, after breakfast together, she and Henry joined dozens of other cozy young couples for a midday movie but suddenly there was no movie. The screen flashed white, and as the projector clicked pointlessly somewhere above them, an officer said what hundreds of officers and air sirens and ringing phones were saying coast to coast at that very moment: "WE ARE UNDER ATTACK."

Phyllis pushed through the throng and, uncertain where to go or what, if anything, would be attacked next, she got on a train back to New York City and into a cab at Grand Central. Maybe something happened to her in the crush exiting the theater, or perhaps the news itself had been enough to upset her equilibrium. In any case, she had enough time to say "Take me to the hospital" but not enough time to get there: She had her baby right there in the back of the cab.

It was as perfectly shaped as the model in her doctor's office. But it never cried, and she only held it once before the hospital took it away and produced a form for her to sign. There was no possibility of a funeral, no grief counseling in those days. An orderly pointed to a grimy phone that could be used to call for a ride. Phyllis was decades older, a grandmother, before she could talk openly about the loss. And in the intervening years she always hesitated when asked how many children she had. Was it four? Or should she say five? Henry never said anything at all, certainly not while the war was going on, which was a period that lasted more or less the rest of his life.

His character changed after Phyllis lost the baby. His aspirations seemed to drift. The army saw him as a machinist, a uniformed mechanic who banged out the dents in planes and made their engines hum. But he pushed back against those expectations, asking to be relocated to Miami and put into the planes themselves, where he most likely toured the gin-clear waters of the Caribbean, tracing the same path his son would in the decades to come, albeit as a man concerned with bombers not bales of marijuana.

Henry must have felt like a real soldier, whatever he was doing, because Miami mattered at that moment in the war. German and Italian U-boats were attacking Allied tankers and oil refineries, sinking ships and taking lives. He was promoted to corporal, then again to sergeant, and again through two levels of seniority and into a mentoring role for junior officers.

At last, on February 10, 1944, he left the tropics, taking the *Queen Elizabeth* from New York to England, to the airfields on the North Sea. He became part of the 702nd Bomb Squadron. The big boys. The B-24 heavy bombers. The Wings of War. He joined the crew of a plane called *Bodacious*, and he took flight with much the same spirit that would later send his son into a bodacious professional life of his own. From the day he got his transfer papers Henry felt like a man in the movies.

His week at sea marked the start of the most intense Allied bombing of the war: the three months before D-Day, the deepest, most sustained assaults on Germany. The flight path of the 702nd was known as "flak alley," where the antiaircraft bullets came in great undulating streams, black from guns on the ground, orange and green tracers from the German interceptors. The bombers were always losing pieces of wings, rudders, windshields, propellers, landing gear.

Whatever came, Henry's job was to keep the bird's feathers on and the beak working, and when German fighters were thick in the air around them, he fired a machine gun, too. He was an engineer-gunner, the most mobile member of a bombing crew, bouncing from the top turret to the ball turret, to the bomb bay, and even below it to an exterior catwalk, miles above the earth. If the shells got stuck or the doors froze shut, his job was to drop the bombs manually, and if the pilots were killed, he was responsible for cranking down the landing gear and flying the plane home.

The average lifespan of a B-24 was twenty missions. After *Bodacious* survived twenty missions, the army added five more, and then five more, and five more. In six months, Henry logged more than two hundred hours of combat air time, and *Bodacious* bombed thirty-three cities; Henry stenciled each onto his bomber jacket in black marker. He won three Oak Leaf Clusters, a Distinguished Flying Cross, and an Air Medal for his efforts. Each citation pushes some version of the phrase "cool under pressure," which is another trait he surely passed on to his son the drug dealer.

A picture of Henry taken overseas shows a happy young officer riding a bicycle in the English countryside. But something happened in August 1944 on the thirty-fourth mission. Henry's complete military records were destroyed in the St. Louis archive fire of 1973; the only remaining army paperwork, besides what he kept, is his final pay stub, which records his discharge from the Army Air Corps' mental hospital in St. Petersburg, Florida. The other nine men on *Bodacious* are still on mission thirty-four.

The Don CeSar Hotel in St. Pete Beach, Florida, is a pink stucco wonder. It opened to the great parties of the Jazz Age, died out with Fitzgerald, and was reborn as a military convalescence center specializing in "operational fatigue." It was the best the army had to offer at the time, which isn't saying much. One common procedure was "barbiturate narcosynthesis," a drug-aided flashback. It was based on the idea that it might help a soldier to relive his most traumatic war experiences, thereby giving him a second or third or fourth chance to "process" his worst nightmares. This didn't work.

But the doctors at Don CeSar had an insidious way of placing blame on their patients. Symptoms appeared to be caused by combat, as one Don CeSar study of men suffering hallucinations concluded in 1944, but "on further study proved related to the character and personality conflicts of the patients." In another paper, doctors took a close look at the case of a man much like Henry: a young white sergeant who flew thirty combat missions as an engineer-gunner aboard a B-24, and ended up at Don CeSar with rashes and related signs of mental distress. These represented "the heavy burden of his marriage," the paper concluded, plus a "loss of parental attention and affection."

The year after Henry was admitted to Don CeSar, the director and his assistant published *Men Under Stress*, the official textbook on flight fatigue. They concluded that what patients really needed was "replenishing affection, consideration and attention, as a small child needs to be praised and comforted after a particularly strenuous and exhausting activity."

This was the army's best thinking on the subject: that scores of unwell bombardiers needed fresh soup, and not, say, relief from their scribbling minds. As far as I can tell, there is just one positive scrap to come out of Don CeSar, a single reference in *Men Under Stress* to a soldier who meets a girl on the beach and feels mysteriously relieved. Unfortunately, this man wasn't Henry.

There are a couple of versions of Henry's story. Both involve him getting sick before mission thirty-four, but in the first version he was forced to sit out the flight and *Bodacious* was shot down. In this version, Henry was brave but the darn army held him off that flight, and he came to Don CeSar wracked by survivor's guilt, the noblest kind. This is the version that makes all the awfulness that would come after the war a sign of Henry's deep, deep worthiness. The more he went on to drink, the darker his moods, the more honorable a man he truly was.

But there's another version, one with the heavier feel of truth to it. It holds that Henry blacked out on the thirty-third mission and broke out in a rash before the thirty-fourth, and that was what put him in the infirmary. *Bodacious* still goes down, and Henry is still the sole survivor. But he no longer deserves any of his medals because he is not a man who is "cool under pressure" but a man with rashes on his legs and a need to apply a useless brown salve and wear house slippers because his feet are too swollen for boots. In this version, he is hardly a man at all. He's alive because he was fragile; his friends are dead because they were not.

A month after he was sent to Florida for treatment, thirty-three of the remaining thirty-six planes in Henry's squadron were shot down, and dozens of men spent the next seven months in prison camps eating a diet of dandelion stew and waiting for the Allies to rescue them. I often wonder if Henry knew about this, and if it felt like he had lost his shot at valor for a second time. If he had gone bad in the prison camps, he would be a wounded warrior. Instead he was just wounded.

After three months of Florida sunsets and sedation therapy, a panel of psychiatrists diagnosed him with a "nervous condition," and he was honorably discharged on April 3, 1945, four weeks before V-Day, the biggest party in the army. His disability was rated at 30 percent.

The army sent Henry away with a standard letter recommending him for civilian work as a mechanic, inspector, or engineer. It declined to mention that he now had a hard time with loud noises and flashing lights, but no matter what "pre-memories" my father may claim, Henry kept his injuries hidden for years. He worked for a manufacturer of commercial jet engines on Long Island, paid for family vacations on the Jersey shore, and pushed his three boys to succeed in school. In 1953, when he was thirty-eight, with a fourth child on the way, Henry moved the family to the suburbs of northern New Jersey, a middle-class Catholic area with Madonnas on the lawns, candles in the windows. The boys hopped from one private school to another, part of a pipeline to Notre Dame and Loyola.

But 1953 was a turning point for the Dokoupils in other ways as well. It was the last year the Dokoupil family went to the shore. I have a picture of Henry from that year, his head shaved, his hand paused on the way to pounding a shot of liquor, three friends around him, two whiskey bottles already half dead on the picnic table. It was the beginning of Henry's decline.

My father's and grandfather's professional lives were utterly different except for a singular fact: They both dropped a foreign object onto strangers and never saw the crater themselves. By the 1950s Henry would have been forced—through press reports and people talking—to confront the fact that he wasn't only bombing military bases and soldiers but towns and civilians. Likewise, in the 1980s my father would have been forced to consider the fact that his product was a poison, like the press and his president were always saying. It's not a poison, of course, and Henry was no war criminal. But both men went through a war, both men were demonized, and both men lost their minds in the process. They were even the same age when it happened: thirty-eight.

Henry ruined a series of jobs, and his prospects dwindled. It was as though something inside him that had pulsed and pulsed, exerting the same pressure in the same spot year after year, burst entirely. The new Henry was violent and abusive. He would shout at Phyllis until his brother Jack could get there, take him out for a drive. Jean and Phyllis stayed behind to reassure the kids, and hours later the men would return to a quiet house, the kids asleep. Henry would hug Phyllis and say he was sorry. But that was only if Jack could make it over in time. When he couldn't, it was the cops who arrived, usually because the neighbors would call. A few times, however, my father called the police. Anything to stop the yelling.

Henry hated his father but he became him. David was the favorite son, Joseph and Carolyn were the babies. Anthony was the whipping boy, the Henry of his generation. Fathers often expect that their sons will be do-overs of themselves, perfect versions with all the cracks and fissures puttied and smoothed. But this never comes to pass, and the disappointment can be so fierce that in a curious way the boys end up feeling both impossibly loved and utterly unwanted.

That's what happened to Anthony. He was beaten and abused by his father, and as it happened he felt that this man who had dreamed of him, had met him and instantly regretted everything: the marriage, the suburbs, the years at the shore. Like a good little boy, my father tried to change his ways. He tried to improve himself, which of course meant acting more like his father, who offered a model of manhood that made my father one helluva drug dealer, one monster of a dad.

For years Henry balanced ale and whiskey against soup bowls of coffee that kept him awake, and the man who in his thirties looked like Aldo Ray now in his forties looked like Aldo Ray's corpse. His face became gray and lined, and took on the strangely desiccated look of the chemically unwell. Sometimes he would rehab at his parents' house a few towns over. Anthony could never predict how long he would be gone or if he would stay sober. Church Sundays, holidays, birthdays, and graduations were always hit and miss with Henry, just as they would be with my own father in years to come.

Henry (and later Anthony) would not show up, or would show up late, or would arrive on time and be an abusive wreck. Henry (and later Anthony) called his family members names, shitting dogs and bitchin' bastards. And he delivered these lines like God on Judgment Day, with such deep conviction in his voice, taking the time to look into his children's eyes and souls and then point his finger and emphasize that they were all the things he called them. Even David, who loved his father and defends him—and says, "Sometimes I feel like my brothers and sister and I grew up in different homes"—admits that the man struggled with confrontations, "had no patience and was very nervous." That, and "he had a pretty volatile personality." That, and he was "a loner and somewhat antisocial."

The Dokoupil household had at least two shotguns in it. They were used for sport hunting in the Meadowlands, two or three blocks from the house. The Shotgun Incident, as it's known to some in the family, could be treated as several separate incidents, since the shotgun was brandished several separate times. I could go into each one. The time Henry chased his wife off the porch, for example, or the time he lined the three youngest kids up and gave each a sip of the muzzle. I could try to find some rational reason for them, too. But none of it would matter, because all that matters is this: He pointed the gun. Once you point a gun at your family, you can lower the barrel, wrap the weapon in blankets, and throw it in the swamp, but you can never get rid of it. The gun is pointed forever.

After a series of jobs as an airline mechanic, Henry continued to create a path his middle son, Anthony, would eventually follow. He worked as a plastics cutter and a night watchman, and he later retired as a short-order cook. Long after that, years and years after the Shotgun Incident, a new panel of army psychiatrists diagnosed him with post-traumatic stress disorder and schizophrenia, and awarded him 100 percent of his military income as disability. Around the same time, in a different city, a different doctor would diagnose my father with post-traumatic stress disorder and schizophrenia. It reminds me of that old playground threat, "I'll hit you so hard your mother will feel it." A war so bad, the son got PTSD.

"Oh, how I love you little boy," my father wrote to himself after the diagnosis. As he continued, his words became a procession of broken mechanical scratches until the paper's edge was reached, and he had to write up into the margins, filling the corners with messages to his former self. "How I want to comfort you. How I ache to hold you and talk to you and soothe you and kiss away your tears. I cry for you now little blond boy, that day, those days, this day." My father was writing about himself but the problem is ours.

Perhaps what's hardest to understand in all this is where was Phyllis. Where was the mother, and why didn't she leave? This is also the hardest part of understanding my own mother, Ann, whose similarity to Phyllis was one reason my father fell in love with her, and one reason both women faced the special problem of pulling a son off the path of their father. Phyllis and my mother were kind, softhearted people unable to resist a genuine apology. And yet both women were also strong, stubborn, and savvy. They knew that leaving was more complicated than simply walking out the door.

The war had taken Phyllis's first child, and the effects of the war were threatening to take the four children who followed. She wasn't going to let that happen. She worked the assembly line at Economic Laboratories, a since-vanished soap and sanitary-products company in Manhattan. She'd given up her dream of being a designer, but the mannequin in the Dokoupils' basement was constantly dressed in children's clothes and draped in new slipcovers and curtains.

She also transferred some of her pent-up creative energies onto her children. Her sister-in-law Jean came over one day, let herself in, and found everyone in Anthony's bedroom, where Phyllis was standing, arms crossed but beaming. "Come here," she said. "Look what my kids did." She pointed to a wall of wild crayon scribbles, colorful patches of construction paper. The wall looked like the face of a clown who had tried and failed to stanch his shaving cuts. Jean covered her mouth with her hand. "What?" said Phyllis. "They're children. They're expressing themselves."

So don't think for one second that Phyllis had given up on her kids; on the contrary, she was invested in them more than ever. Henry flew into rages, waved around a shotgun, and on occasion even ran off with other women, just as Anthony did to Ann. Phyllis could have filed divorce papers. She could have gotten them approved by a judge, too. But only the daughter would have been hers. The sons, a helpful lawyer friend explained, would go to their father. Those were the rules in the 1950s, so she stayed with Henry. She stayed and tried to be a positive influence, and whenever it got hard she reminded herself of why she was doing it. She repeated a simple phrase that became a mantra: "Not my boys."

It must have helped that they loved her for it. "My refuge and safety zone," my father confided to his journal. He cried on his first day of kindergarten, begging his mommy not to go, hoping she would keep her word about coming back. She did, of course, and she tried to do much more than that for all of her children, but especially for her three boys. And she succeeded.

She saved two out of three.

The Dokoupils had family in Katonah, New York, a bedroom community north of the city. And it was here that Anthony Dokoupil's great-uncle—whose name was also Anthony Dokoupil and who evidently didn't work much—showed his young nephew that the straight world was for dummies. The Dokoupil kids and their cousins would caravan up in Jean's green Jeep station wagon, surfing the special wicker seats as affluence gathered outside their windows. Shrewd Uncle Tony lived with his wife in a large and quiet home, perched on large and verdant grounds. They had no kids of their own but an endless tolerance for the chaos of other people's offspring.

Among my father's earliest memories are sock-sliding on Tony's oak floors, swinging by the low branches of a giant weeping willow, the pleasure of plenty, and the sensation—as unforgettable as his mother's love—of resting his grubby grade-school head on a large soft pillow until a single thought buzzed like a bee in a jar, an idea that he would ruminate over with adolescent intensity for the rest of his life: Don't be a sucker.

As for the teenager my father would become, it was a more distant uncle on his mother's side who shaped him the most. Uncle Cecil lived three houses away from the Dokoupils in New Jersey. He was the big man in the area: the first on the block to have a pool, the first to have a color television, the first to drive a Cadillac, with seats so firm you could safely rest a mug of coffee on them. He owned a bar called the 440 Club, situated on what was then a vein for trucks heading to New York City. He also operated his own long-haul company, which somehow landed national contracts and government accounts, and meant that Cecil's garage was a wonderland of fur coats and federal satellites.

Cecil was not exactly like the other businessmen of his day. He was a little less orthodox than the average entrepreneur in the 1950s, even the average bar owner. He couldn't count, for one thing. He would call one of the Dokoupil boys to help him do his payroll, which consisted of a box of money, a list of names, and some envelopes. He also organized meetings in the loft space above the bar, accessible only via an attached staircase. It was a big, creaky room with bare bulbs and curtains that gave it the look of a grand hotel gone seedy. On unpredictable days a fleet of black cars ghosted to the curb, and the stairway played host to a procession of dark-coated men, coughing into hankies and hugging the railing as they made their way skyward.

One Sunday my father, then seventeen, happened to watch them from the front seat of an ice-cream truck. The vehicle's freezers were packed, but it was summer and he was a teenager and they didn't pay him enough to be ambitious, so he hadn't refilled the dry-ice supply and now the treats were melting.

He thought: *I'm fucked.*

He thought: *Cecil can fix this.*

Miraculously, Cecil did. He called a friend at Dow Chemical, who delivered a few pounds of dry ice. Joy returned to Lyndhurst.

So, yes, my father idolized Uncle Tony and Uncle Cecil. They gave him a future, just not a reputable one.

Henry gave my father his peculiar energy. Dad was the goofiest, giggliest, happy-go-luckiest kid in his part of the county. He was a boy who danced for company and told jokes for the neighbors. When my great-aunt Jean thinks of Anthony, she thinks of him arms in the air, butt wagging, legs spread out. The casual observer would say he was the loudest little man because he had the largest wounds, and the casual observer would be on to something.

As a teenager my father walked around his community in cuffed jeans, a white shirt, pomaded hair, spouting theories on girls that involved chatting them up while prancing backward and emoting a lot. Or else driving by groups of them very slowly and leaning out the window, panting, banging on the door with an open palm, maybe whistling.

In class he was a good student and a bad disciplinary problem. He felt entitled to jerk around. "I already know what this guy is talking about," he'd think to himself, "explaining some simple bullshit, A plus B." He would play with the teachers, bait them, and try for a reaction. Sometimes that meant standing up and throwing his shoulders forward, stretching his back like a cat. Other times he would stroll over to the window mid-lecture. He wanted to make them call his name and scold him, and when they did he would act surprised: Ooooooh, you don't let people do this?

The principal's office was on the girl's floor, so sometimes he got reprimanded just to make the visit, just to slouch in a swirl of perfume, swinging hair, and popping hips, just for the chance to clutch his heart, say, "Ooh, ooh, it hurts, you're looking so good today," and then spin away, pushing off football players on his way back to class. He was a theater geek without being in the theater.

Three months into high school, my father and some friends walked to a patch of trees behind a used-car dealership, and many coughs and splutters later, they started laughing and giggling and pushing one another around. They were high on their first high, but they were definitely drug high, too. An older brother had given them a wrinkled little joint, and they blazed it down to their fingertips.

But mostly they drank. My father and his buddies bought home-made wine from a spinster and hey-mistered their way into pints of Schaefer beer. In the early spring of sophomore year, when one of his friends got a driver's license, they drove to the city for the first time, sipping from sixty-cent bottles of Colt 45 malt liquor. Along Bowery, they took shots that tasted like two twists off a wet bar rag and went outside to laugh at the bums. One bum was too sick to even wash windshields. He was an old black guy with swollen feet.

Even then my father had an innate sense of himself as a redeemable figure, the kind of guy who could still see right from wrong when he was blind drunk. He couldn't always walk this line, as my battered mother will tell you, but he challenged himself to do so. And while his friends laughed, he gave the man a quarter.

Later in Miami, when it would be $20s and $50s, and the bums would be wearing tank tops, it was the same gesture. My father gave money to them because they gave back to his traveling show, his life as performance art, just as surely as if they had stuck a chewed piece of straw in his mouth and made a breeze blow through his hair. He felt a certain kind of kinship with the homeless because he saw them through cataracts of sheer romance. They never traded freedom for stability, adventure for the everyday, and my father never would, either.

By his senior year in high school, my father had kissed girls, done drugs, won fights. He had broken laws and literally leaped over tombstones to escape punishment. Yet for all his misbehaving, he was also a member of the National Honor Society. He was a student delinquent. And to the people who knew my father in high school—to the boys who cruised with him and the girls who folded his picture into their pocketbooks—his ticket was stamped. His whole demeanor suggested glorious get-it-on fun.

But in fact my father felt the opposite of glorious. He was a boy who grew up in a cash-strapped family with a war-broken father, and that made him doubt his performance. He felt best during the school day, when he had things to do: check his schedule, find a desk, locate pens and paper. He dreaded the still moments when pleasantries were exchanged and character was revealed. When drugs came along they were a way to script himself into life, "to prove myself one of the crowd, to show everyone I belonged, that I could joke and swear and please."

Until then he still had normal dreams. Please-your-parents dreams. Kennedy dreams. He thought of a career in chemistry, maybe engineering. He told friends he would work in research and development. He liked the way people responded to that idea. And when he graduated in 1964—third in his class—any of those futures were still open to him. His graduation pictures show an almost military young man: brushed hair, bright eyes, square jaw.

In the fall, with a $400 gift from his grandmother, my father took his first plane ride, a flight to Los Angeles to begin college at Loyola Marymount University. Why LA? The sound of it. The reactions it elicited from guys on the block. Tony from the corner in LA? Get out of here. Also, the Beach Boys. "Surfin' Safari." "California Girls."

The Fonz had yet to come along to introduce New Jersey to the rest of the country, so at Loyola my father looked like a visitor from outer space. He felt like one, too. At his first dance he found a seat all alone and stared at his palms. The next thing he knew he was surrounded by a clump of boys. "Hi, my name is Tony," my father said, raising himself to shake the hand of the boy in front of him. My father was wearing a red cabretta leather jacket, perhaps the only one in Los Angeles. Someone's fist banged the side of his head, and after he crumpled in shock, my father walked home past strange houses and people, feeling the first stirrings of what he believes was his fate to become a lover of drugs.

When the school year was over, he drove cross-country and spent the summer chain-smoking in Greenwich Village. It was then, through the big square window of one bar or another, that he saw men doing a slow nod, a loose smile on their faces. He watched as one man lit a cigarette that burned to nothing before he could get around to taking a drag. On his way home, he passed these same men at the top of the subway stairs, paused there, peering down into the gloom for what seemed like hours. He was looking at his first heroin addicts, the lowest rung of the '60s drug experience. But he thought: I want to try that.

Addiction is ravenous: It devours people, families, communities. Oddly, however, addicts are often among the most gracious hosts. They take from the straight world, but if you're interested in joining them in their world, an addict will happily give you a free tour. Which is how my father found himself in his childhood bedroom with two old high-school chums taking a free hit of heroin. His little sister, Carolyn, listened at the door.

Carolyn was thirteen, a rising high-school freshman, and Anthony was nineteen. He had moved home to finish school among his own kind, the local boys at St. Peter's College in Jersey City. She heard the leather squeak and a buckle clatter as the boys made a tourniquet to bring up Anthony's veins. She heard the scritch-scratch of a lighter and the hungry crackle as someone cooked the dope, flash-boiled the white powder and water in a soda cap, held with a bobby pin. Silently, a ripped cigarette filter fell into the clear, syrupy liquid, the syringe filled, and the needle slipped into her brother's arm. She heard someone yelling, "You're gonna kill him!" Then the creak of the bed as her brother was laid out like a corpse, not dead, but a little closer to dead than he had been before.

"I feel like I'm floating," he said from behind his bedroom door, and maybe he was.

When his friends left, he came downstairs and sat in his father's easy chair while dinner was cooking. Carolyn came down and joined her mother on the couch, and they stared at Anthony, who looked like he was goofing them, with his eyes unfocused, his mouth hanging open.

"Anthony!" Phyllis said. She snapped her fingers. "Anthony! Stop that."

Soon my father had a "chippy," which meant he had an internal dope clock and when his dope clock called for another hit, he had to get another hit or his eyes would water, and his nose would run, and his bones would ache. He learned what junkies learn if they mean to beat the clock: the cheapest dealers, the quietest places to shoot, the best pawnshops. When Joseph went to Vietnam, his fiancée bought him a gold watch, a piece of civilization to come home to when he was done being a soldier. Anthony pawned it for a few dozen nods.

It's simple, really: When you're high, anything seems possible. The unforgiving physics of family are suspended. You fall far from the tree.

Walking by a travel agent's window in the spring of 1968, Anthony stopped at a picture of white sand and bikini-clad girls. He would graduate in a few weeks, and he had a summer to fill before entering a master's program in English and philosophy at the University of Detroit. He would fill his summer there, right there, in the picture, on the white sand, with the bikini-clad girls. He did not invite a single friend to join him on this graduation trip. Instead, with the money he'd saved by living at home, he bought a copy of *The Playboy Book of Mixology* and a one-way ticket to St. Thomas. Specific plans: sand, girls, bartend, quit drugs.

The trip did not begin well. My father failed to crack his drinks book as his plane gurgled and smoked its way to the Caribbean. On the ground, no one wanted to hire a pale New Yorker with only the most transparently fictitious experience behind a bar. And my father was on the brink of going home when the navy chugged into the harbor of Charlotte Amalie, the capital of the U.S. Virgin Islands. As white-suited midshipmen disembarked from the gunship, he scampered alongside them, asking, "Where are you headed, where are you headed?" He asked every third or fourth man, and the general consensus seemed to be the bar at Caravan's, a ticky-tacky hotel across the harbor.

Only the head bartender was behind the counter when Anthony arrived, out of breath. As he had at other bars, he invented a fake work history. He used his hands to cut the air into great dancing advertisements for himself. But as at other bars, the manager was unmoved. Until the navy arrived. For the next six hours, Anthony made big sloppy pineapple daiquiris and banana daiquiris, and vodka and gin martinis. By 2:00 a.m., his pockets bulged with tips, and he had a job for the summer. He even went home with a girl from Southern California.

Take that, Los Angeles.

At the University of Detroit my father read hard philosophy, but he and morality began to permanently part ways. He fell back into heroin use. Trying to cop in Harlem, he was robbed twice. Once by three kids with knives. Once at gunpoint. By then, his mother and sister knew what was going on, having overlooked the marble glare but not the white church shirts blood-spotted in the crook of each arm. They sent him to his first rehab, an in-patient clinic on Long Island.

When rehab didn't work, Uncle Cecil intervened. He got his nephew a three-day supply of methadone, a doctor-prescribed synthetic high that's supposed to alleviate the pain of withdrawal, and hired him for a job down in Puerto Rico. Cecil checked them into separate rooms of a nice hotel, and they went to the casinos, where my father was given $50 to have himself a good time. The next day they went to the job site, which turned out to be a massive old brewery with a bar attached. My father wore work clothes, and didn't think about why Cecil was not dressed the same until they swung open the doors. The bar was stripped clean.

"What the hell happened?" my father asked.

"Relax," Cecil said. And he shut the door.

For three weeks, Cecil locked my father in the brewery during the day. He lay on the cool concrete floor, staring at the skylights, watching the light change, and feeling his bones ache for heroin. At night Cecil freed his nephew, and they went to an Italian restaurant in the hills owned by Cecil's son, Michael. After three weeks without drugs and with good food, my father seemed to improve, revivify, and Cecil left. Anthony stayed on, working at Michael's restaurant and living in an apartment overlooking old San Juan.

Before long, however, he started to get that old romantic feeling about himself and went for a walk, stepping his way over cobblestone streets until he found himself in La Perla, a candy-colored slum, with chickens in the street and no doors on the houses. He thought of handing out some money to beggars, as he had in the Bowery. Then saw some guys nodding in the shade, and he knew he was in the Dopeville of old San Juan, and his rehab was over. The relapse had begun.

My father dropped out of the University of Detroit the following spring, a couple of months and a thesis paper away from graduation. At the end of the semester he accepted a ride from a classmate who was going home to Milford, Connecticut, a little beach town ten miles from the state university.

There my father found his calling as an outlaw. He became a marijuana dealer because otherwise what would become of him? He was always moving, always devouring new experiences, because he was afraid that if he ever sat still the transformation into Henry would begin.

That kind of life is exhausting. It's a life of pure performance, and my father knew it and that drove him deeper into drugs and crime, further from the main thoroughfare of life, where most kids drive along feeling free, never realizing that their wheels are fixed on the track, their destination determined at birth.

You could even say my father took drugs preemptively, as a way to give himself something, anything, other than the destiny of his old man. But there was no real escape. My father took stupid risks because he wanted an intervention, cosmic or legal, but instead he got what he feared the most: genetic destiny.

In his late thirties, my father became his father: violent, foul-mouthed, rambling, totally absent, perpetually there. As I've said, I am not an Anthony on my birth certificate or so far in my life. But I turned over his pictures, cursed his name, and imagined that I was my mother's son and no one else's. It seemed to work until I had a boy of my own.

One day in an elevator I noticed him beaming at me, age three, his legs crossed at the ankle like mine. He echoes what I say to his mother: "Love you, babe." "See you later, babe." He recites the banalities I offer to cabdrivers, cashiers, or friends I see on the street.

"He is you," my wife often says, and at this point I have to agree. Paul to Henry to Anthony to me to my own son. Five little blond boys, the sickly-sweet prophecy of the "Footprints" poem coming true. Even my son seems to understand on some level. When I show him pictures of me as a toddler in Florida feeding a sheep, he sees himself.

"It's me!" he says. "I feed the sheep!"

"No, no," I say. "It's Daddy. Daddy was once a little boy, too." But there's no changing his mind. He knows what he sees. And I do, too.

6

The Pirate Life

My father walked into a thirty-day rehab in January 1985, feeling like a man one step ahead of the falling piano. It was a group therapy program somewhere in pine-tree Mississippi. He fished on a lake named after a racist and played volleyball every day at four thirty. He also did some thinking, some "work," as the counselors called it.

During the past year he had sliced and knotted all the nerve endings between high and unconscious until he could feel nothing anymore, not even the shame of leaving his four-year-old son in the care of Walt Disney's in-room entertainment center. So he was happy to be in rehab, pleased to be restacking the blocks of his life. He needed to be reminded of his potential. That was always important, a sense of another possible reality for himself. To throw away a life, one needs a life to throw away.

The fact that he was a professional drug dealer must have added a layer of unspoken hilarity to his in-take papers.

Has your reputation been affected by your drug use?
Yes, I broke the pirate code.
Have you found that it takes more drugs to give you the same high (or low)?
Yes, as a matter of fact, every year I need to sell more weed.
Have you ever neglected your obligations for two or more days because of drugs?
Indeed, I left my son in a hotel room at Disney World.

Rehab succeeded in turning my father back toward the goal of being a better man. At the end of the month he walked the small path to our front door, which led into a living room. It was sunken with wall-to-wall white carpet. A plush violet couch and love seat covered one wall; a big-screen television, heavy antique marble-top tables, emerald green stained-glass lamps covered another; a mirror—teeming with light from the picture window—covered a third. The fourth was open and included the space for a baby grand piano I would never learn to play.

That night at dinner with my mother and me, at a frosted-glass table surrounded by chairs with shiny golden arms, my father used words like *promise* and *cherish*. He said he had a surprise, but we had to close our eyes. When we opened them, my mother saw a three-piece diamond jewelry set—two earrings and a necklace—and three round-trip tickets to New York City for Valentine's Day weekend. I was too young to remember, but I must have seen shiny rocks and paper and my mother's smile, which I hadn't seen in a while. My father smiled back at her, and he was sure there had never been a more beautiful woman.

We stayed at the top of the Plaza Hotel, a room my father reserved with a credit card plucked from a wallet bulging with an unusual amount of cash and unorthodox forms of identification. In a slot behind his Florida driver's license, for example, he had his other life. He changed it every few years. This one included a social security card, vehicle registration, and employee photo ID from an air service company in Los Angeles where he was registered as a mechanic.

His own father had been an airplane mechanic, so when his contact— West Coast guy named Glen, the friend of a Connecticut wholesaler— offered the identity, my father grabbed it. The whole package cost him $500 and included a few pleasant hours in Los Angeles with the local professional girls.

It would be hard for me to lead such a double life. I can't imagine opening my wallet for ice-cream money and finding a reminder of my two-girl weekend in another state. Even if I wanted to try for such a weekend, my good time would be blotted out by an internal monologue, a nagging alarm that said: I am a father. I have a family.

That's what's amazing to me, in a darkly macho sort of way: My father evidently never had this experience. He never found himself standing in the light of a new day, looking at his wife and son, and then at himself in the mirror and thought: Can I really be the same man I was last night?

The lobby of the Plaza was thronged with men in suits, clean-shaven, chins lifted toward the future; wives in dresses so recently dry-cleaned they crackled with each step; mistresses with chopsticks in their hair and high heels that sounded like the click-click of a toy train set. Against all odds my father was still free, and on such a day it was possible to believe he always would be—incarceration less a reality than a rumor, an idea discarded with the morning paper.

The governors of five Southern states were at that moment begging the military to start targeting drug smugglers like my dad. "We're literally being invaded by land and sea," Mark White, the governor of Texas, had told reporters a month earlier. Bob Graham of Florida said he had begun to organize residents in a "civil defense" effort against smugglers. The phrase called to mind women who water their shrubs at midnight, watching and waiting, prepared to give Oliver North the signal to take down Anthony Edward Dokoupil and tear apart his family.

But my father was enjoying himself too much to care. It made him happy to flash his plastic at the desk of a place like the Plaza, where he appeared winterized and rugged in a black leather coat and gray corduroys. My father's credit cards were all in his real name, the fruit of his years as "president" of his two front companies. He paid taxes on six-figure earnings and that put him on all the glossy solicitation lists. "The credit card companies love me!" he used to say, bouncing back from the mailbox in the morning, pleased with his little caper.

Our room had a view of Central Park all the way to Harlem. The ceilings were gold and the beds squeaked like living things. I bounced over one and then another, then bounded to the window, my mother snapping photos, which show me wearing a cycling hat with a Porsche logo, a gift from Connie on Long Island. We had forty-eight hours to play.

We took it slow at first, a carriage ride through Central Park, followed by a visit to St. Patrick's Cathedral, the archdiocese of my father's boyhood, home to all of New York City's Catholics. Inside my old man stood calm as a skyscraper, never kneeling or praying but obviously consumed with feeling. Catholics believe God contains a kind of "Footprints" poem himself, a trinity of equal and divine persons, each born in the image of the former in the way of all fathers and sons. "This is my beloved Son," says God the Father, at the baptism of Jesus Christ, as the Holy Spirit is said to hover on the horizon, "in whom I am well pleased."

We exited in a blissful daze and when we turned the corner, the street opened into a cheerful square, the courtyard of a different hotel, the Palace, one of my father's favorites. And there was my mother, sitting on the edge of a low wall. She was still looking in the direction of the cathedral, but when she turned and saw us, there was serenity in her face. She stood and took a few steps, arms outstretched.

Then we were off again, expected at a heliport on the West Side, where we rose higher and higher, sailing over the city and the river, the roof of every skyscraper dribbling steam like a balky cloud maker, the Hudson ablaze in the slanting light of the day. When we landed, we rushed uptown. We had orchestra seats at a kids' show at Symphony Space, a performance that matched our mood. It was called *Whoop-Dee-Doo!*

We flew home the next day, flew home to a city that itself had become the subject of cartwheeling exclamations. Miami was no longer Vietnam South but the new Casablanca, darling of *Esquire* and *Vogue*, *The Washington Post* and *The Wall Street Journal*. No less than *House & Garden* called it "one of those magical American places."

Drugs ruined the city, then saved it. They pushed up the murder rate, sent three mayors to jail, then rebuilt the skyline and drove the nightlife. Drug money was present in every paycheck, piled on every church plate, stuffed in every wallet. Statistically speaking, drugs themselves were unavoidable in this new Miami. The urban legend about trace amounts of cocaine on hundred-dollar bills originated in our town, and it was largely true. In 1985 a local pharmacologist tested bundles of randomly selected cash from seven mainstream Miami banks and found "large amounts of cocaine" on all of them. If you handled more than $1,000 in a year, in any denomination, you had drugs on your hands.

The previous fall, Miami's sex appeal had gone national. The sounds outside were still the normal noises. The gunshots and the screeching tires, the girls on West Thirty-ninth dancing beneath the neon signs. All that carried on. What changed was the orientation: The iconography of the city, already recognized subconsciously, was pulled together and splashed across the screen in the most dramatic fashion. *Miami Vice* debuted.

Afterward, the city of Miami started talking about itself differently. Otherwise serious, sober people dropped $2,300 on dinner, $1,600 on shoes. They went out every night then slept it off under gradually turning ceiling fans in immaculate fruit palaces. Suddenly it seemed all of Miami was on the same page as my father, who did more than look on from the banks of Babylon. In fact, he acquired his own longed-for Vizcaya, the luxury dream home or, at least, the luxury condo version of it, a mile north of the real Vizcaya along the shore of Biscayne Bay.

The condo was high in a just-completed four-tower complex with six tennis courts, a clubhouse, two pools, its own fake beach, and the pedigree of being located along the Millionaire's Row of old Miami, where William Jennings Bryan might have borrowed sugar from his neighbor, the artist Louis Comfort Tiffany. It was across the street from the Atlantis building, the blue one with the fifty-foot hole in the center, a "sky court" with a red spiral staircase, a palm tree, and a whirlpool, all of it made famous by the opening credits of *Miami Vice*. Turn right out of my father's front gate, and in five minutes you were in Miami's banking district, and the new downtown.

He was home most nights, but he felt entitled to play around some, and my mother didn't stop him. She had become like the wife of any ambitious professional. She put up with long hours, big trips, presumed affairs, potential swings of fortune, and all with good cheer, because of what she got in return: money, freedom, travel, and the best education for her son that money could buy.

This was my first year at Gulliver Academy, my mother's top choice for turning drug money into something the federal authorities could never confiscate. Gulliver was one of the best private schools in the country, home to "the big names and big bucks of South Florida," according to a defeated *Miami Herald* reporter who toured the school with her son, "feeling nervous" in her Toyota Sentra. My mother liked the reading program, the cursive handwriting program, and the science lab, which had not only baby chicks but sea turtles and tarantulas, too. She liked the small class sizes and optional extended day care.

She also liked the facilities, which were anchored by a country house and accessed only through a cool oak-lined hall that you couldn't enter without a moment of absolute coal miner darkness as your eyes adjusted from the hard light outside. Pass through that, and the backyard was a warren of flower-lined walkways and cozy classrooms, yielding to fleecy green grass that ran for a quarter mile.

Gulliver was the school of Du Pont scions, members of the Estefan family, the Iglesias family. The grandson of George H. W. Bush was my classmate, and the unsmiling totems of my childhood became Secret Service agents, bearing silent witness as I peed on a fire-ant hill. At the end of each day, when the agents would finally move, they were somehow never stiff when sliding into a limo with "The Bushes" emblazoned on the door.

The tuition at Gulliver was more than the University of Florida, but many parents, my own included, paid in cash, benefiting from a small discount that encouraged it. A joke circulated, a wry one-liner about what all the school's fabulously wealthy Latino fathers did for a living. "They aren't doctors or lawyers," it began. "They must be Indian chiefs." At some point my mother admitted her situation outright to Mae, my best friend's mother, and the news didn't damage their relationship. It deepened it. The two women began to pop wine and trade Miami stories while us kids played.

Mae's stories kept pace with my mom's. In the late 1970s, she and her husband had moved out of Coconut Grove, concerned about raising kids in a tropical Gomorrah. They felt confirmed in their sound decision-making when a naked lady jogged past their moving van. Later, as the office manager of her husband's medical practice, Mae grew accustomed to patients—even fellow Gulliver parents—paying huge bills in cash. And on Fridays, she walked out with some of it in her purse, treating Clay and me to a cart-filling shopping spree at Toys"R"Us. The only reckoning was "Just Say No to Drugs Day," when everyone's parents rode around town wearing red ribbons, soft smiles floating above steering wheels.

This was also the year I started to act more like my father. Family is an important part of the recovery process, the doctors told my mother, and after all, he is the boy's father, they explained, so as crazy as it sounds, I was allowed to spend more time with my father post-rehab than before. These were long, strange hours of bonding. A season of broken baby teeth, knocked out when Dad pitched me a basketball and the bat exploded back toward my mouth. It was also the season of the alligator.

We were at Matheson Hammock, a local beach and freshwater estuary, when the beast emerged from one of the pools leading up to the shore. This wasn't surprising in Florida, and if the gator stayed there for long, park rangers would wrap the pond in yellow tape and put a cone nearby, as if nature had just spilled itself. The message seems redundant. Go away, you say? I think the gator already made itself clear on that point. But my father edged toward the alligator, and brought me with him until the gator flinched and we ran, laughing.

Around the same time my father took me and a friend from Gulliver out for a madcap fishing trip. My father's occupation as a boat captain was bogus but his yacht was real, a beautiful vessel with two outboard motors, a big, proud bow, and a cockpit that made a man feel like a chariot racer on the high seas. We etched white waves into the middle of shipping channels, jumped wakes that would have swamped us broadside, and wove through Stiltsville at a rate that would light the cherries on a police boat if one were ever around.

My sharpest recollection is of the steady thwack of the hull on the waves and the hum of the engines suddenly giving way, replaced by a new sound that reminded me of a headfirst dive into third base. I remember the shock of the boat actually stopping, and rocking to its side. I looked over the hull and saw sand. We had hit a low-tide island, and apparently a pretty popular one because when my father got out to push us, he cut his bare foot on a broken bottle. The blood mixed with water and turned the whole deck red. And that was before we started fishing the flats for barracuda, the man-size predators with razor teeth. Dad had me pose with two meat-eaters bigger than me.

This was our shared Miami: riotous, swarming, unpredictable. The city averaged six feet above sea level, which meant when I touched bottom in our Miami swimming pool I was deeper into the sea, in terms of elevation, than when I was already bobbing in the Atlantic chop. It meant I could strike water with a few plastic shovel blows in the front yard, and we had to board one of those cruise ships before putting any meaningful distance between ourselves and mother ocean.

Our Miami was a place where a single giant wave could sweep the land clean. It was a city where teenagers canoodled in the glow of television weather reports and hedged against drowning as virgins, while kids like me wore strainers on their heads and stood like Washington on the prow of their couches. It was bracing to live with that kind of sword dangling overhead. It added to the intensity of existence in Miami, where Life and Death seemed to be roommates rather than neighbors.

Our Miami was a place where canals clogged with bags of drowned kittens and headless farm animals, the dregs of a voodoo prayer; big snakes crossed roads, encircled toddlers, and squeezed dogs. At a playground one day, my mother yanked me off a jungle gym because a coral snake was sunning itself on the play mats. We were told not to retrieve balls we lost in the river, after an animal—probably an alligator, maybe a panther—remaindered the neighbor's poodle.

Every day in our Miami it rained in great slashing curtains, heavy water skating around, pelting one location, leaving the next untouched. At my Little League games the rain turned infielders soppy and left outfielders dry; this father running for cover, that one licking his pencil and keeping score. It put one in mind of a cartoon God somewhere above the thunderheads slouched in a lawn chair, a finger looped over the long neck of a beer bottle, flicking the hose.

Our Miami was life as shipwrecked fantasy: a place where people ran away to live on squirt cheese and crackers, sleeping on their boats or way out in the ocean in houses on stilts. In our Miami a lightning strike could burn a forest and reveal an ancient burial ground, and pirate's treasure wasn't abstract and lost offshore but liable to wash up after a storm. Or appear in the folds of a pull-out couch, as $10,000 did one night when Aunt Carolyn came to visit.

My father and I once walked to the end of this shared Miami, or one of the many ends of America's only entirely unnecessary city. We came to the end of a sidewalk in our neighborhood, where the road was paved and then dirt and then just a path. We took it past bullet casings and painted rocks and empty beer cans. We saw condoms and dung piles, and we pushed on until the vines crowded in, and the mangroves enveloped us, and it was easy to imagine the palm fronds slapping a dinosaur in the face. Eventually there was no more landfill, just half-deluged fields and impenetrable swamp, alive with unseen possibilities, like my own darkened room or my father's unfolding evening.

Miami was an exciting place to a drug dealer or a little boy.

It was barely a place at all.

Every night at bedtime my father told me a story. One of them, *The Wreck of the Zephyr*, I read to my own son. It's the legend of a boy who briefly learns to sail above the waves, his boat flying through the clouds, until he gets too cocky and crashes on a bluff, breaking his leg. The narrator is skeptical when he first hears the tale, relayed by an old man sitting next to a broken boat high on a bluff. But on the last page, the wind picks up and the old man walks off with a limp, and you know in that instant that he has spent his whole life trying to fly again, searching for that perfect wind, the one that got him high and made him crazy.

My father always said that he'd quit the drug business when he made his million dollars. "Almost there," he told friends in 1981, like a man a few payments away from owning his car. He repeated the claim the following year, and the year after that, and soon it was less a reflection of sentiment than of superstition, a perpetual retirement process.

It's not that my father was lying to people—or to himself. He really was "almost there." What he didn't say is that the million he was working on wasn't his first, which was lost in the penthouses of Biscayne Bay and downtown Miami, where the cocaine came in softball-size mounds and the prostitutes stayed for days. It wasn't his second either, which was lost in much the same way. The million he was working on was his third. And for the first time in his career my father felt genuinely afraid of losing it.

As drug traffickers glowed with ever more perceived evil, they lost many of the federal protections enjoyed by murderers, rapists, and some of the more run-of-the-mill defilers of society. Every arm of the U.S. government was reaching for them. Uncle Sam could search bags and vehicles without a warrant, snatch property without a trial. Prosecutors took anything they believed was bought with drug money or equal in value to the drug money they believed was earned.

All they needed was probable cause, the belief that something was an ill-gotten gain. And on that alone federal agents took hotels, ranches, planes, boats, and topless bars. At the same time, in an effort to halt what *The New York Times* called the "annual invasion" of weed every summer—an invasion my father had a starring role in—the Coast Guard started racking up busts: twenty-eight tons on a cargo ship off the Massachusetts coast, thirty-two tons on a shrimp boat near the Florida Keys.

So many bales of marijuana were hastily thrown off planes and boats, usually when the authorities were in pursuit, that Floridians developed a nickname for this floating contraband: square grouper. It washed up on the beach like driftwood, or bobbed like cork and was swept around the nose of Florida by the Gulf current. Fifty-seven bales were found off St. Lucie, thirty-eight bales drifted ashore on Jupiter Island, another thirty-four landed on Vero Beach. The Gulf of Mexico became a kind of medicinal tea, flavored by thousands of bales.

Once you know what waits for him, the details of my father's life take on a fated quality. It's hard to imagine him ever doing anything else, which may be true of any life you study closely, but it feels particularly true in my father's case because the factors shaping his life were so much bigger than him. He might have dropped out of the drug trade in 1985, much as he might have done in 1976 if history had not given him Jimmy Carter. This time the gang was kept on course by a smaller but no less profound gift. It came when Charlie took a trip to Portland, Maine, where he met a Coast Guard commander, a very drunk and very sad-seeming man.

"How's it going in the Coast Guard?" Charlie asked him, and the commander looked at Charlie's bronze skin and sun-bleached hair.

"Are you a sailor?" he asked.

"I sail whenever I can," Charlie said.

"Well we must know a lot of the same people," the commander suggested.

"I bet we do," Charlie said, and they talked on, whiskey taking both men captive, making Charlie bolder, the commander more maudlin. The man said that he was planning to retire from the Coast Guard. He said the Coast Guard had lost its way. Six fishermen had drowned in the seas off the coast of Maine while his ship was in the Caribbean, hunting for pot. "I love the sea," the man said. "I want to save people from it. If I wanted to stop pot, I would have joined the DEA."

Without saying more he reached into his briefcase and handed Charlie a map of the East Coast and the islands. To Charlie's astonishment it had summer routes for the Coast Guard and the placement of stationary radar balloons. Charlie folded the chart into his coat pocket, paid the man's tab, and walked away with the deed to an uneventful season.

How could my father quit then? One more year, he said.

That summer Charlie and Willy confirmed their own plans to exit the business. Bobby was still keen to work, and my father's other source, John, forget about it, he wasn't going to stop for nothing. But if the principal band was breaking up, the last show should be a doozy, their biggest yet. And it was: twenty-two thousand pounds of Colombian delivered and sold from August to October 1985.

My father took his final cut from a stash house in Connecticut: $500,000 (the equivalent of twice that much in today's money), which he packed into two suitcases, each one heavy enough to tear a man's rotator cuff. He didn't party or dawdle; he got a ride to Katonah, New York, where he took $5,000 from a safe-deposit box, and continued on to New Haven, where he bought a $20 road map from the bookstore at Yale. He rented a car and set off for Albuquerque, New Mexico, his back end sagging ever so slightly.

The journey took four days and three nights, which my father spent in Columbus, St. Louis, and Oklahoma City. He was clean the whole journey. Even without the paranoia of cocaine, however, he was constantly checking for a tail. The White House boasted of arresting ten thousand "traffickers" a year and pot culture itself was shriveling amid what Nancy Reagan proudly called "an atmosphere of intolerance."

Her Just Say No campaign was one of the most unsophisticated anti-drug slogans ever. It suggested that drugs are evil but you can quit them any time. Side by side those concepts set the table for pleasure as surely as the phrase "diet vacation." And yet the Reagans were reaching their goals: The number of annual pot smokers fell by nearly ten million from the Carter years, and two out of three Americans supported throwing smokers into prison, let alone dealers and smugglers.

It was a reversal of public sentiment, especially among the young, who no longer viewed pot as the drug of creative types and rebels but of wastes and dropouts, people who couldn't succeed. Professionally. Socially. Sartorially. At Manhattan cocktail parties during the Carter years joints were smoked down to a finger-singeing ember, smoked until the remains fluttered to rest on the toe of a penny loafer. In the age of Reagan, the same joint came back full length, cold, untouched, and never to be passed again. If pot was once a light on in the attic, the light had gone off.

At each stop on his journey my father selected nice hotels near the city center, places where he could feel relatively secure with his precious cargo. He paid for his room for multiple days, hoping to give the impression of a man with business in town. Then he hung out a sign and disappeared before dawn, making sure only the rising sun was in his rearview mirror.

On the fourth day of his journey he called ahead to let my aunt and her husband know that all was well, and he would be arriving soon. They lived in a grinning McMansion on Indian land outside the city, a place with an indoor pool and arrowheads in the garden. Her husband worked in finance; she was a homemaker. My mother had set up the location because this was supposed to be our money, a security account, as my father explained, "in case something happens to me." I have no idea why my aunt and uncle agreed.

My father arrived around noon, bearing an Igloo cooler, a new caulking gun, and hundreds of plastic baggies and rubber bands. With my younger cousins at school, he set to work on the kitchen floor. He would count a stack of $5,000, slip a rubber band over it, and bundle it into a baggie like tomorrow's lunch. It took two hours but he confirmed the full half million, including a lot of fives and tens—which told my father he was holding street-corner money, the most evocative kind. The stacks fit perfectly, the lid just barely locking into place.

He had less than an hour to dig the hole before the kids came home from school, so he picked an easy spot in the freshly turned clay near the foundation of the house. He used a tree as his marker, moved four feet of dirt, dropped in the cooler, and anchored it with a big flagstone.

And that was that. Of all the decisions my father made, this was not among the worst. He expected my mother to tip out her family, but whatever the future held, he felt sure that she and I would be taken care of, and that left him feeling light and free. He heaved the suitcases and caulking gun into a clanking-big gas-station Dumpster and returned the car to the local rental office. He spent the night in an airport hotel, and the next morning he was flying home, flying toward her, toward me, aloft on his first full day of official retirement.

His career had spanned four presidents, survived two campaigns in the War on Drugs, and pushed the Big Green Elephant deep into the 1980s, a preposterously late date for something people can grow on a windowsill and the Coast Guard will sink you for. Many of his peers, maybe even most, had long ago switched to cocaine, flamed out, grown up, gone to graduate school, or been confined to reading *The Odyssey* in a federal pen. To stay on top all he had to do was precisely nothing.

But precisely nothing was the only thing he had never done.

In Boston the Organized Crime Drug Enforcement Task Force began referring to my father's crew as "the confederacy." They knew this confederacy had small-time roots in the early 1970s, but that in the first half of the Reagan administration, it had grown into a multiform monster. They knew the ring was really two rings, and then three, depending on the year, the job, who was in rehab, and who was trying to buy a new boat.

They knew that the men of these rings worked on one of two essential tasks, procurement or distribution, taking turns in different roles. By design, however, no one knew the ring's entire structure and neither did the task force. That meant job insurance: Neither the buyers nor the sellers knew enough to cut the other side out of the deal. It also meant legal protection: People can't testify about what they don't know.

One configuration of the ring began with John in the mountains of Colombia, where he would select his product and ship it to my father and Bobby. A second configuration began with Willy in the same mountains, who delivered directly to my father, along with another distributor he kept to himself. During more than a decade these rings combined to push easily half a million pounds of marijuana into America, more than any confederacy ever uncovered. But they didn't consider themselves "organized" crime.

They were men who peeled fruit, owned woks, and knew all the rules of fondue. Many of them gave to charity. They thought of themselves as artists, and to varying degrees they were. They played guitars, sang, acted. Mostly they wrote ballads in their heads and with their lives. My father and his crew were not The Last Smugglers. Until weed is legalized, no one will be. But their retirement did mark the end of a certain kind of criminal era.

"No matter what happens, drinking and drugging is not an option," begins a notebook my father kept in the 1980s. The text has no date, and my father doesn't remember it. But it reads like the jottings of a man on the other side of rehab, which would mean they were made sometime in the spring or summer of 1985, which is my best guess. One whole side of the page is filled with little urgings, reminders, and admonitions. The last line reads simply, "I must be concrete and specific about how I intend to stay sober." Flip the page, however, and it continues in a different pen and a blend of rougher block lettering and ornate cursive. Someone has sketched a goblin with its legs crossed in the left-hand margin.

It begins: "I have made a very big decision."

My father tried to settle into a normal middle-class existence, but it was like exiting an athletic career or work as a soldier. It turned off a certain kind of chemical in my father's brain, and he felt cut down in middle age, sick for another round. Every morning the alarm would echo for decades. It would ring down the long, drab corridor of his life, the years stretching ahead, filled with nothing but regular-strength life. It's sad, of course, that he could not survive on that, but it's also understandable.

It's not that my father and men like him had no skills, it's that the straight world didn't know how to value them. After a lengthy federal prison term, one wholesaler tried to bridge this divide: He circulated a résumé entitled "Ex-Marijuana Kingpin Needs a Job." It generated national news but little work.

To fill his day my father volunteered as the "Daddy aide" in my kindergarten class. Apparently he just wheeled in a cart of milk and apple slices one morning, introducing himself to the teachers and creating the job. He must have mentioned some long-ago experience, his almost–master's degree, maybe, and the real teachers let him stay, at least until he started hitting on Ms. Alvarez, the headmistress.

She felt compelled to call home about the incident, which got my mother's heart thumping. The previous year I had bitten a teacher in my pre-K class, and my mother was braced for more bad news, some of the worst kind: a diagnosis of this or that, more difficulty, the ruination of her plan to turn drug money into scholarship money. She cradled the phone and waited.

"This is about your husband," said Ms. Alvarez, and my mother about collapsed. She had a sudden image of a kidnapping, or an extortion scheme, or armed men in the classroom, blood spraying, the kind of unforgiving kill-your-child Latin American nightmare she clicked past on the television. "He's been showing up to class," Ms. Alvarez continued, and though the subtext was scandalous my mother began to relax. "It's disturbing the learning environment," Ms. Alvarez said, ever so gently, and Ann had to stifle a laugh. "I bet he is," she thought. And that was the end of my father's volunteer work.

For Thanksgiving we all went to Connie's house on Long Island, a neat and cheerful home on a wooded lot with a nice fireplace. The wine went down in gulps and the adults stayed up telling stories, which served as a kind of stand-in for logic, a narrative explanation for all the crazy years—because sometimes a good story is logic enough.

Connie told one story, about a weekend a few years earlier, when my father paid her to disappear, leaving him and Bobby to use the house for a job. She came home early to find him counting out a million dollars on the kitchen table, right where we all sat for Thanksgiving. That was a good story. And it was a good story to know the land outside was dotted with buried coolers of cash. And a good story about the time my father and Connie's first husband went out for milk and disappeared for days, claiming they hit an anvil on the highway.

"I smell a movie," my mother said, and everyone laughed and agreed. They talked on until all the wine was gone and there were no regrets.

The following month my father flew to New York for lunch with one of his old wholesalers, a nice guy named Alan, who wore a gold dolphin ring and a rope bracelet. They had a tradition of sharing a winter drink at Tavern on the Green, the polished three-star restaurant in Central Park West. They also talked about the good old days, because everything is funny in hindsight.

They roared about one time in particular. It was a year or two earlier, when Alan and Charlie broke the pirate code and got themselves into a tussle that put everyone on some sort of a hit list. The way Alan told it, he took Boston Mob money and tried to put together a load of Thai Stick, a legendarily potent strain of Far East dope. It was made by lashing marijuana to bamboo sticks and dousing each stick in opium or hash oil for an extra kick. If it were candy, Thai Stick would be Fun Dip, a flavored sugar wand dipped in stronger flavored sugar and served to people who really, really like sugar. After the fall of Saigon and the rise of Reagan, Thai Stick became popular, rare, and profitable.

Alan sent a guy to get the load out of Turkey, then he met the load in Maine, after it had been tacked across the Atlantic on two sixty-foot ketches. He was shocked by what he found in the hold. Not Thai Stick so much as stick stick: kindling, ten tons of marshmallow poles with some kind of wet coating, maybe drugs, maybe poison, maybe nothing. My father sent Bobby up from Brooklyn to take a look, who missed his kid's basketball game just to state the obvious: This isn't marketable to anyone in any form.

Alan went into damage-control mode. He paid a local farmer to feed the load to his pigs; six of them died so Alan paid for the pigs, too. Then he paid his sailors and off-loaders. Finally he called Charlie to request enough cash to cover the Mob investment, which was totally lost. Charlie refused. He and Willy figured it was Alan's deal, Alan's problem.

A few weeks later a man known as Ice Pick, a pale hulking Mob enforcer, walked into Horsefeathers on St. Thomas and asked for Charlie. He intended to kill him or at least kidnap him for ransom, but Charlie was visiting Willy in St. Barts, where he was tipped off to Ice Pick's inquiry and irate at Alan, who ended up squaring things with the Mob—and going after Charlie and Willy himself. In Alan's memory Charlie pulled a gun, and Alan yanked it from him. In Charlie's memory Willy had the gun, a .38, sitting on a table when he and Alan walked into Charlie's living room. Either way, it was a glorious goddamn good time.

And the story helped my father realize he hated his new life, hated being an ex-somebody even if he had money and time. Back home my father's worst routines reasserted themselves. He woke with a line of cocaine off the cuff-link shelf of his antique dresser, which stirred him like a memory box. The flip blade he used, sentimentally, to slice open every bale he ever sold, was there next to his father's brass U.S. Army buttons, which were next to the gifts my father received from grateful partners. The presidential gold Rolex Billy had given him. The gold cigarette case Charlie had given him, supposedly once owned by F. Scott Fitzgerald.

At midday he went off for breakfast at a diner in Little Havana. On the way he picked up *The Miami Herald* and *The New York Times*; pocketed an Almond Joy to get him through the late afternoon. When he got tired, he took another hit of cocaine, a toot from a modified nasal spray. One of my father's last distinct pleasures was to peruse national drug coverage, which amounted to a newsletter of his competitors' woes.

He felt utterly invincible reading these tales of intrigue, adventure, and personal woe on the trail of the Big Green Elephant. There was the dealer who failed to latch his briefcase and had bricks of marijuana fall out of it onto the feet of a cop. The pilot who landed his dope bird in a field where local politicians were hosting their annual Turkey Run. The pilot who was found floating in the Atlantic, clinging to a bale of dope he claimed just happened to be bobbing nearby, a story the police believed until they found him in the same condition a month later.

The captain of a marijuana-laden freighter who flew the Panamanian flag upside down. The driver of a hardtop pickup who forgot to tint his back window, and another driver who pulled into a gas station behind a cop, who immediately smelled the dope. Two more kingpins couldn't make their drop because a canal that looked dredged on the map wasn't dredged in reality.

The most tragic case involved a pilot who clipped a power line as he approached an unfinished portion of I-95. He lost a wing and cartwheeled down the asphalt while his ground crew scrambled to recover six measly bales thrown clear of the inferno. They drove off—success!—only to be pulled over because of a minor traffic violation: Their muffler was dragging, throwing off sparks.

As it happened, at that very instant, Charlie and Bobby and Willy were themselves struggling with life as ex–professional drug smugglers. The four of them had begun in this business young enough to believe that life would only get better, weed only more legal. Instead they were approaching middle age in the darkest hour in modern marijuana history, halfway through a nearly two-decade stretch without the passage of a single pro-marijuana law, state or federal, and mass incarceration at every level of the drug culture.

Worse, their profession itself was being pushed into history. Marijuana was here to stay but the business of marijuana was undergoing a profound shift toward domestic suppliers, the era of high-end home-grown reefer, which was an easier business to enter and carried less risk than a multiton sea smuggle.

My father and his friends could see the shift manifest in the pages of *High Times*. Those long boastful features about "Wheeling and Dealing" were replaced by short, knowledgeable tear sheets on how to make your marijuana plants love you. The ads for counterintelligence equipment were replaced by kits to detect the sex of a plant and traps to stop rabbits from eating your crop. The magazine even hired a companionable green thumb—the Ann Landers of pot—to answer readers' questions on soil acidity and light density.

At first this confused men like my father. For most of their careers homegrown weed was the vegetable smoke of last resort, not unlike bathtub gin during Prohibition. That changed in the early 1980s, in the same parts of the country where moonshine was once distilled. In

California, Oregon, Hawaii, North Carolina, Oklahoma, Tennessee, Florida, Kansas, Georgia, Missouri, and South Carolina, just to name the big ones, more than a hundred thousand mostly rural Americans discovered they could make a living growing marijuana.

And they grew it well, using more than just bravura to coax gorgeous green tops out of the ground and cart them to market. Unlike my father, who never did figure out acorn farming, the new domestic-grass farmer understood tractors, trade journals, and serious botany. Their weed was at least twice as strong as what my father gathered from Colombia. And production tripled between 1980 and 1985, according to federal estimates; by mid-decade NORML was calling it the market leader.

As individuals these farmers were often aging hippies, hermits, and freaks, about as sexy as the old couple in *American Gothic*. They marked time on a Druid calendar and lived like *Wall Street* wasn't about to become the number-one film in America. Some wouldn't pluck dead leaves because they said it "traumatizes" the plant. But despite these oddities their work took on its own romantic glow, earning the name "guerrilla growing," and to be fair it was a lot more than just gardening.

Furry naturalists who wouldn't hurt a fly became tie-dye soldiers, slung rifles over their shoulders and slipped on ski masks to intimidate trespassers. They defended their plots using spiked boards, bear traps, moats, punji sticks, pipe bombs, hand grenades, and old-fashioned armed conflict. In the days of illegal whiskey stills, a code of conduct developed that when you found someone's still, you drank a little to let them know that you weren't about to tell the sheriff. In a weed field, you didn't dare roll a joint.

When it came time for harvest, the guerrilla growers booked every bad hotel room from Florida to Oregon. There, in the glow of *Diff'rent Strokes* and *Family Feud*, they trimmed and packaged enough weed to push all of South America toward irrelevancy, my father and his team along with it.

My father's confederacy might have been forced into retirement earlier, in fact, if not for an assist from the federal government, which shoveled enforcement dollars toward arresting growers. In 1982 the DEA eradicated more domestically grown marijuana than was previously believed to exist. The year after that "Ronnie's Raiders," as they were known, arrived in full force. They used military helicopters, U-2 spy planes, and thermal imaging to spot crops from the sky. Then they moved in using "mobile eradication units," hundred-man crews that cleared the land with three-foot machetes called bush axes.

The national effort was called CAMP (Campaign Against Marijuana Planting). And it worked all too well. The year my father retired the raids were the largest ever, a series of D-days in the war on pot. Armies of bug-cussing doughnut-shaped sheriffs claimed to uproot some thirteen million plants, which they hauled away in giant "Dumbo" nets below their helicopters. They made the Big Green Elephant fly, but in doing so they created an opening for the old smugglers, men who were dying for one more chance to play pirate for a grateful nation.

As 1985 rolled into 1986, word spread that many pot farmers were planning to take the summer off rather than hassle with the law. Many others—in a preview of the future—were moving indoors. They were buying extension cords and generators, and trying to re-create the equatorial sun with thousand-watt bulbs. By 1987 they would flood America with marijuana again, and the pot world would never be the same.

But for the moment my father's talents could still be used. America's stashes were actually empty. Weeks and weeks went by without new loads, and shortages were reported coast to coast. As America's remaining potheads—proud protectors of the marijuana culture in its darkest hour—got more and more frantic, the price of good pot began to rise again. Between 1981 and 1986 the price of an ounce of pot doubled from $200 to $400, according to the DEA. That meant each ton my father could secure was worth at least the soaringly, effervescent street value of $12 million, more than $20 million in today's money.

Bobby relayed the outlines of this new market to my father in Miami, and my father called Charlie and Willy again. He explained that it was last call at the bar, and as any barfly knows, you always order a last round. When he explained what it could mean financially, Willy proposed they go bigger than they ever had before: thirty-five thousand pounds, the exact amount that the feds used to throw around as a single day's supply of dope in America. That's probably a bogus estimate, the way everything else is in the War on Drugs. But it's better to think that it's true, and to imagine it as my father and Bobby did, as a last scam for one day of dope in an America that was gasping for it.

7

The Last Scam

Every smuggle is makeshift and freelance. The people involved are the people available, which is not the same as the best people, the ones you would pick if a decade of your life depended on it. The cocktail-napkin version of the job hadn't changed since Charlie and Willy first teamed with my father and Bobby back in 1979. What changed was the rest of the team: a cast of oddball pirates plucked from Central Casting, or as Charlie often put it, "The finest group of intellectual, pragmatic men I've ever known."

There was Scrimshaw, a British-born cabdriver from London who sailed to Antigua in the 1970s to work as an artist. He carved whale bones, shark teeth, and driftwood into cane heads and jewelry. His job was to find and manage a summer apartment for money drops in Manhattan. For this, he would get $75,000 and, with luck, the anchor he needed to look forever through a magnifying glass, turning Moby Dick into a wedding ring.

There was Inga, a pretty sailor with straw-blond hair down to her collarbone and a tomboy's penchant for boating caps and khaki shorts to mid-thigh. From her base in Massachusetts, she was to relay radio calls between Colombia, the sailboats, and the ground crew. She would also be paid $75,000 for the work, enough to refill her cruising kitty so she could sail to the West Indies every winter.

Daniel was a freshly divorced sailor from Camden, Maine. He gave his wife everything but $25,000 for a small ketch that he promptly moved to the east end of St. John, an island hop from St. Thomas. He was to broker the job, gathering contributions of almost $100,000 to help Willy make his down payment to the Colombians. Daniel expected a three-to-one return on his investment.

Pierre was a silver-haired French braggart who claimed to have sailed with Jacques Cousteau. He worked for years in the Caribbean as a treasure hunter before he met the vacationing daughter of an oil executive in 1973 and pillaged her as well. After "I do," he had control of an eighty-slip yacht harbor in Urbanna, Virginia, a tobacco port older than America itself. There, he hung an American flag from the back window of his pickup, and presented himself as super-dad, heading up soccer carpools and taking the team tubing on the Chesapeake. His contribution was property: For a fee, he rented out his marina to smugglers, charging $25 a pound and even helping with the off-loads.

Last but not least, there was Timber Tom, the quintessential sailor with squinty eyes and a romantic soul. The Caribbean was once full of such men, for whom sailing will always mean sextants and stars, not cell phones and global positioning; for whom new sailboats are fiberglass Clorox boxes compared to an old wooden schooner, whose hull is as close to a living thing that man can make with his hands. When they see indictment papers coming down the dock, men like this are known to pull up anchor, smile wanly, and disappear for twenty-five years.

Tom came to this vocation relatively late in life. He's a craggy, good-looking artist, who spent his twenties in big cities, acting and performing. One summer he saw the coast of Nova Scotia, however, and decided that the only sane response to such beautiful water was beautiful boats. He bought one, learned where all the ropes go, and relaunched his life as a guitar-picking charter captain. His job in this smuggle was to pay off the Colombians, pick up the marijuana in whatever they secured for him, and make sure the dope was loaded safely onto the sailboats, which would take it to America. For this he would get $35,000, less than almost everyone else but the farmers, because Tom would have done it for free.

There were other players involved, including a thirty-something carpenter named Jimbo who helped Willy in Colombia, and a sailor named Corky who hired the crews for all six sailboats that made the trip. But these were the core players along with the original quartet.

My father met Bobby in New York for the planning phase, which began about March 1986, six months before they expected a payday. So much of smuggling is waiting that it's important to have a good watering hole, a place where the pay phone is inside, preferably above a barstool. For my father and Bobby that place was the Landmark Tavern, a century-old saloon built on Eleventh Avenue when that still meant the waterfront.

When my father first found the place, around 1978, it was a dangerous corner of Hell's Kitchen, a red-brick Irish pub in an area controlled by a red-knuckled crime family that knew how to make bodies disappear. In the gathering spring of 1986, however, the silver smoke of the bar mirror told a different story. It contained Bobby and my father, and over their shoulders a room of young professionals, open-faced and bright, their ten-speeds locked up neatly outside. They sat remarking on the tin ceilings and oak beams, chomping bangers and mash, and making my father and Bobby feel like wax figurines from the golden era of pot. They were not meant for an era when two of the Top 20 songs in America were called "Jump."

They had $300 worth of quarters on them for the job. There were no cell phones, no discount international calling plans. Colombia cost $12 to reach. The Caribbean about $10. Either way it began with a few rolls of quarters torn open and fed into the slot. Popopopopopopopopop. Hold. Ka-ching. Popopopopoppopopopopop. Bobby could reach Barranquilla before my father got to the bottom of his beer.

As my father continued his dream of nonconformity, I was in kindergarten at Gulliver, where his tuition money funded a regime of cotillion rigidity. He spent days in a state of unshaven bliss, while my hair had to be short, natural, and brushed. He wore white pants and plumage, while I had to be in khaki and navy shorts with a tennis shirt bearing the official school crest. In a concession to geography I could choose lime green, turquoise, pink, or tangerine, which simply meant I looked like a well-scrubbed piece of fruit.

My mother was pleased with such a discrepancy, because after my father's false retirement, she knew the nature of his relationship to the business. She didn't suspect it or fear it: She *knew* he would never quit these insane adventures, never stop until he was in a coffin or a jail cell, and she knew both were waiting for him. She started teaching again, since I was in full-time school. She started phase two of her plan, plotting to make her final break.

In March Inga and Willy found winter coats and flew to Richmond, Virginia, where they met Pierre at the airport to talk through the use of his dock. They made a quick tour of the site, and then flew to New York City, where they joined Charlie and called the pay phone at the Landmark. Bobby picked up, and my father called out a meeting place, a "splendiferous" locale near St. Patrick's Cathedral: the Palace Hotel.

He then used the line to hire a limo as a not-so-subtle fuck-you to the more down-at-heels Willy, who was always playing his guitar as though he were some sort of heroic bard. The fivesome talked trucks and transportation, resolved a few minor questions about the Virginia drop point, and had the deal done before the appetizers came. Afterward, they drank away half the night, becoming pirates by midnight and little boys by dawn.

Imagine subterranean meetings, recon missions, counterintelligence strategies, and deep planning, replanning, and contingency planning. Imagine blowups about leadership, scuffles over money, and close calls with the authorities even before the job started. Imagine the movies, in short, and then bang it all out of your ears like seawater.

Willy returned to St. Barts, where the planning itself was a groovy time. He threw parties, and under the guise of casual conversation talked to Inga, Scrimshaw, Daniel, Charlie, and his other players. It wasn't hard algebra, after all, just simple x's and o's, and big round numbers. What's the weight? What are the payouts? When? Where? Who? This wasn't anyone's opening night on Broadway. They all knew their lines.

Later that spring my father and Bobby went to Urbanna to shake Pierre's hand, see the setup, and start thinking about the transfer. They also traveled to Maine, where they rented a cabin near Seal Cove, since you couldn't rely on hotel rooms on the coast in the summer. Back in New York, their operation moved to Avenue X in Brooklyn, where Bobby had a mechanic prep the gang's two trucks and my father bought new scales.

Scales were the only way to figure out the "shake mistake" in every bale, the percentage that isn't smokable because it's all dust or stem parts. When buying scales, most dealers would pay in cash, use fake IDs, and park their cars blocks away. But they all bought from the same egg-shaped shopkeeper, who watched the same clowns come in over and over. One year they buy a triple-beam scale. The next they buy a medium-bar scale and a big trolley cart. Finally, they get the mammoth scale used for bales of hay—in the middle of Brooklyn!—and, hey, they weren't selling counterfeit jeans by the pound.

Last but not least, my father rented the stash house, which was an art in its own right. The house could never be a commercial place or have a retail vibe of any sort, but neither could it be somewhere too residential, too community-focused. You didn't want people wandering over, wondering what's up at the old McLean place. And you made sure the landlord was out of state. You don't want a retiree popping in, checking on his carpets.

My father settled on New Canaan, Connecticut, one of the most affluent towns in America but also one of the most anonymous. It's forty-five minutes from Manhattan, about equidistant from Richmond and Portland, with a housing stock that's rich in attached garages and hardwood flooring (the best for dragging and sweeping). It also has a local population of movers and remodelers, people who hire other people and who have an utter lack of curiosity about things not themselves. People who spend their summers elsewhere. One of my father's gophers rented the actual place, telling the owner he needed it to work on a photography book, which wasn't untrue.

In early June my father came back to Miami for my kindergarten graduation, where he was celebrating more than my little white graduation hat, flooded by more than fatherly pride. Gulliver organized a big ceremony in a packed off-campus auditorium. In the crowd there were tears of parental affection, suits and dresses made for church. As my turn to walk approached, my father took a camera and prepared to record the moment. But he was so coked up he couldn't get the lens to focus, couldn't get the machine to match reality as he saw it.

"Give it to me," my mother said, with increasing agitation, "and sit *down*."

But my father had another idea. Rather than adjust the lens, he decided to adjust himself. He climbed the bleachers until the image was in focus. He climbed and climbed, stepping on people's hands, crushing sunglasses, cracking plastic cups of water. He would later deny anything more than "a little toot" in the bathroom, but there's the matter of the pictures: There are none. Just a studio shot of me in a white hat.

The next day my parents hosted a graduation party for the entire class at the Falls, a new open-air mall built like a pirate's hideaway on a series of man-made lagoons. It was a weekend, early afternoon, and as moms, dads, and grandparents walked into the restaurant, they saw bottles and bottles of booze. Behind them was a man pouring drinks, trying to pull people into his state of mind: my father, of course.

That same month, his weed was secured in Colombia.

The northernmost country in South America, Colombia has nearly two thousand miles of coastline. Almost all the marijuana smuggling, however, happened on a sparsely inhabited peninsula shared with Venezuela. It was officially known as the Guajira Department, better known as the badlands and not only because of its scarred stretches of desert. The terrain, inhabited by one of the only indigenous peoples who never fell to Spanish rule, was bloody even by the blood-soaked standards of Colombia in the mid-1980s.

Bogotá and Medellín were civilized, downright posh environs compared to the Guajira, where death was omnipresent. When friends asked Willy about the conditions, he would shake his head and say, "Barbaric and dangerous," a world of "jungle warlords and uneducated men," a place "where everyone is subhuman and treated as such."

Some of that is bombast, but the fact remained that in a typical year in the 1980s, American authorities recorded dozens of missing gringos in the region, none of them likely to turn up in a morgue. One drug lord was busted with an in-home crematorium and a lot of ash in the pan. The DEA found a cave near the Venezuelan border with at least a hundred bodies in it, all presumed smugglers. And the countryside was pocked with fresh holes, the last signs of drug dealers who were sometimes treated like lame racehorses, shot dead and buried if their plane would not take off, their boat leaked, their truck failed to start.

Willy's Colombian adventure lives in the rum diaries of friends and the notebooks of federal agents. Where memory and prosecutorial necessity breaks down, it lives in the tales of other smugglers who have followed the same gringo trail into the jungle, come out with their bales, and recorded their story for posterity.

He spent June 1986, the month of the smuggle, on the Dutch side of St. Martin, doing cocaine and watching the World Cup from a storm-damaged suite in a grand hotel. The grounds were closed to the public while repairs were under way. Willy found someone in management who was willing to let a drug dealer in while tourists were locked out. Then he found a generator and a satellite television.

He was bored with Colombia, bored of ten years on the same trails, the same roads, shaking the same hands. There was a sameness to smuggles out of Colombia in the era, just as there was a sameness to smuggles out of Mexico or Jamaica. A gringo who wanted to buy the country's reefer could just fly into Barranquilla, a Colombian port city scouted as a place that makes the Wild West look like Club Med.

He could stay at El Prado Hotel, the watering hole for visiting white guys who travel light and hope to have a conversation. By walking in and lying by the pool, his intentions would be as well known as those of a man wearing hiking boots at Everest base camp. After a day or two, if no one approached, he could go outside and lean against a taxi: Every driver in town could yank a chain of associations and help an aspiring felon fulfill his dream.

Or kill him on the flimsiest of pretenses.

I often think of this when I hear people talking about the harmlessness of marijuana. Smoking it, sure, but smuggling it was a ticket to death, dismemberment, or a long jail term, quite possibly in a place where electro-shock to the testicles isn't a sight gag. All that carnage has to end up in the weed, and not only in the price. In America, my father would wake up in his stash house and wonder: Am I going to make a million dollars today or am I going to get busted? In Colombia, Willy woke up and wondered: Am I going to make a million dollars today or go to sleep with a sock in my mouth?

After a few days of whiskey and accordion trios, a smuggler would find his way into the backseat of a Ford Bronco, a pile of tires on the cushion next to him, unsmiling men in front. The only road into the Guajira was a ribbon of asphalt that hugged the coast from Barranquilla to Santa Marta, a city of white beaches framed by abrupt snowcapped mountains, the highest in the country. After Santa Marta, the roads got bad, the spare tires became necessary.

This was the drive Willy had taken dozens of times by then, and every time the view from his window was Third World romantic: zinc roofs that catch the afternoon sun, stray dogs with swollen tits and strange bumps. After a four-hour climb, a State Department billboard warned U.S. passport holders that continuing into the countryside may be fatal. Then Willy reached Riohacha, the capital of the Guajira. It was to marijuana what Medellín or Cali are to cocaine. The local disco had a marble dance floor.

Smuggling became big business here in the 1860s, when enterprising boat owners realized they could get a better price for coffee if they snuck it to Aruba, a free-trade Dutch port ninety miles off the coast. For a century, boats would leave with beans and return with black market liquor and cigarettes. When American sailors in Aruba began to request marijuana, it slowly pushed coffee from each load until weed was the whole load and the return trip was nothing but money. By my father's day, there was no need for the boats at all. The gringos came directly to the source.

The Colombians called it a *caleta*, which literally means "a hole." Some of the fancier cartels had holes outfitted with generators and mini-fridges stocked with Heineken. Others operated out of warehouses, and kept the gringos out of the jungle altogether. But the luckiest smugglers—Willy included—were offered the magic of a behind-the-scenes experience. They were brought through the "staff only" door of America's marijuana factory, as close to the source as white men would get until they started growing their own. A stream burbled nearby, camouflage scrub nets hung as insulation against military helicopters, and cartel members in dusty street clothes lazed about on crates, cleaning guns, spitting.

High Times called the Guajira "pirate paradise."

But to appreciate what this must have felt like for a smuggler, remember that before marijuana became an over-the-counter experience, the very process of securing a single joint was an ecstatic challenge, a high before the high. Then multiply the feeling of a score by all the levels between a joint in your bedroom and a crop in Colombia, all the dealers between a ten-gram baggie on a corner and a ten-ton boatload on an ocean, all the miles between evading American parents and evading international law enforcement, all the hours and the years of freedom at risk if you falter, and then square that number to account for the sheer economic power of it all.

The patriarchs of local farms presented samples of their finest crops, hoping Willy would buy the field, feed their family, make the year a good one. Willy, for his part, would smell the product, roll it between thumb and forefinger, check the tops for the fine red hairs that told him it was ready to smoke. It was that moment, as the farmer waits and America waits, that hooked smugglers on the life.

That, and cocaine. Willy was so lit up by cocaine that he sent Jimbo to negotiate with the Colombians. At the same time, Charlie pushed Daniel out to find investors in the smuggle. Scrimshaw looked for that apartment in Manhattan. Corky looked for sailors. As an insurance policy against Willy's load falling apart, and out of sheer professional duty, my father agreed to sell a load of John's dope that was coming into Massachusetts in October.

John spent his week in the mountains sleeping in a hammock and working to refine his load down to the bare essentials. With a team of locals helping him, he rose at dawn and worked until dusk, until his fingers cracked and the bugs bore into him. He helped remove three tons of stems and leaves, cutting the size of his load in half, making it pure bud.

"See the little blisters here, here, and here?" he later said to a friend in the lobby of a hotel in Boston. He held up his hand for inspection, business travelers marching around him, smoothing their ties. He might as well have returned from some sort of adventure travel package aimed at rich, corporate types. Journey to the heart of the Colombian badlands to clean just-pulled ancient herbs. Start the bidding at $5,000.

By late June, Willy's load had been selected from the source with no problems, but Jimbo had bad news: The Colombians wanted more money to move it. He learned this in Barranquilla, where he visited the gaudy compound of the cartel leader. The house was part vacation villa, part prison, and entirely self-conscious. The armed guards wore polo shirts. The hallways were lined in riding trophies. There was even a book on the coffee table, put out by a vanity press, entitled *103 Murders*. It carried the byline of the cartel leader himself.

Timber Tom was dispatched to Barranquilla with a top-off sum: $60,000 taped around his thighs. His first thought, as he looked at the aquarium in the living room, was that he had somehow slipped into a Fellini dream. He was reminded of why he had taken this job: not only because his coffers were down but also because it was a pure act, and if you succeeded, no applause was needed.

When Tom got into the compound, he peeled the cash off his legs and tossed the money at Jimbo, who blanched at the sight of it. The money wasn't for the Colombians, as it turned out—it was for the Americans, local DEA agents who wanted $10,000 apiece to accept and perpetuate a false story about the travel plans for the boat Tom would take from Barranquilla to the Guajira. There were twelve of them in town, not six.

"We need $60,000 more," Jimbo said.

Days passed.

Willy tried to sober up, scrounge some more dough. In the meantime Timber Tom went to the roof, where he had a view of the city, a bustling port at the mouth of the Magdalena River, the biggest in Colombia. He tried some of the weed he would be carrying, feeling his skin start to tingle, and he watched the sun fall toward the horizon, setting windows ablaze and plunging side streets into darkness. He could scarcely believe his eyes as soldiers appeared, closing down intersections, waiting in parked trucks, surrounding the compound. He looked at the joint and back at the street. But it wasn't a hallucination, and it wasn't a bust. The pope was in town, bringing a message of, what else: Don't do drugs.

Later that week or the next, Tom walked to the river, where he hoped to get a glimpse of his ship. The cartel had rented it to Willy, who of course requested that the boat be fresh and clean, rather than recently boarded or busted by the Coast Guard. One vessel in particular he said was hot. "Whatever you do," Willy had stressed to Tom before he left for South America, "don't let them give you the ocean-going tugboat." Tom was looking at the ocean-going tugboat.

More delays.

As Tom went to work on the boat, my father and Willy languished at the Landmark. They nibbled cold shepherd's pie as their ice cubes melted. It was face-rakingly boring, absolutely typical, and kind of a blast. Time froze on the brink of something worth the wait.

At a hardware store, Tom bought a dozen cans of white paint, a dozen cans of black paint. Over the next couple of days he turned his boat into a replica of the striped service tugs that pulled fresh water between the islands. When Tom finished, the cartel's Colombian captain of the boat came on board and shrugged at the labor. He was a big man with a limp hand. "Sorry I'm late," he said, not sorry at all. The rest of the money had come in, he continued, and it was all-aboard time.

The next morning Timber Tom, the fish-handed captain, and twelve Colombian nationals left port. They traveled fifteen miles south to where the silty brown of the Magdalena dumps into the Caribbean. They headed straight out, as though taking fresh water to Guadeloupe, roughly the midpoint in a necklace of islands that runs from Puerto Rico to Caracas, Venezuela. At Guadeloupe, Tom veered south again, following the arc as though still on a water route, which the DEA in Barranquilla had been paid off to confirm, before making a night dash toward the coast of the Guajira. The move added a thousand miles to the journey, but that's a small price to pay for an alibi.

The meeting point was a tendril of land that created a little lagoon, a brackish pond of river water and churn off the Caribbean. Tom found it without a problem but he didn't see anyone waiting for him in the tree line. Still more days passed. No word from shore. No word from Willy. No one to call, nothing to do but scan the tree line, leave, and scan it again.

Tom guided the tug back out to sea, where he let her drift a while to save gas. When he returned to the spot, he saw vibrations in the leaves and then a mule appeared and then another and another. He saw multiple bales of pressed marijuana lashed to their sides and backs, each mule rocking like a railroad car as it approached the lagoon, led by farmers, followed by gunmen. Tom lost count after two hundred and fifty animals had gathered along the stunted shore, where Wayuu Indians waited in hand-carved canoes.

In the early days of Spanish rule, the Wayuu taught themselves firearms and riding, recognizing what was needed to survive. In the quarter millennium that followed, they continued to improvise, profiting from guns, gold, emeralds, pearls, sugar, coffee. Every thing was sold with their help, or their hostility. This time it was help. They moved the marijuana from shore to boat, splitting the sea with new outboard motors lashed to pieces of old-growth tropical rain forest.

The switch point was to be Île Fourchue, a quarter mile of wildflowers and rocks. John used Guadeloupe and St. Kitts for his meeting points. The truth is, just about anywhere on the map would do. Caribbean narcotics "squads" were usually a single constable with a billy club and a set of jangling keys. If he caught you, he was as liable to ask how much for ten bales as to put you in his one-room jailhouse. And don't worry about the locals saying anything.

During the golden age of piracy, 1715 to 1725, sympathetic crowds rescued men from the gallows and offered refuge from assault. More than two hundred and fifty years later, during the golden age of pot and beyond, similar crowds assisted the smugglers. In the Turks and Caicos, when American authorities arrested the president, who allegedly let smugglers refuel on his islands, his people booed. In the Bahamas, the DEA pursued a smuggler's boat onto a crowded beach, only to be beaten back by crowds hurling bottles and rocks. Marijuana paid the bills there, too.

It was the open water, not land, that got smugglers into trouble. The Coast Guard alone had twenty-one vessels a day searching the Caribbean, and averaging a bust for every four patrols, usually the result of a chance run-in (Hey, a ship!) and a gut feeling (Doing what, exactly?). Tom reduced his risk by following the semicircle of islands northward again, well out of his way. But as he curled the tug around Guadeloupe, he saw it on the far side of the island: the *White Horn*, a hundred-foot Coast Guard cutter, prickling with antennae. It seemed to be waiting for them.

"Everybody down below," he yelled to his adopted crew. "Come up and I'll shoot you."

Tom walked out of the boat's towers and stood on the bow, the picture of counterfeit ease. He lit a cigarette, and as he puffed, he couldn't help but count the number of gold marijuana leafs on the hull and smokestacks of this mammoth cutter. Each one represented a million pounds of confiscated dope, dozens of busts. One, two, three, four, five . . . He almost went slack in the knees. The *White Horn* had fourteen leaves on her. He waved at his fellow captain, or to whoever was behind the tinted windows of Reagan's warship. Then he turned his back, casually, he hoped, and prayed.

Tom waited for what he felt was an unsuspicious interval, then slid the tugboat alongside a neighboring cruise ship, blocking the Coast Guard's line of sight and giving him a cloak of radar coverage. Then he peeled off around the next uninhabited island, into a cove where he spent the night. At dawn he was out again, making good time to Île Fourchue.

In the 1970s, Charlie used to sit on the peak of that island with night goggles and a flashlight. Coast Guard cutters were always circling the area, seeing nothing, when in fact the sea around every bend was hot with activity. This time, no man waited for Tom atop the mountain, so no one was there to tell him not to bother showing up for the transfer. A chartered yacht had anchored in his drop spot for a cocktail party.

He called yet another audible and arranged the drops to happen off the coast of St. Barts. The captains of the sailboats he was meeting balked at the idea, citing the seaside dining spots. Tom insisted that from a well-lit area the patrons would not be able to see into darkness. "We'll be ghosts," he said.

One by one, as fat and happy diners gazed at their own reflections in the windows or else a vague ocean of seamless black, the six sailboats navigated to Tom's "mother ship." That's what big dope boats were universally dubbed, in a beautiful blend of Cold War and *Star Wars* lingo. Inflatable Zodiac rafts shuttled the dope from the tug to the sailboats. After the last transfer, Tom left the ship to its Colombian owners and hitched a ride on another Zodiac.

A few feet from sand, he hopped out. Damp and reeking of weed, he walked up the beach, through a murmuring French restaurant, glowing with that special energy that comes from a quantity of adrenaline dissolved in bliss. Willy was waiting for him on the main street, and they drank champagne until dawn, their reefer sailing on toward America.

Dope is a terrible first mate. It consumes all the living space, all the food space, all the bed space. At night, the captain sleeps topside or on the bales themselves, waking with watery bloodshot eyes at best and to a tarantula that has crawled out of the pile and into his stomach hair at worst. All the dope is good for is curing seasickness. That and boredom, which was inevitable during the three- or four-week journey north with little more than crackers and canned cheese to eat.

The timing of the smuggle was perfect. It was mid-July—the height of the sailing season. Tens of thousands of boats would be on the water. That meant tens of thousands of boats nettling the Coast Guard with incompetence. Inga was in a hotel room in Fredericksburg, Virginia, with a VHF radio and a single-sideband radio. As soon as the boats were within nine hundred miles, she could communicate with them, clearing their path with bogus SOS calls if needed. A week after the boats departed St. Barts, the first three turned left at Bermuda and made radio contact. Inga relayed progress reports to my father and Bobby, who by now had another driver with them.

My mother and I had spent the rest of June on Cape Cod, where she won $500 playing scratch-off lotto and I breathed the air of affluence at a summer camp. We drove to New York in early July, where my father squinted and stumbled his way a block west to meet us at the Intrepid Museum, a decommissioned aircraft carrier on the Hudson. One picture tells the story: a shot of us on the deck, or rather on a shelf dug into the side of the deck. I'm five years old and a "big boy," as they say. And yet my father has hoisted me in his arms, and his smile is this strange blend of clench and calm, like the smile of a bodybuilder in full flex on the cover of a muscle mag or a paunchy man sucking in his gut as he passes a pretty girl.

Days later we flew home to Miami, and my father drove his truck to Richmond, where he padded around in his element: an anonymous high-end hotel. The theme was the Old World tobacco trade. When men like my father get busted as "organizers" of a smuggle, defense lawyers often deploy the same tired line, scoffing at the notion of an organizer driving trucks, working the docks. They ask the jurors to see the ridiculousness of the idea. "It's like the CEO of General Motors down on the shop floor kicking the tires." Sometimes juries even buy it, not knowing that kicking the tires is exactly what these men are in the business for in the first place. They didn't become criminals to keep their hands clean.

His phone rang as the first ketch slipped over the submerged middle third of the Chesapeake Bay Bridge-Tunnel, ceding to the weary authority of passing freighters. The crew trimmed sails and yanked on a small outboard motor as state parks passed in darkness on either shore. My father and the other driver slid into their trucks, the vinyl seats imparting a predawn chill. As the first sailboat followed a finger of the Chesapeake toward Urbanna, my father exited I-64 and crossed the York River, passing farms and forest for thirty thought-provoking miles until the road forked again at Old Virginia Street, and he was in Urbanna.

Some smugglers get cute on their journey toward American shores. If they own the boat, they paint a high-water line around the hull so at a glance the vessel appears to be riding empty. Others hang a foreign flag when in international waters, in hopes of deterring the Coast Guard, and run the Stars and Stripes near the shore, in hopes of deterring customs and everyone else. Still others hang a sack of getaway scuba gear off the stern—praying they won't have to use it.

This crew kept their running lights on to avoid a "safety check," the maritime equivalent of being pulled over for a missing taillight, but they hewed to Charlie's principle of invisibility in plain sight. Besides being a tobacco port, Urbanna had once been a schooner and steamship dock, with its tiny creek dredged and widened repeatedly over the years, enough to accommodate sailboats with relatively deep keels.

The boats sailed right in, as though returning home. They hung a left into the Rappahannock River, then another into the creek, and sidled up to an outcropping of Pierre's inherited marina, a covered structure called the Oyster House, because that's what it was usually for: unloading oysters.

A century ago the sons of Urbanna stretched the necks of pirates on a wharf across from Pierre's marina. My father parked the Mario's Fish truck in an alley. His colleague backed the Global Moving truck to the edge of the water, and the men got to work. With help from Pierre and two friends, they unloaded the bales, about a hundred and twenty-five of them.

Each bale was about the size of a large sofa cushion, and it arrived pressed and triple wrapped. Like hay or mulch, marijuana has a tendency to warm up in the center and leech potency. So each bale was wrapped once in brown paper, which absorbed some of the moisture and sweat; once in plastic, which kept oil or bilge or seawater from spoiling the load; and, lastly, it was wrapped in a burlap sack that was thrown over the bale and sewn shut, so men like my father could heave and toss the stuff into trucks and onto the scales.

My father shut the back of the truck as silently as he would the door to my room as I slept. When the first truck was gone, he backed his up to the water's edge. This was the unnerving part: the wait for boat number two, staggered miles behind the lead vessel. The off-load crew and my father waited and waited, burning cigarettes and staring at the pay phone by the dock. They scuffed their shoes on the wood and spit and watched the moon lose and gain clouds. They were cold and scared and thinking, Man, this is fun. It was almost sad when, around 5:00 a.m., my father's big bony elbow was poking out the window, his foot on the gas. He turned the radio on, whirling the dial in search of a road song.

As a precaution, a premonition either Inga or the captain had, the third boat was diverted to a private off-load spot in Maryland. The other driver, a friend of Bobby's, was radioed to meet it. There were no chase cars this time. The Global Moving truck was alone at the drop point, and it was alone on the highway. It was also alone at the rest stop near Philadelphia, where it broke down and the driver skedaddled, leaving behind a disabled truck with out-of-state plates and more than a million dollars of marijuana inside.

My father made it all the way to the stash house in New Canaan, Connecticut, some ten hours north, before he heard from Bobby, who was frantic. They only had two trucks, after all, and Global Moving was one of them. It needed to be in Maine in a day, and, anyway, it couldn't sit there and bake in the sun. The last that Bobby had heard from their deserter was that the truck was drivable but risky: The gas pedal was sticking, and the vehicle kept lurching and jerking, which would make it a cat toy for cops—if the truck had not been searched already.

My father was cooking up some classic stash-house vittles in New Canaan when Bobby called and told him to get back on the road. Instead my father took his time, filling his belly with yellow mac and cheese from a box, canned tuna, and frozen peas. He downed a can of Miller High Life and had Fig Newtons for dessert, and still he didn't leave. He chatted with his two helpers, more friends of Bobby's, who flipped a coin to see who would take my father south.

If you plotted the job on a matrix where the vertical axis is exertion and the horizontal axis is fellow feeling, working a stash house would rank near couch moving and television installation: a bit of sweat, but lots of smiles and beer. The pay was always $2 a pound, which was good money for a pleasant night's work with like-minded men.

My father filled an attached garage and living room with the bales, each of them tagged with a weight and a price, then numbered, so the count in the room always matched the count on his clipboard, which matched the count that comes in from the buyers, who were due within the next twenty-four hours. With hundreds of bales to unload, this process could take half the night, especially if the quality varied wildly, which it often did because a multiton load was usually drawn from multiple Colombian farms. But this load was exceptionally consistent and high quality, and it had been cleaned first, so it was almost all bud.

The only problem was the two bales that had been hit with waves or plucked from the sea. My father set those aside as shrinkage. The ocean changed the way the weed burned, it was said, which is why sea bales were known as "headache" weed. No one seemed to know why this happened or what could be done about it, and over the years it became a genuine smuggler's conundrum. A few years ago, Uncle Dougie and his partner had stayed up half the night in a stash house like this one, trying to solve it.

What about hosing it off with fresh water? It's not a head of lettuce.

What about setting it in a cube of good bales and letting the steam evaporate the salt? That will contaminate other loads.

What about sugar water?

They settled on sugar as the antidote to salt, and filled a kiddie pool with water and a pound of the sweet stuff. They dragged the bale and the pool to a barn on the property, and tossed the bale in. They doused it and went to sleep.

When they woke up the bale was gone, or almost gone. A few chunks floated in the sugar water, surrounded by ragged pieces of twine. The floor around the kiddie pool was clean except for a few dropped stems and seeds from the larger stash. Then they saw a kind of nest above the double doors, and another nest in a knothole near the floorboards. Their eyes followed the bones of the barn upward, and they saw more and more nests—almost every flat or dug-out surface was now a bed of marijuana. Saltwater weed may disagree with humans, but roof rats and deer mice don't seem to mind it—especially if it's coated with sugar. Even a trace of marijuana is enough for authorities to confiscate property, so it cost them a day's labor to clean out the barn.

That was my father's parting advice as he left to retrieve the broken-down moving truck: Don't use sugar water.

He hitched a ride south, closing his eyes for the first time in more than a day. He awoke near Philadelphia, early the following morning, the hour when night and day noises overlap. He got out, took a piss, smoked a cigarette, and sized up the situation. He didn't know the exact time—since wearing a watch always made him feel slightly off-balance—but he calculated that at least half a day had already passed, which meant the truck could be staked, bugged, followed, robbed, you name it.

He sent his ride home and smoked another cigarette. The rest stop was little more than a hollow where the state parked heavy equipment when building the road. One or two picnic tables, a dozen old trees, fifty yards of blacktop, and a tennis court–size patch of grass you just knew was covered in little piles of dog art. The truck was parked alone near the edge of the surrounding forest. It looked quiet, but quiet was how people got caught.

He began walking toward the truck, thinking he was surely going to be the leprechaun caught with his pot of gold. The door was open and he climbed in. As my father turned the key, he closed his eyes and opened them, expecting to be squinting into a flashlight beam. He waited for a second, still expecting to be yanked down to the curb. Instead the truck started up fine, and that was that; no one seemed to follow him. The gas pedal even wiggled back into place.

A few days later, Bobby and my father were in Maine, near Seal Cove. It was the kind of place where you might write narrative history, sew fishing lures, or try to bond with your son. The kind of place you would bring a mistress. And since Inga was there, too, fiddling with her radios, waiting for word, my father figured she might make do. He had just played the hero, and she was beautiful, a girl who knew how to wave to somebody from the end of a dock. Inga did not want to wave to my father, however, and I'm reminded of my father in high school, messing with his teachers, trying to bait them. More than a few times, they called him to the front of the class and slapped him. Inga did the same thing, long before dawn. But he didn't care. It was kind of the point.

The Maine smuggle went off fine, smoother than the Virginia leg, which meant that the men had just secured the biggest score of their lives, one of the biggest single scores in marijuana history. My father was prone to a crash after a big job, and those crashes became ever more severe as the jobs themselves became ever more extreme. During this job he had succeeded in working clean, and yet as the work shifted from smuggling and sales to the simpler work of receiving boxes of cash, he shifted into the celebratory fugue he thought he deserved.

In the middle of this good time, on the evening of September 14, 1986, Ronald Reagan preempted Sunday-night programming with "something special to talk about." He was dressed in security-guard gray slacks and a blue jacket, and sitting on a flowery white couch in his private living room. Beside him was Nancy, dressed in a red skirt with gold buttons. They were holding hands and looked both tired and worried, as though America were out way past its curfew, doing God knows what, and had just come home smelling like cinnamon gum.

"Good evening," Reagan began, the camera tightening on his face, which had aged in office. There were now cords of flesh at the corners of his mouth and a gobbler beneath his chin. "Nancy is joining me because the message this evening is not my message but ours." He mentioned some of his successes, rebuilding the economy and serving the cause of freedom in the world. Then he turned to the focus of the evening: drugs.

Drugs are "threatening our values and undercutting our institutions," he said, before a weighty pause. "They're killing our children."

Since early August the idea for this joint speech had been floating around the White House. It was being drafted and redrafted as Bobby and my father sold seventeen tons of marijuana to eight wholesalers. Each man drove a truck up from New York City, meeting my dad at a busy rest stop off I-95, where he left them to use the vending machines while he drove the truck to the stash house, unloaded their down payment of some $300,000 a ton, and loaded their dope.

As Reagan's speechwriter processed the president's thoughts and bundled his ideas, my father and Bobby processed more than $11 million in mixed bills and bundled them for shipment to the Caribbean and beyond. Scrimshaw was set up for deliveries, sitting in an apartment he'd found on Manhattan's Upper East Side: an eleventh-floor two-bedroom in one of those big prewar buildings. He figured the doorman and the laws of probability would limit the risk of a random robbery. His cover job was art trading, which he actually did part time, spending weeks in and out of Sotheby's, Christie's, MoMA, the Met, the Guggenheim, and the Frick. If you consider that $1 million in hundreds weighs almost exactly twenty pounds and gets heavier with each drop down the denomination ladder, we're talking about at least half a ton of cash, probably more.

The night Reagan delivered his biggest drug-policy speech since declaring the War on Drugs, my father and Bobby were splayed out beneath the fourteen-foot ceilings of a Plaza Hotel penthouse—a reward after couch-surfing at the stash house. They had between them $1.5 million, $750,000 each. The rest was already out of the country, on a journey around the world and into banks in the Channel Islands, Switzerland, and Hong Kong, as well as more local and less distinguished holes, including deep into the bilge of a few sailboats.

My father and Bobby didn't watch the address, but if they had it might have confused them. After all, the night Nancy Reagan accused drug dealers of "destroying the brightness and life of the sons and daughters of the United States," my father and Bobby were having a bright and lively time indeed. She said that drugs take "the dream from every child's heart," "the vivid color that God gave us," but in their come-down room, my father and Bobby had a childlike money fight and did lines off of the mahogany side tables until they were catatonic with joy.

They would have been most mystified by the president, however, who found the camera for his dramatic closing statement. He used the word *crusade* six times in the next ten minutes. He compared the fight against traffickers to the counterpunch that followed Pearl Harbor, dubbing it "another war for our freedom." And he brought good news from the front lines.

"In four years the number of high-school seniors using marijuana on a daily basis has dropped from one in fourteen to one in twenty," the president said. What's more, he continued, "shortages of marijuana are now being reported."

Forgive him, he didn't have the latest figures.

All smugglers are dreamers. They live for their last big job, the mother of them all, and they talk endlessly about what they would do if they actually pulled it off. In this way they are a lot like teenage boys who talk about all they would do if they could just get this or that pretty girl undressed. In both cases success is the first step to failure, the dream come true is the demise in waiting.

My father did not take well to his success. I remember a beautiful day on Virginia Key, collecting seashells and driftwood, Dad and I playing Wiffle ball until our shoulders still felt warm in the shade. In the afternoon, we headed back to the car, my mother's maroon Volvo, planning to buy some roadside key lime pie or add another plastic baseball helmet to my collection of sundae bowls from Carvel. The passenger-side window was shattered, and the radio was gone.

My father went wild, slapping at the exposed wires and reaching his hand into the slot as though the machine had merely fallen in. He prowled around the car and scanned the lot, like a man who had just lost a briefcase with his soul inside, not a radio and a hundred bucks or so to replace a window. I think he must have had his drugs behind the radio.

In early October, my father's bender got so bad that Bobby and his other supplier, John, came to physically retrieve him and put him back in a quickie rehab program. They needed him to help handle John's three-ton load, which was still coming into Martha's Vineyard that month, so they knocked on our front door.

No answer.

They kicked on our front door.

No answer.

Finally, they banged on our picture window and then stood back to see the blinds part.

Two red-rimmed eyes stared out.

They took my father to upstate New York, where Bobby found him immediate placement in a fancy rehab center with complimentary massages and twenty-four-hour racquetball. My father went willingly. He loved those guys, after all. They were his best friends and he knew he was putting them at risk. They had a week before he was needed in a stash house for John.

In the middle of the night, however, my father went to the front desk with a packed duffel bag and asked the guard to call him a cab. When the guard made a move to call the night staff, my father made one of his own, telling the guard he was going to piss in his face and tell him it's raining. The next day Bobby called to check in on his friend, and he got the surprise message: Tony Dokoupil is no longer a patient here.

It ended up making no difference to John, whose load arrived on a single forty-foot ketch named *Calliope*. The boat only got as far as Martha's Vineyard, where the captain mistook one island for another and ran into the rocks of Nashawena, just across the sound. The crew escaped, and no one was arrested, but the Coast Guard counted 144 bales of finely cleaned reefer in the hold, telling *The Boston Globe*: "She was full from the decks to the top of the ceiling."

That December the gang met for a celebration in St. Thomas, where my father and some friends were supposed to mark their exit from the catastrophe business. Charlie and Bobby were there, along with a long-retired smuggler named Brandy, Bobby's girlfriend (a former hooker), my mother, my father, Bobby's son, Brandy's son, and myself.

Before we all set sail, my mother and father and I ambled around the island. We patted old cannons, paused over the iron information placards, and yo-ho-ho'ed our way around the ancient warehouses of the capital, Charlotte Amelie, which once supposedly held the bounty of Bluebeard, Blackbeard, and Captain Kidd. Before we returned to the hotel, my father got the idea that he would start stockpiling man stuff for his little guy. You know, passing on the wisdoms of a life lived in obeisance to romance, as the star of his own epic.

The tradition actually began with that baby-blue Stones T-shirt in 1975. It continued with a small watercolor of a saloon in Key West. It ended in St. Thomas, when my father bought a carved and painted coconut, depicting a pirate holding the hand of a little monkey, which of course stood for my father holding the hand of little blond me: happy and free.

Our hotel was holding a "pirate hunt" down by the water. It was only a few doubloons buried by the hotel staff and a treasure chest disguised by a few well-worn palm fronds, but I was a kid and fantasy is easy. I dug up the money, popped the lock on the treasure chest, picked up handfuls of yellow plastic—the "treasure"—and let it drizzle into a pile, which I rolled through and defended against the encroaching fantasies of other little boys.

Two or three days later, my father was gone. He walked off the boat, down the pier, and disappeared into myth, where he has lived ever since. No one could really find him there. It's a place where my imagination is a spinning instrument panel, and even now with all my research I feel like I can only just find the horizon line, maybe make out a few shadows. I have big questions. Where did he go? Why did he go?

He flew back to Miami and moved out of our house, officially this time, and into his place on Brickell Avenue, which I never saw until recently. It became the high board for his swan dive toward the asphalt and down through it, deeper, to the very scummy bottom, past the rock, and into the sludge and the swamp.

During this stretch of his life, he thought a lot about the 150,000 books he claimed to have read. One of his all-time favorites was *Death in Venice*, a book about growing old in a young world. It seemed to deepen his blissful tragedy, allowing him to feel his body shrivel and his mind reel and to revel in the loss of whatever powers he'd once had. It was sublime. It was dying.

My mother thinks my father was addicted to the partying. That's probably what most people would surmise. The good times got him. But I think the opposite was true. I think he was addicted to the bad times, to the foxhole. When he had money, my mother, and me, he lost his god, so he created a new foxhole, a low stinky place where he could find a new god. He created problems for himself, so he could have problems. He was miserable without them.

What he never considered, and seems incapable of considering, is the other side of the equation. The simple, sad possibility that we might be miserable without him.

III

Coming Down

8

Busted

Plenty of pot barons self-destructed in retirement, but no one did it quite like Anthony Edward Dokoupil. For weeks at a stretch he lived in hotels, upended kilos of cocaine, and hired naked strangers by the squad. The girls were in the phone book under E for escorts. One night my father started dialing, and the agencies somehow knew it was him. Every one refused him service. And his life was only just beginning to get ugly.

My mother supported him through a long series of thirty-day rehab programs at as much as $10,000 apiece, and no refund if the patient decides to piss in the guard's face before the month is over, which one way or another my father always did. He ran away from mud huts, hot stones, and heated pools. I visited him once, and we fished from the landscaped banks of a stocked pond while my mother waited in the car, polishing off a Tupperware bowl of homemade pasta. She gained more than forty pounds in 1987 and 1988, telling friends that food was her medication.

The phrase "no way" reoccurred in my mother's life. She first said "no way" when she was dating my father and he called her names. She said "no way" when he slapped her around, too, and "no way" when he disappeared for days. She said "no way" that night in Connecticut, the night my father became his own father, throwing a knife instead of pointing a gun.

She said "no way" again in early 1987, after she gave me *The Brown Bottle*, a kids' book about addiction. I was six, the target age, and together we read about Charlie, "a fuzzy brown creature who leaves the caterpillar kingdom to follow the bright, invigorating glow of life inside a discarded brown bottle." Charlie gets drunk, in other words, likes it, and never becomes a butterfly.

It was simple enough, and at first I seemed to show a new understanding of Dad and his demons. A few days later, I pointed to a chocolate bar in the rack next to the checkout at the supermarket. "I really want that," I said sagely, "and that must be how Daddy feels when he wants drugs." But of course this was not how Daddy felt.

To get an idea of what Daddy felt, I would have needed to smuggle that grocery-store chocolate into my first-grade classroom, stash it in my desk, sell it on the sly, and use the proceeds to consume a big bag of Doritos every day on the calendar. Eventually I would need to promise myself that I will stop such behavior, and then do it all again with *two* boxes of chocolate bars, *two* bags of Doritos.

Because I didn't really understand my father, I was free to adore him. I continued to try on his mannerisms, just as my son does in my shadow today. I crossed my arms like him, groomed my imaginary mustache like him, read the *Herald* like him. When it was time to go somewhere, I dolphined a hand through my hair and led my mother through the door. He was gone from our lives but present in me, and that hurt my mother more than his fists ever could.

It was these echoes of my father, not the father himself, that gave her the energy she needed to end things, formally and completely. She said "no way," and for the first time she meant it. My grandmother Phyllis would have understood if she knew: "Not my boy," my mother was saying. "You have gotten me, but you won't take him."

In early 1987 Ann sued Anthony for full custody of me, hiring a $200-an-hour Coral Gables lawyer to do the job. She alleged—accurately, I might add—that my father "calls or appears from time to time," showing a "propensity for violence" and "consuming controlled substances in substantial quantities." Because she worried about how he would respond, she filed a restraining order against him as well, and she secured Gulliver's cooperation against the man paying the tuition: I was not to be released to him under any circumstances.

This trickled down to me in the form of one bizarrely tense and tearful goodbye. When we arrived at the top of the school drop-off circle, my mother captured both of my hands in hers and turned me toward her, delivering a message of doom. I was not to go with my father if he comes to the fence during after-school play, she said. My father never did.

He was too far gone, so far in fact that his memory of these years is spotty, like a series of subterranean tunnels, the entrance long since hidden in a rock slide and discoverable only by a fall through the ceiling when you are on your way somewhere else. He remembers a four-day binge with a girl he'd never met before, a girl he trusted like a Swiss Bank. He remembers giving her $75,000 to hold because the registration on his Mercedes had expired, and he was afraid he would be pulled over and caught with the cash. He remembers losing the Mercedes. He remembers losing the girl.

He remembers losing his boat, too, but he can't recall how. He definitely stopped paying slip fees. That realization came to him in a high-rise hotel, one in the endless, almost monotonous procession of luxury accommodations he consumed and then forgot. Inside the elevator he met a man who seemed higher than him, a man who was flying, swinging his arms and rearranging his stances. He said, "You got a boat, because I just got a boat, a nice boat." As far as my father was concerned it was his boat. He knew it was.

In addition to rehab bills, my mother paid medical bills. She wrote checks to Harbor View, North Miami Medical Center, Dr. Cope, Dr. Keeler, Dr. Nelson, Dr. Kahn. One doctor found an incurable infection lodged somewhere near my father's heart. He called my mother and told her to prepare for a funeral. She laughed in his ear, and my father simply racked up another bill, another debt to be paid. All year my mother watched her accounts dwindle.

By Thanksgiving she was broke enough to worry. We traveled to Connie's house, kicking through the leaves and "exploring" (as I understood it) the property. No luck. My father had already dug up and squandered the two known stashes, and we couldn't find others. My mother did snag two classic cars she had stored in the Florida Redlands, one of which she ended up loaning to the makers of *Miami Vice*. But two cars were never going to cover tuition for private school for another dozen years. Two cars weren't going to break the chain. So in the lonely quiet, while I was at school, my mother planned a mission in search of the richest prize: that cooler in New Mexico.

She bought a map, rented a Winnebago, and cleared the visit with her sister out west. But she needed time. It would take ten days to two weeks to drive a mobile home the four thousand miles round-trip with an incontinent black Lab and a kid on board. She was teaching again, so the trip couldn't be until summer break, and she knew summer might be too late. Every day she changed the date on her chalkboard, and she thought maybe this is the day the money is gone.

When June 1988 arrived our motor home swayed westward without incident, and we returned home with our hidden cargo of illicit cash. I lazed on the big bed in the back, oblivious to the real purpose of our mission and listening to one oldie station fizzle into the next. The songs were the same as they always were, a singable mix of antiwar melodies and folksy drug ballads from my mother's youth. The difference was that my mother did more singing along, and I joined in, mumbling toward the chorus when our voices rose and flattened, and everything flew right out the window with our sound.

My mother was making her break. She called my father at his Brickell Avenue apartment, and they agreed to meet just over the causeway, in the Art Deco district along Miami Beach. My mother didn't want to be alone with the man, not ever again, so she picked a side road near the ocean, arrived early, and waited in the car until she saw my father.

He looked so old, she thought, as she watched him walking past teens in Jordache jeans and broad-limbed Cuban men in guayaberas. He was forty-two years old, but when he took off his sunglasses, he had the eyes of an old man, and his belly, which once felt like a warm stream over hard rocks, looked stuffed with feathers. She handed him a contract. My father signed it, his signature such a palsied, coked-up mess that the *E* in his middle name, Edward, came out a bit like a cartoon stink line.

The document confirmed my mother as "a single woman," and it gave her possession of the house, which she paid for with $30,000 in a suitcase. It was a nothing sum, but my father was getting desperate. He'd lost his identification somewhere, so he could not get access to his safe-deposit box no matter how many times he told the guards that his code name was Plato.

In his telling of this story, my mother handed him the money and drove off yelling to any thief in earshot, "He's got $30,000 on him! He's got $30,000 on him!" This doesn't sound like my mother. Then again I've never treated my mother the way my father did, so I won't pretend to be able to get to the bottom of their traded barbs, except to say that whatever began in the Beachcomber during the Nixon years was over.

My mother bought herself a makeover of mind and body. She went back into therapy, cut her hair short and streaked it blond. She commissioned a new ring: two fourteen-karat-gold dolphins swimming around a smooth piece of turquoise, which she said represented power, freedom, and peace. She also invested a large portion of the money, buying into a shady apartment project in North Miami. And she secured her own Vizcaya, or at least the property for it: two waterfront lots in the Turks and Caicos, an island chain that once harbored Mary Read and Anne Bonny, the lady pirates who sailed with Calico Jack, Captain Kidd, and Blackbeard. In symbolism it doesn't take an English professor to point out, she used drug money to pay for a graduate certificate in drug and alcohol counseling from the University of Miami.

For New Year's she hopped on a cruise from Miami to Mexico, traveling through Jamaica and the Cayman Islands, including two midnight celebrations, as the boat raced from one time zone to another. Lastly, she bought a deep purple Mustang convertible, the color of a bruised apple, with a little chrome horse galloping on the hood. She took me for a ride, touching a hundred miles an hour on a straightaway in the Everglades, where she felt uncatchable.

My father didn't respond kindly to this turn of events. As with the rest of his violence and abuse, he did it around corners, behind doors, and when I was out of earshot. But I do have one solid memory from the middle of 1988, when I was seven years old. Like all true tales of heartache it begins with the New York Mets. They were my dad's team, and therefore they were my team. We saw them together in New

York and followed them together in the local paper. Once I turned on a game when they were playing the Yankees at the moment after Darryl Strawberry hit a home run. It gave me the idea that I was a jinx, a ruiner of things. When I wasn't watching, the team did well. When I watched, the team did poorly.

The Strawberry homer represented a balance between these two positions. It happened because it was allowed to happen almost entirely without the weight of my waiting for it, watching it, jinxing it. So for all of the 1988 season, that's how I watched the Mets—by not watching the Mets, except for the moments when I would sneak up on the TV and surprise them in the act of winning.

This required subterfuge and guile. I would wipe boogers on the wall next to my bed or throw parachute men into the air in the front yard until I got the feeling that winning was happening. I would run over the cool smooth concrete of the garage and fling open the door of the living room.

As I did so this particular time I heard a kind of whoosh, almost a cheer. And I saw my father on his knees, fists poised over the table, glass entirely shattered. My mother appeared from the kitchen, her face melted by emotion. The game was on, but I shut the door and only later learned that she was trying to throw him out.

"Why are you doing this?" my father had asked.

"To break the chain," my mother said.

I never saw my father again, not as a kid, anyway, not when it mattered most. He disappeared from our lives and the lives of his friends. And he edged toward nightmare.

A funny thing about drug dealers: many of them live low-rent even when they have enough money to live lavishly. The contrast is richest with coke dealers, guys making tens of millions of dollars, buying mansions in the Bahamas and Miami, fellas who own tigers, helicopters, and racehorses, fleets of fast cars, and every other cliché of the narco rich. These same guys often live in squalor, and not just metaphorically. There's the emotional squalor, sure, the wretchedness of perpetual wish fulfillment and the wreckage of broken relationships.

But there's honest to God squalor, too, the traditional stuff: dirty house, dirty car, dirty body. Time and time again, when a coke dealer was busted in Miami, the cops were shocked to find, in a ten-thousand-square-foot property, piles of steaming tiger shit, banisters plastered with exotic parrot scat, stained and torn furniture. The dealers could pay someone to pick it up, of course, but they don't. Maybe they think it matches the squalor on the inside, or maybe it makes them feel safe, or never mind why, because it's simply true and my father was such a dealer.

He was always interested in the other side of a situation, the opposite pole. If he stood before you in a brass-buttoned blue coat, lean-jawed and proud, happy and healthy, bright and shiny, he began to play a little game in his mind. He began to toy with a question: How far can I slide? What he wanted to know—what he wondered in a way that screamed undergrad philosophy student with a substance abuse problem—was what's the value of my life absent . . . everything? What's the weight of just . . . *me?*

In this my father was not unusual among big-time dealers. In 1979, Larry Sloman, the soon-to-be editor in chief of *High Times*, published *Reefer Madness*, a book billed as the first social history of marijuana in America. It was a hit and remains a well-reported classic of pot studies. But people were confused by Sloman's portrait of drug dealing as a sad, walled-in business of easy money, thin friendships, and existential despair. He sat down with a ton-level dealer who turned the interview into a gin-and-tonic therapy session in the corner of a dark bar.

The source acknowledged the top notes of dealing: the glamour and girls, the fanfare and rituals ("Are you high? I'm high. You high?"), the pleasure of being trusted and giving trust in return, the simple pride, the post-job smile, the feelings of power, and the pain of hand-counting a million dollars. But he pivoted hard into the dark stuff. He hammered the way dealing makes you climb the ladder or get off. The way it drives up the need for thrills, until you're running red lights and goading cops, anything to give the nerves a tingle. Above all he admitted to the loneliness of the business, the way you hang out with people who want your drugs, not you.

"It's not the dope hero that has been portrayed in *High Times*," Sloman's source said. "Out of all the people who make all the money, none of them are happy."

The founder and publisher of *High Times*, the original dope hero Tom Forcade, was himself a cautionary tale, a window into the calamitous mind of a dealer, and a much sadder case than the average marijuana smoker would know. He was described in his own pages as "a flying ace of the dope air force," who ran marijuana jobs "like a military operation with overtones of religious fervor." But here's how Forcade really spent the last years of his life, after a pipe burst in his Washington Square Park apartment and firemen found two hundred pounds of dope in his closet.

He fled to Florida's Gulf Coast, where he secured a nine-ton load of marijuana that a friend smuggled into the Everglades. He neglected to hire help, however, and it took him twenty-four hours to load the bales into his Winnebago. By then he was spotted by a wildlife officer. Police soon blocked the only road to Miami, forcing Forcade to jerk the camper into the swamp. Three days later he emerged undiscovered but mosquito-mauled, determined to liquidate *High Times*, presumably to cover his losses.

He was talked out of doing so by friends, but Forcade returned to smuggling in 1978. The job called for a pilot to fly to Colombia, pick up a load, and kick it out over a remote location in southern Florida. Tom had no role in the actual smuggle, but he needed to be part of it, to be able to say, "Hey, man, we did it together, didn't we?"

Forcade took up a second plane to "guide" the first plane to the drop point. Everything worked perfectly until Forcade radioed instructions for the pilot to "Get lower! Get lower!" The pilot got lower, hit a tree, and died. The gang lost its load. Forcade lost one of his best friends. And six months later Forcade killed himself with a pearl-handled .22 pistol.

"Tom died like a soldier," wrote Albert Goldman, another former *High Times* editor, in a retrospective published on the magazine's twentieth anniversary. "He didn't flinch, he didn't fail. His hand was steady, his aim was true. He died without a cry or even a complaint. He was alone, wounded, cut off from his comrade. But he was in supreme command of himself. Such have been the deaths of men who cared less for life than they did for the Great Adventure."

There's only one serious long-term ethnography of my father's peers, and it too confirms the sad arc of the average dealer's life. Between 1974 and 1980, the University of Colorado sociologist Patricia Adler followed sixty-three "jet-setters of the drug world," specifically marijuana smugglers and wholesalers in Southern California. She revisited her subjects in the 1990s and was unable to locate many smooth transitions into a post-dealing career, amid dozens of tales of arrest, addiction, and abysmal living, much of it uncannily similar to my father's own experience.

Dad had more than a million dollars to his name in 1987, and that's not counting his gold-mine investment and his safe-deposit-box money, neither of which he could access. Less than three years later he had nothing. Where did it all go? The missing million: that staple of family history. The difference in my family is that this is not a story of missed opportunity—a stock not bought, an idea not pursued—but of actual cold, hard cash that was lost, sometimes literally misplaced, sometimes disappeared up a nose, into a vein, or under a hooker's mattress, sometimes just gone.

The $750,000 he made in his last job? My father could not find it. He thought maybe my mother had the bulk of it, or possibly even me, age eight and untrustworthy with lunch money. He wrote to her in 1989, outraged, saying: "I am still $30,000 short of having received my 1/3 of the $700,000 you took." But of course she didn't take it, and I didn't take it. It was just . . . gone.

And my father was gone, too. He went out again and again with $100,000 on him, partied until he passed out, and woke up broke, until one day he left his apartment with his last box of $50,000. He hailed a cab for the ghetto, where, in the manner of Tom Forcade, he might die like a true soldier of dope.

As my father sank into the mud, my mother flew to St. Thomas, where my father's partner Charlie had also recently left a long-term relationship. This was the summer of 1989, and I went with her, bringing along a friend. We stayed in Charlie's house for about a week, touring the island by day and playing Connect Four by night.

Charlie wooed me with soldiers' dirty old folk songs. To this day, as I wipe up spilled apple juice or change a diaper, I am liable to mindlessly sing, "On Friday I had my fingers in it. On Saturday she gave my balls a wrench." He added an inheritance of obscene limericks, and a nasty habit of unrestrained burping and farting, along with a picture of a woman's naked derriere as she walks down the beach. This was a painting, he explained solemnly. It was not pornography, it was art. Har-har. Our joke. I liked him, of course. I was a boy and he spoke my language.

My mother liked him, too. He had blue eyes like my father, but he didn't seem mean or abusive. Looks were no longer a major factor. So he was short? She didn't care. Their overlapping past made the present instantly comfortable. Nothing needed to be said. They already knew each other and where each other had come from, and Charlie was smart—or at least responsive enough to chat through bottles of wine and throws of the Yahtzee dice. People in the islands are serious about their board games.

By the end of the week they were already acting like a couple. By the end of the year, they were in love. It was good timing for Charlie, because in September 1989, Hurricane Hugo ravaged the Virgin Islands. It destroyed Charlie's home and his restaurant, and with the money habits of a typical brother of marijuana, he arrived in Miami with nothing but the clothes he had on the night of the storm. That, and some psychedelic mushrooms, which were a nice accompaniment to the cocaine he'd shipped ahead in a hollowed-out chess set.

Shortly before he started dating my mother, Charlie ran into Alan, the old friend who had shepherded in that disastrous load of Thai Stick, the one that almost got them mown down by the Boston Mob. The two laughed and talked, and at some point my father's name came up, and Charlie talked about the Old Man's insanity: the buried money, the lost loot. He pointed out that if Tony were busted it could get everyone in trouble, and there was really only one way to guard against that possibility: marry Tony's girl, my mother, Ann.

There's no doubt that Charlie loved my mother, and she loved him, but it's also true that he knew she could be a bulwark between him and prison. He knew that if he married my mother, he could take my father's money, win amnesty for himself, and lock her off as someone who could rebut his testimony.

Through the first half of 1990, Charlie lived off my mother's cooler money and some money he had managed to get refunded from the Yukon gold investment. Tony was God knows where, maybe dead but certainly not busted, so Charlie didn't propose to Ann just yet. Then one night the phone rang, and Charlie's reason was on the line.

It wasn't my father. It was Willy. Charlie hadn't seen Willy since 1986, but the old bastard said he was around the corner, sipping a Greenie in a bar along the same strip where we bought our groceries: a block from my Little League field, two blocks from Uncle Frank's pizzeria, where my father and I used to play endless games of Frogger and Track & Field, celebrating in super-slo-mo to the instrumental sound track from *Chariots of Fire*.

It was a short drive away, in other words, but Charlie had enough time to realize that this call was bad news, probably the worst kind of news imaginable, because how else did Willy get this phone number and address and find this little bar years after the last job when he and everyone else disappeared into the wind?

Willy did not walk away as planned after the 1986 job. He did one more job for what amounts to his second family, a ring of three brothers in Boston. They were dumb with their cash. They bought cars and boats and ran a mortgage company that, upon closer inspection, seemed to only loan money to friends and family. In 1988 the criminal division of the Internal Revenue Service called the Boston branch of the Organized Crime Drug Enforcement Task Force. A year later the three brothers were charged with importing more than a hundred tons of Colombian dope since the late 1970s.

Willy had been one of their biggest suppliers, but the brothers didn't know Willy like Charlie and my father did, or else they protected him exceptionally well, because on the indictment Willy was identified as "LNU"—last name unknown. Even when the feds got his full name, they couldn't find him and as a new decade dawned the task force turned its attention to more pressing crimes.

Federal prosecutor Paul Kelly and DEA agents Damian Farley and Joe Desmond were exceptions. Kelly was five years into a job as the assistant U.S. attorney for Massachusetts and had just become acting head of the task force. Cocaine was the new public menace, but from what Farley and Desmond were showing him in the DEA's files, Willy was the biggest East Coast pot smuggler of all time. The drugs had all been sold, and the principal ring long retired, but these three were old school, even if they were all under thirty-five. A fugitive is a fugitive, they figured.

Besides, like most law enforcement, they rather enjoyed marijuana dealers. No one condoned what they did, but when you catch them, they're good company. So the case grew and grew and in early 1990—after a DEA search that included a visit to Jimmy Buffett—a U.S. marshal named Bill Degan found something: a tall American guy in Portugal. He was living in some tiered mansion on the sea, driving a Ferrari. It was Willy Terry. He was living on the southern coast, near Vilamoura, the largest purpose-built resort on the Continent.

The Portuguese authorities busted him at the dentist, no less, and then waited for the team to arrive from Boston. Kelly says he knew right away that Willy would cooperate. His girlfriend was pregnant, for one, and for another, the sooner he opened up, the sooner Kelly could get him free again. Not two months later Willy was on a flight to Miami to bring Charlie into the deal.

"It's all over," Willy said, even before Charlie sat down at the bar.

He explained that he was cooperating with the feds, and he urged Charlie to do the same. "There's a pay phone there." He pointed to the end of the bar. When Charlie looked back down at his beer, he saw that Willy had slipped a number to him on a napkin.

"And if I don't use it?" Charlie asked.

"They'll break down the door," Willy said.

"When?" Charlie asked.

"Tonight," Willy said. "They'll break it down. They'll arrest Ann.

They'll put Tony in foster care. You don't want that. Here's the number, Charlie. Turn yourself in."

Charlie did.

Summer turned to fall before the government announced its next move: a sit-down proffer session with Charlie and Willy. Kelly's team was flexible about the location. They were also getting chilly in New England, so when Willy suggested Fort Lauderdale, the team agreed. Charlie and Willy checked into ocean-view rooms, where they spent their last night as respectable pirates.

In the morning they met Kelly, Farley, and Desmond under blue umbrellas in the sand. Charlie remembers everybody was in bathing suits. Anyone walking by would have seen the outlines of a team-building corporate retreat, a session of man therapy, not the drug war. The crew even had virgin drinks with the funny straws.

There are two types of snitches. The first kind will shake hands, sit down, talk patiently and politely, and then go away without any sign of remorse. That was Willy, who met alone with the feds first. The second kind won't shake hands, delays sitting down, bites the questioner, and tries to insult the process. That was Charlie. When he arrived for his turn with the feds, one of the DEA agents called the blue umbrella a cabana, and Charlie corrected him: a cabana is thatched. Then he started in with the ethnic jokes. Irish wedding this, and O'Brien twins that. "How do you make a seven-course meal for an Irishman?" he asked Kelly, as though by clapping his backside at the passing royal yacht he was still a pirate and not turning state's evidence. "Boil a potato and hand him a six-pack."

The meetings lasted three days, and both men were called back for meetings in Boston, a total of more than a week of questioning. Kelly's office started looking like a psychopath's bedroom, the walls papered with leads. He was sharing reports with multiple federal agencies and multiple local departments. By the end, they had more cases than they could possibly pursue, but my father's name had floated to the top of a list, along with Bobby and eight other men attached to Willy and Charlie's side of the smuggle. It was a case the feds pursued for the next year, from the fall of 1990 to late 1991.

Now Charlie was in the marrying mood. He insisted on it, in fact, arguing that I was wild and needed a father. My mother relented. She later said she knew the legal strategy behind it. Either way she always seemed game for going along with someone else's story.

One sunny Saturday afternoon in December 1990, as the task force continued its investigation, I poked my head out of a blue limousine and flashed peace signs to the Miami skyline. That evening my mother married Charlie on a small sailboat in Biscayne Bay as a red sun set the city ablaze. She wore a white dress. He wore flip-flops, white shorts, and a blue shirt, which he unbuttoned to the navel. I was the best man and I wore the same.

My mother walked down the aisle with two of her oldest girlfriends, Connie and the second wife of my father's old partner, Billy. Charlie's post-informant entourage consisted of a ten-year-old boy and a teenage runaway my mother—who was now a school counselor—had volunteered to work with on the weekends. I stood by Charlie's side during the ceremony and handed him the ring for my mother's finger. I shook his hand after he said "I do." And later he gave me sips of beer and taught me how to fart downwind.

Charlie was a conscientious objector during Vietnam and a self-styled dealer in the movement, but in the end he got a get-out-of-jail free card for his service to his country's War on Drugs. Willy almost got the same deal. He pleaded guilty, in February 1991, to conspiracy to import ten tons of marijuana into Seal Cove, Maine, in 1985 and 1986, a fraction of his career total, which, to the outrage of DEA agents up and down the coast, was totally overlooked. According to the deal he struck with Kelly and company, he would get ten years in prison for this crime. He would not serve that time.

His records were impounded and sealed, and have most likely been destroyed. Neither I nor a lawyer I hired could find them, or anything at all about William Terry except for a short press release about his arrest, and a judge's unstated understanding that Terry could not be called to testify in a civil dispute between two old friends. Willy was released into a "witness protection–like" program, according to Kelly, who arranged the deal. He was given a new name and social security number. And that was the end of the Terrys who came ashore with the *Mayflower*.

As the task force continued knocking on doors, in the summer of 1991, my mother and Charlie moved our family to Maryland, telling everyone on my father's side of the family that we were just going to Tallahassee for the summer. The story was that Mom had a temporary teaching job that might turn permanent. If it did, she promised, we'd be sure to invite everyone over to our new residence. But of course we never did.

At a going-away party at my friend Clay's house, four pals and I had a cake fight on the patio. We washed off with giant cannonballs from waterfall to pool. As the sun set, we unhitched Clay's boat and in the light wake of the bay took little-boy oaths of fidelity, and forgot each other by middle school.

Before he vanished, Willy paid Charlie and my mother a visit in Maryland, just to say goodbye. I wasn't home the night Willy came over, although I can't imagine I had a friend's house to go to. I was protesting the move by wearing orange and green Miami Hurricane T-shirts every day for a year. But I must have been gone. Charlie and Willy drank their fill of Grand Marnier and Heineken at my father's antique table, beneath my father's ugly jungle painting, in a room of my father's things or things he paid for. Willy was invited to spend the night in my room, the room of the son of the man he betrayed, and he accepted.

I wonder whether he looked around before turning in. On my corkboard was a picture of my father sitting on the steps of our house on Cape Cod, his black Lab, Captain, between his legs. He would have seen the pinholes where I'd stabbed the picture dozens of times, rearranging it on the board but also needling it like a voodoo doll. And he would have noticed that the only picture in worse shape was my own picture on the same steps.

Whatever the case, Willy did not sleep well that night under my blue comforter, because in the morning he and Charlie eyed each other uneasily, emotional muscles sore. They argued briefly but fiercely and then Willy was gone. In the wastebasket in my room he left his old license and identification cards, along with a letter from the federal government, bestowing on him a paperwork makeover, the freedom to run.

In October 1991, a few weeks into our first fall in Maryland, two dozen of my father's peers gathered in secret in Boston. This was his grand jury. The voice of the American public. Grand juries are where the federal branding iron gets hot. After the grand jury, government agents get to come through the pantry with weapons drawn, and the next day the paper boy gets to run through town with news of what the Bill of Rights called "infamous crime."

Kelly made his case against my father and his coconspirators, and the jury agreed, returning a three-count indictment, which Kelly had sealed out of concern that my father and company would run. It was unbelievable timing. The law had five years to make this case, the clock ticking from October 15, 1986, which was considered the day of the last criminal act, when the last dollar of drug money was laundered, and the last door was locked against the night. They made it after four years, fifty-one weeks, and a day, returning the indictment on October 9, 1991, less than one week—six measly days—before the statute of limitations was set to expire, freeing my father and his partners for life.

Three additional, overlapping indictments followed, along with a global manhunt. With an assist from Interpol and local law enforcement, U.S. marshals pursued suspects in Canada, England, Thailand, the British and U.S. Virgin Islands, Virginia, New Jersey, Maine, and, of course, New York City, pouring through Bobby's door one day before dawn while his son was in the house. In all, they would seize more than $4 million in cash and assets, including a marina in Virginia, a restaurant in Maine, two houses in Massachusetts, and several six-figure sailboats. They located drug money in Zurich, Hong Kong, Guernsey, Curaçao, London.

John was arrested at Boston's South Station and the authorities found him sitting on a pair of $250,000 homes, a mint-condition antique Jeep, two MG convertibles, and an ivory 1978 Mercedes. In his wallet, they found a license and ID cards in the name of Stephen

Crea and a passport in the name of Edwin Lugo. Occupation: pizza man.

Pierre was busted at his home in Virginia, where authorities commandeered *The Phantom*, a sixty-six-foot racing yacht. Later they shoulder-tapped two of his local partners in a Canadian airport, trying to smuggle $200,000 in rare rubies.

Timber Tom was arrested in Canada as well, where a few weeks before the authorities got to him, his car was hit by a bus near Nova Scotia, almost killing him. He had been planning a sailing trip around the world.

Jimbo was handcuffed outside a Waffle House in Miami, arrested after climbing into a U-Haul truck that undercover agents had led him to believe had a ton of dope in it. The rest of the busts were routine. They got Scrimshaw in England, where he had once been a cabdriver, and Inga in Martha's Vineyard, where she was working as a boat captain. Daniel was busted in St. Thomas.

After an exhaustive eight-month search, most men were in custody. But a few remained "elusive," as federal prosecutors put it in a request for an extension. They wanted more time to hunt suspects before the indictment was made public, potentially sending people further into hiding. Among the men they couldn't locate was one of the sailors, who had fled to Thailand, and the man atop the indictment, a certain Anthony Edward Dokoupil, who had the best hiding place of all.

A DEA agent called my mother in Maryland. He told her he was going to ask her something very important, and that before she answered she should remember that lying could mean they would take me away.

"Do you understand?" he said.

"I do," my mother said.

"Where is Anthony?"

My mother threw a cloud of guilt over our house simply by telling the truth.

When my father left his apartment for the last time in 1989, he took his $50,000 to Overtown, the palm-fringed black slum near downtown, a place where less than a decade earlier mobs were beating and burning white people. It doesn't get seedier than Overtown, and as a result the slum imparted a certain status to those who navigated it. But my father never got too far into the ghetto. In the back of the cab, he passed out.

He woke up on the floor of an old wood-frame two-bedroom house in North Miami, his box of money intact beside him. The bed in the room had three women in it, Carol, Sylvia, and Lauri, each of them hookers working a stretch of the South Dixie Highway, and marching for hooker's rights each election season. The owner of the house was the owner of the cab: Lou.

Lou was a salty, white-haired man with a pension from some maritime union, who worked as the driver for these women, ferrying them from john to john and running the meter the whole time. They never paid. But they stayed in his house rent-free in exchange for sexual favors. My father also stayed rent-free because he did pay the meter. Lou would drive my father all over Miami to buy cocaine, which by then was mostly sold as crack, then drive him to some fleabag hotel on South Dixie. Sometimes the girls would join him, accepting crack as payment for sex. This continued, off and on, the whole year.

Against all odds, as a matter of fact, I'm drawn to this image of my father chauffeured around the city by a maniacal old sailor turned taxi driver, who keeps his fares, his sex, and his friends in-house and cruises Miami as if in a flying boat. I even get a weird charge out of just how awful that house really was, if you strip away the fever-dream romanticism. My father buried his cash behind Lou's house, in what he describes as a "rotten-egg spot" that collected runoff from the outdoor shower. That was his ATM.

By the end of the summer, he started cadging money from family. He called his siblings and his mother late at night with sad stories about a bed at the Salvation Army for the weekend until his bank opened again on Monday. He would have wiring instructions ready: names, addresses, phone numbers. His mother died with $17,000 worth of Western Union receipts between her and the boy who got away.

But the money was useless. Each dollar was a needless word in a book, a slack minute in a movie. It created extra scenes in my father's story, but it didn't change the ending.

Sometime late in 1989, my father slept for the first time under the I-95 overpass, next to the Miami River. It was extremely abnormal for a white man to sleep here, of course, but that was a redeeming quality. My father was marooned, living the kind of extreme existence he could always love, if not enjoy. He dribbled away his days, mooching hot-dog stubs and hamburger buns from teenagers at the arcade. He arranged himself, as though in a series of self-portraits: on a bench on the bayside, in front of a street musician, on a patch of city grass, rejoicing at the sight of a smokable cigarette butt.

In the evening, he joined Huck-and-Jim hobo teams that fished the river for food using found nets and rods liberated from the yachts nearby. Usually all they caught were minnows, good for just one bite of meat, prepared in a soup can with river water boiled by a scavenged Sterno torch. After dinner he slept in a box. His only change of clothes had been stolen, and he would wake up with palmetto bugs nibbling his eyelashes or resting on the plateau of his cheek. It got to where he always felt like they were on him. And bugs are bigger in Florida, novelty size. When a Miami cockroach catches a bit of streetlight it looks almost decorative, a work of elfin craftsmanship and design.

And yet even here my father would claim he was happy, a fact I found astonishing until I learned the story of Captain Tony's Saloon, the one in the watercolor my father bought me when I was five. He'd never explained his attachment to this saloon; he can't even recall if he ever paid homage in person. But when I researched it as an adult the attachment had a way of explaining itself.

Captain Tony's real name was Anthony Tarracino, and according to lore of his own creation, he dropped out of high school in the 1920s to help his father bootleg whiskey. After World War II, he turned to professional gambling, won big on horses around New York City— and fled south, freshly beaten by angry bookies. He arrived in Miami with a pink Cadillac, a blond girlfriend, and $10,000. Not long after, he fled farther south to Key West on the back of a milk truck, homeless and $9,982 poorer.

This was the kind of life my father loved, one that swung to rock bottom, as they say, which to my father felt like a catnap on God's own carpet, the ultimate rehab from the pain of being a man. Each night in his box, if he got home in time to get one, my father would lie completely still until he would swear he could feel the planet spin like a Ferris wheel. He wrote me letters during this desolate period. Each one was on a different kind of paper, written in a different pen. The content varies, filtered through a mind cocked this way and that. But the return address was usually just "Daddy," as though his next-door neighbor were "Santa."

My mother saved many of these letters and I have eight of them spanning 1989 and 1991, with a gap in the middle, when my father's life hammocked most dramatically. The hardest part about the letters is the confusion about just who I am and how old I am. The first letter begins "Hello." Full stop. "I hope this letter finds you happy and healthy." Full stop. Years later I would recognize the same tone in the letters federal prisoners sent to me as a journalist.

"Do you like the boy scouts?" the letter continues. "What Rank are You? I would like to know the name of your patrol and your troop number. I was a patrol leader of the Wolf Patrol, Troop 81."

I was never in the Boy Scouts.

A follow-up letter references some pictures of me in my baseball uniform. I am a catcher and so he sends me a page and a half of questions about playing catcher. He wants to know if I signal the pitcher, tag guys out at home, catch long throws from the outfield, run down foul pop-ups, chase bunts. He asks me to write about the most exciting plays that I've been in, and then, just when his interest begins to warm a little part of me, to make it glow, the whole charade is revealed in a small loss of the plot.

"I figure your arm must be pretty good if you play the outfield," he writes, reassigning my position mid-letter. "I figure that you must be pretty fast, too. Have you ever been playing outfield and had to make a running, jumping catch to 'steal' a double or triple or even a homer from some long ball hitter? Did you ever throw some runner out at home plate? Wow, I am asking a lot of questions, aren't I?"

He always would. He would ask about summer plans, friends, teachers, tests, sports, clothes, food, weather. Some letters were more than 50 percent questions. The other 50 percent was demands. He wanted more calls. Pictures. Videos. The neediness was intense, endless. And what he gave back was cringe-worthy. He sent me two mushrooms from the woods. One had "a turtle bite out of it."

His thoughts drifted from one genre to the next. The result could be funny, like when he downshifted from the high diction of fatherly advice into the coy flirting of a summer love letter. "I'm lonely for your sweet smile and warm hug. XXX." It was more painful when the slip revealed just how far away from us he was.

He "heard" that I went on a trip with Mommy, the trip to St. Thomas to see Charlie, but he didn't know where. He wrote "woof, woof Captain" in the margin, and "give him a pet for me," and never knew that the dog—who at thirteen or fourteen could no longer see or hear or hold his bowels—had been put down. He said he was praying to God nightly, and he asked me to say the Lord's Prayer before bedtime, and thank God for what I have, which was well and good but not at all how I had been raised.

Other passages show him waking up to what he has lost and will never get back. When I got an A+ in fourth-grade social studies, he wrote, "Tony, I'd like to tell you that learning to make friends and having friendly behavior is maybe just as important as studying hard. Both learning and being a friend are very important in being happy and successful in life."

He referred to himself as "your daddy and your friend." And he signed every card "your loving Daddy," or "all my love," or "Remember that you are my special boy like I always used to tell you. I love you with all my heart and all my strength. Kisses, hugs, love. Daddy." Scrawled across one letter was a note, an apology for not giving me a birthday present. "I don't have money for a present now," he explained, "but let's just say I owe you one."

One of the last letters is a Shoebox Greeting Card. It arrived in the summer of 1991, three years since I'd last seen him and mere weeks before we left Florida for good. The front of the card is a *Tyranno-saurus rex* sitting in a director's chair, legs crossed daintily. The beast's head is turned coquettishly, thumbs twiddling. This is the character my father had chosen as his stand-in: a predator trying to look harmless. Inside the card said, "Haven't heard from you in ages."

Eventually my father signed himself into Dade County Jail for a spell, making use of a special detox program that offered three hots and a cot for recovering addicts. Afterward he moved from under I-95 to Miami Beach, where he slept in the lifeguard stands and bathed in the ocean, in another achingly romantic self-portrait. If my father could fish from the crook of a crescent moon, I am sure he would, just for the imagery of it.

One day he walked into a regional convention of Narcotics Anonymous, held in one of the old hotels on Collins Avenue, and as he had done before, he buttonholed his way into a job. This time the job was with Miami-Dade County Beach Operations, as part of a trash crew on Miami Beach. It did not pay well, just $128 a week, and could not be called a good job by any stretch.

But it was a new experience, and not permanent, which was the same way my father viewed the first flophouse he could afford, and the little black-and-white television that only let him down during electrical storms. Work began each morning at seven, and my father walked to the beach from his little room a few blocks away, joining a three-man crew.

His job was to walk behind a flatbed truck for a hundred blocks, from 100th Street to South Beach, pausing to hoist metal cans to a man on the truck bed. At eleven, the crew would break for lunch at the interesting end of the beach, near the cold-water showers the girls use to wash sand off their feet. Then they would drive back, three abreast in the cab, bathed in air-conditioning, watching the surrounding animals like rich tourists on safari in Africa.

There was always extra money to be had. Film crews would pay to have the beach cleared of seaweed, and my father learned the catch points for valuable debris, the places where stray cash would blow and stick, turning fetid groves into money trees. Some days a kind of beach Zamboni would skim away the top layer of the sand, revealing fresh white beneath it, then dumping the gray stuff near the operations shack. To the beach operations team, these were like dredgings from the treasure coast.

Mixed in with the six-pack holders, crates, plastic tarps, and odd pieces of lumber there were goodies: rings, watches, smashed ciga-rette packs, which almost always had a crumpled bill or two. My dad never told his friends on Mount Trashmore—men who celebrated a dented pack of Camels and a diseased dollar—that just a while back he had been a millionaire. Like the government, they would never have believed him.

In the months before he was indicted, my father was accepted into a federal program for people with "mental disabilities." He was referred to Orlando J. Valdes, PhD, who produced a report, stamped and filed with Florida's Mental Health Unit. The nine-page document begins with a recap of my father's life, including his career in "the antique business" and "construction." "Mr. Dokoupil did live with a female for approximately 14 years, which resulted in a 10-year-old son," Dr. Val-des notes, but this "lady friend" recently left him, taking the boy. My father has since found himself in some "unorthodox" living arrange-ments, the good doctor noted, including "under the bridge" and "on the beach."

"I hit rock bottom," my father told Valdes in conclusion. "What I have are the clothes on my back."

To assess my father, Dr. Valdes gave him the Wechsler Adult Intel-ligence Scale—Revised (WAIS-R), the most popular IQ test of all time, defined by its maker as a gauge of "the global capacity of the individual to act purposefully, to think rationally, and to deal effectively with his environment." Purposefully . . . rationally . . . effectively. Not exactly the three words one might associate with Anthony Dokoupil. A perfect score is a 150. Mensa eligibility begins at 130, and anything above that level is termed "very superior." The word *genius* is popularly attached to scores in the 140s and above.

I was thirty when I found this report in my father's papers, and while I do not feel like my father, not at the moment, many scientists say there is no meaningful distinction between genetics and personality. DNA is not destiny but genes are spookily consistent, uncannily cumulative. The battle between nature and nurture is over, in other words, and nurture has lost. The "Psychological Report of Tony Dokoupil" is, according to the best science of the moment, exactly what it sounds like: a psychological report about me.

What I read started off promising. My father's full-scale IQ score was recorded at 142. His verbal score was even higher at 148.

"Cognitive difficulties are not noted," Dr. Valdes wrote. "Anthony Dokoupil presented himself as a pleasant, highly intelligent, 44-year-old male." He "possesses a keen ability for details, common sense and expressive vocabulary." And, yes, the doctor concluded, he "appears to be intellectually gifted."

I considered the possibility that Dr. Valdes was describing the wrong patient. There is a stray reference to a man of a different name in my father's report, which gravely imperiled the whole document. But Valdes also administered the Minnesota Multiphasic Personality Inventory exam, a popular gauge of "abnormal" mental health. What follows can only be described as ominous, at least if your name is Tony Dokoupil.

"His overall profile was suggestive of low frustration tolerance and much impulsivity," Valdes concluded. "Similar patients are often seen as having self-centered tendencies, adventurous and unreliable manners. They tend to disregard the potential of actual consequences and may minimally profit from experience. Even though Anthony created a good first impression, it is apparent that the subject may have many interpersonal problems, particularly with authority figures."

Valdes was bullish on my father's chances for rehabilitation. A second government therapist concurred. He need only to "leave his past behind," she wrote, recommending him for work in a library. Yes, Anthony Dokoupil was on his way up when Charlie and Willy conspired to keep him down.

My father himself seemed to sense that the time had come for some final sentiments. His last letter to me—our last communication of any kind for a long, long time—arrived a few months before he rallied into his job as beach cleaner. It was written on thick-stock, high-quality paper and would pass as a professional man's paper if the top were not emblazoned with the logo for Gables Cats, a Jaguar repair shop.

He told me that he loved me, always and unconditionally. He told me that I was strong and handsome, and he warned of puberty, an "exhilarating feeling," "a busy and tireless time"; he told me to eat my fruit and vegetables every day and to drink orange juice; and he told me to pray. Lastly, like a man about to embark on a very dangerous mission, he adopted a man-of-the-house tone, suggesting that I give my mother a kiss on the cheek for him.

Near the bottom of the letter, he got to the point: "There is not one hour of the day in which I don't think of you, and want to be with you," he wrote. "But perhaps God has other plans."

My father was arrested on July 7, 1992, a payday, as he sat with coworkers at the Miami Beach operations shack at Seventy-ninth Street and the Atlantic Ocean. It was early afternoon and the men were waiting on their checks, ribbing Leon, their boss, about his yellow jalopy. A black sedan pulled up and a pair of Windbreaker-clad men walked over to my father. They presented a glossy photo for his inspection, not a mug shot but a snapshot, something a friend must have taken. It had been blown up to the size of a sheet of paper, and it showed a young man with brown hair streaked corn-cob yellow by sun. The table went silent.

"Are you Anthony Dokoupil?" one of the U.S. marshals asked.

"You know I am," he said.

"You're under arrest."

"For what?"

"We'll get to that."

A few hours earlier my father had cleaned South Beach, emptying metal trash bins into a truck with a piece of stale pizza crust in his mouth, day-old watermelon juice on his chin. It was a pleasant day and he was looking forward to the weekend. But instead he was in Miami's federal detention center, where a woman took down his personal history in a perfectly round bubble script, the handwriting of someone who chews gum at the office and smells of hand lotion. I can see my father leering at her as she records his vitals: Anthony Edward Dokoupil, five foot eight, a hundred and sixty-five pounds, forty-five, blue eyes, brown-blond hair, complexion "tanned." The rest of her report is a portrait in negative space, the history of an unemployed "schoolteacher," with a rented room in one of the vacancy-sign hotels along Collins Avenue. No phone to call. No identification to show. No money owed. No money saved.

In his mug shot, my father is wearing a polo shirt, suavely unbuttoned, his mustache neatly groomed. He looks like a man roped for drunk-driving his Porsche through Coconut Grove, not a laborer arrested from work at a trash shack. His eyes stare into the camera like it refused him a quarter for bus fare.

These are the sworn entries into his affidavit:

Have you any cash on hand or money in savings or checking
    account: NO.
Do you own any real estate, stocks, bonds, notes, automobiles,
    or other valuable property: NO.
Debts and monthly bills, please list all: Apartment: NONE.
    Creditors: NONE.
Total number of dependents: ZERO.

Only that last line was a lie.

9

Big Tony, Little Tony

Before dawn on the morning of August 24, 1992, a year after we had hightailed it to Maryland, a hurricane crushed Miami along with what remained of my father's legacy as a drug dealer. The storm swamped my mother's antique cars and blew away her black market slum investment. It reduced our old house to a drained aquarium, which my mother paid to have bulldozed. She sold the lot for less than $30,000, or roughly what my father once had stashed under the washing machine.

She also started to think of my father as a dead man. She had a vision of him facedown in a rising tide, a shark no more. She didn't know he had been arrested six weeks earlier, taken off the very beach where television anchors began their tours of Hurricane Andrew's destruction. If Charlie knew of my father's arrest he didn't say, which resulted in the family's strange middle position on my father's mortality. On a long drive to one of my summer baseball games, my mother delivered the halting and indirect news that my father was probably no more. I nodded and agreed and exuded the straight-spined sobriety only a twelve-year-old boy can summon in the presence of a chance to act like a man.

Without those cars and the rental income, the high life was truly behind us. We scraped by in the summer, cutting costs by only air-conditioning the living room and using old sheets over the doorways to keep in the cold. Our house in Maryland looked like it had arrived on a flatbed truck. It had no basement or attic and, with the exception of the porch—a slab of concrete covered with a moldy square of putt-

putt grass—nothing obviously predated the beep-beep of a wide load in careful reverse.

Someone's sailboat was slowly collapsing near the property line. A basketball hoop was tacked shoddily to a pine tree. The white siding was dirty and the flagstones wobbled after rain and spit mud on your clothes. The house always seemed to be narrowing the distance between itself and you. It was not on the wrong side of the tracks, but the tracks were in our backyard, transformed into a bike path I wasn't allowed to walk at night.

At school I felt the way people feel when they walk into a high-end clothing store: unkempt. My new public-school friends took to calling me "poor boy," the kid with an AWOL father and a mother working three jobs to get by. Charlie, meanwhile, resigned himself to a kind of malingering that made him a famous neighborhood character.

His back bothered him too much for regular construction work, and our dinner-table talk was about a high-risk surgery that would either fix his vertebrae forever or kill him outright. My mother got him jobs as a substitute teacher, but he came home fuming about "kids these days." He became like a feckless older brother who smoked in the good chair, monopolized the remote control, and filled the septic tank with beer piss, because he could not get his act together.

I spent a year collecting, without irony or even a nimbus of parental discouragement, thousands of "Marlboro Miles," tiny proof-of-purchase labels (worth five miles each) from the side of cigarette packs. I successfully redeemed shirts, a wallet, and a dartboard. I regret not holding out for the pool table, maybe the canoe. I ran up our cable bill buying dirty movies, and Charlie's response was, "Hell, Tony, why didn't you call me out to watch?"

My strongest memories of him as a father are all auditory. The exuberant *ksssh* of his newly opened can of beer. The happy thwack of a bottle top flicked free with a Bic lighter. The needful suck as he tilts the booze to his mouth. Then the unrestrained belching and the lip farts, which stood in for all manner of explication. "Charlie, what do you think of Operation Desert Storm?"

"Braauppt."

When he inevitably bounced off the doorframe or bumped into the table, he made a sound like "Iccccccce!" And then the night dissolved into howls and guffaws, asinine stories and Charlie's spontaneous imitations of a panther. Why a panther? I've never known.

"So, anyway, the doctor asked, are you a diabetic, and, uh"—here he pauses to cover his eyes for a moment and gather himself—"No, no, I told him. I'm a Democrat." Roaring laughter, dead silence, panther growl, then a surprisingly skillful wink.

The most terrible sound was when he rubbed his dry, calloused hands in solemn reflection, and with unbearable seriousness, leaned, squeakily, against our cigarette-scarred dining-room table and harmonized with whatever folksy tune he decided was good for dinner. His favorites were Brewer and Shipley, and his old friend Jimmy Buffett, whose music he now adored. "Goo-od times and riches, and son of a bitches, I've seen more than I can recall!"

Charlie could be a positive influence despite himself, more a billboard for clean living than an advert for the dangerous life. For the bad stuff, I still had my father, who might be dead but who lingered nonetheless.

It's the absence of personal history, as much as its presence, that can be damaging to a young person. I had no father, so I made up a father. I built him up from the two scraps of truth I actually liked about him: that he had once sold marijuana, a fact I picked up like stray dog hairs and the smell of cigarettes, and that his whereabouts were unknown. I feathered those bones until I had a father myth I could live with, one that gave me confidence in my genes, confidence in my lineage.

I started telling friends about my dad, the big-time drug dealer. As high school progressed, I elaborated on that lie. He probably lived in Colombia, I told them, because he had fled there, and compared to their dads—federal bureaucrats, scientists, engineers—he was a badass. Compared to them, it followed, I was a badass, too. I had a hidden power, a knack for crime. My life had been cracked in two and the two parts didn't match, the stories did not cohere. Rich then poor, beloved then abandoned. The dissonance was sometimes overwhelming and the outcome was cruel. The more my mother fought to put distance between me and my father, the more she added to his absentee charms.

I had the kiss of student-athlete status, as the starting center fielder on the baseball team. But my friends and I were not jocks but jokers, best known for a line of nonviolent pranks and high jinks. We spirited away faculty bathroom keys, photocopied hall passes, stole and then sold test answer keys. We slipped VHS porn into the video library of the SAT prep class, until the counselor's cliché of "find a fit" never sounded so tawdry.

But my greatest scam was definitely as the high-school bootlegger. It began in tenth grade. My mother went in for a new license and I went with her. There was some sort of mix-up at the counter. We had to shuffle down to an out-of-service window to finish a form. I noticed a stack of licenses. There was no glass between the workers and customers, just raised counters, which meant you really had to drape yourself over to reach the other side. But drape I did. I tried to make it look casual, like I was stretching my lats, mindlessly drumming with my palms on the other side of the line.

I walked out with a stack of licenses as thick as a deck of cards—reclaimed licenses, as it turned out, because they were expired or nearly expired. Half were women, another third were guys over thirty-five. In the end there was really only one license that seemed like a match. I can't remember the name on it, but the face will never leave me: long black hair, pale, twenty-seven years old. I was fifteen, dumb-jawed, fuzzy mustache, pimples, and a stage curtain of blond-brown hair. It was not a match. But I tried it and it worked. And it kept working.

During this stretch my mother was one of the county's alcohol counselors. You had to see her if you were caught drinking underage, which meant I was a prodigious buyer of alcohol for exactly the market that walked through her door. I was also now a minor baseball star, the leading public-school hitter in the county as a sophomore, with no education fund other than the long-shot kind I might win for myself. It's no exaggeration, in other words, to say I risked everything. I risked my mother's job. I risked my future.

We were juniors when it finally happened. The weather was warm and we were drunk on a malt liquor called Steel Reserve. It made us punch glass and bleed into dish towels. We were tending a good junk fire in a pit behind Gordon's house, which was just up the hill from my house and shabbier. I'd known Gordon for a year and had never met his parents. We all understood that his house was the house with not enough money, not enough rules.

His three- or four-year-old sister was always around, up at all hours but always in pajamas. People said she slept in a drawer. I don't think Gordon ever denied it. The squalor of the place attracted a wider ring of friends—jocks, wits, stoners. Never girls, just boys who wanted to hit a blender with a golf club, throw a can of hair spray into a fire pit, and drink. I always bought the beer, the liquor, the cigarettes. I did not do it for the money. I never pocketed more than the change from somebody's $20. I did it for the fun of it. I did it to see if I could. I did it because I was a kid and maturity sucks and, my God, what did the world expect from a kid with a dad like mine?

I read that one of my baseball idols had grown up with an absent father, modest home life, criminal sidelines, and I saw my own situation as it might appear two decades later as a human-interest story aired during a New York Mets rain delay.

"After his father left," the announcer would say, over video footage of me blowing a bubble of pink gum in the brilliant summer sun, "Mets rookie Tony Dokoupil dedicated himself to two things: his mother and baseball." I started taking a hundred practice swings a day, partly so I could tell interviewers later. The narrative grew until it encompassed everything in my life. I was not a delinquent on the road to ruin, but a hero whose story required some time walking the chalk line between good and evil.

One of the kids around the fire pit was Jonathan. He was Jewish in a Christian county, and the Christian kids let him know that. They called him the Juice, but pronounced it as the Jew and rarely got to the "ice" part without cracking themselves up. When the advertising slogan for Starburst candy was "The Juice Is Loose," they got ahold of some stickers for Jonathan's locker, backpack, shirt, hair. Jonathan was one of my best friends. He called me Poor Boy. I called him the Jew. And we were all together at Gordon's, drinking, name-calling, drinking.

We passed a bottle of Goldschläger. We passed a bottle of Southern Comfort. We drank our Steel Reserve. At some point Jonathan decided to lie down in the kid sister's room. She had a bed after all, it seems, because I found him in it a couple of hours later. It was around midnight, curfew time for most of us. His face was smeared with blood from a fall near the fire pit. He had wrapped himself in a blanket, a final act before sleep.

He wasn't breathing.

I rolled him onto his back. I thought that might kill him, make him swallow his tongue, so I rolled him back onto his side. He spluttered. A breath, and then nothing again for a long time.

I had no good options. If I called for an ambulance, I might as well have called for a pair of handcuffs, I thought. I shouted into Jonathan's face as the fire pit burned down in the backyard. We were the only ones left in the house when I finally called my mother, who called an ambulance. It seemed like five of them came, jamming the dead-end street where Gordon lived, bringing out the neighbors.

A few weeks later, Jonathan's parents called me at home. They invited me over, thanked me, bought me a fleece vest from Eddie Bauer, and said I had saved their son's life. They said they were grateful for what I had done for Jonathan. I accepted the vest, said gracious things. No one ever asked where we got the booze. I guess they just figured boys will be boys.

I felt like a murderer for a while after.

But I did not stop buying people booze.

Genes are spooky that way. My father couldn't stop, either. The only difference is, he was running from a monster and I was running from a ghost.

As a center fielder, I was positioned to see not only the whole field of play but also the bleachers and the parking lots, and I studied both at least as closely as the guy at bat. I was afraid my father would show up one day, a cameo by a guy who was more junkie than heroic drug dealer.

Since I did not know what he looked like, every unidentified man was suspect. Everybody was my father.

The day my father finally appeared was one of my proudest. I felt sharp walking through Reagan National Airport, wearing a Windbreaker with my number on it. It was 2001. I had a six-figure college scholarship to play baseball and study, and I was returning from Disney's Wide World of Sports, a name that still sets off a geyser of pride inside my chest. It was the site of our conference tournament, and although we had been eliminated, each member of the team got $120 a day for food and free theme-park tickets, so we came home feeling like champs.

"This came for you at the office," my coach said, handing me a letter. The postmark was many weeks old. I opened it and my knees almost buckled at the salutation: "LITTLE TONY!"

The note inside was from Aunt Carolyn. It said that my grandmother Phyllis's health was fading, but her last wish was to see her long-lost grandson again. Uncle David had found me "on the computer," and he suggested they send this letter to the athletic department, since they couldn't trust my mother.

"CALL ME!" she added.

When I did call, a couple of days later, I learned that my grandmother was dead. I have no memories of Grandma Phyllis, this keen-minded, strong woman who was good for a hat and a savior to her children. But Carolyn had other news. Your father is doing well, she said. He's living in Boston and would love to hear from you. She didn't say what he was doing, or how he ended up in Boston. She didn't mention drugs or addiction, let alone the Organized Crime Drug Enforcement Task Force, U.S. marshals, and federal time. As far as I could tell, in fact, he was almost as estranged from his family as I was.

I wrote down the number, folded it into my pocket, and tried to put my father out of my mind. I reported to play in the New York Collegiate League, giving myself over to the sweet Simon and Garfunkel melancholy of the road, the man-walks-into-a-room anonymity of sandwiches from Subway in ten different counties, the banded weirdness of spending two months in a new town with your exact counterparts at other colleges. I found under-the-table work digging pools for a local company. It's what it sounds like: dig a hole, dodge a backhoe blade, fight the hidden river of clean, cold water when it bursts through the surrounding mud walls.

I was happy with the work and excited about my life, so I called my father, confident enough to think I was ready to replace myth with reality, dumb enough not to know what reality would be. He picked up instantly like a man at a desk, a personable fellow waiting on orders for his workshop full of toys. His voice was singsongy.

"Hel-oh," he said, and I realized I never should have called. When I introduced myself, he uncorked great spraying arcs of champagne about how he loved me and missed me. How he bought me everything as a baby, did everything for me, went everywhere with me. I felt my chest compress, my brain burn, and I hurried the conversation along, pushed it forward like a man swallowing a piece of food it would be too impolite to spit out.

I'll be in Boston over the weekend with friends, I told him. Could I stop by? We could have dinner.

I wanted my father to let me in on the story of his life. I wanted him to tell it to me in the belly of some smoky Boston restaurant, and for me to get angry for a moment before I let him bear-hug me into a golden period of camaraderie and high spirits as "your daddy and your friend." I wanted to feel a shift from the ranks of those for whom the past is blank, the future uncertain, to those for whom all is known, all fates sealed. I wanted the simple, straightforward example of a parent's life well led. I wanted to be him, is what I'm trying to say. But it sounded like he was nobody.

He refused to see me.

"Oh, Tony," he said, "I'm not well." And I felt something shatter inside, my carefully imagined display case containing my father: "Drug Dealer," American. He destroyed it with a few words. I hadn't seen the man since 1987, when he smashed a table in our living room and the Mets lost every time I watched them play. Fifteen years later there would be no reunion. He said no, because he didn't know how to explain his real biography. I hung up, because I didn't dare ask for it.

I might have immediately cut ties with him if not for a hint of his temper, a crackle of interference that seemed to belong to a bigger man. It came across when I told him about Ann and Charlie, their marriage, and the fact I was paying for college with scholarship money and a loan. He growled at the news, hissed about the money, all the Mr. Rogers gone from his voice. "I don't understand," he insisted. "Ann has money."

I was ready to believe it, since how else to account for the abundance of our lives in Miami? It didn't make sense that we were poor, unless I was missing something. And I was: No one ever used the word *marijuana*.

That fall I went back to college in Washington, D.C., where I heard from yet another long-lost family member: my father's elder brother, David. He wanted me to know that my father had inherited about $40,000 from his mother's estate and that he had decided to give me $5,000 of it as "fun money." This news arrived in the form of a check, and a note from my uncle telling me to cash the check *right away*. I thought that was odd, but I did as I was told.

The check bounced.

Frantic, David sent another check for $5,000. That went through, and I blew it on a hiking trip to Colorado and a surfing foray in California. My father spent the remaining $35,000 in five days flat.

Dad and I talked a lot more by phone that semester. After his gift, I felt like I owed him my time. But he reverted into a man striving toward respectability. With each banal anecdote about my crib toys or how I enjoyed the sprinkler, he was desecrating my idea of him, scribbling over the picture. In the summer I reported to play in the Great Lakes League, one of the best in the country, and where I generally swaggered around working in bars and hitting.

Baseball culture was a lot like smuggling culture, and my father and I might have talked about that if he ever took off his sweater vest. He seemed relieved when I told him I couldn't bear to call anymore. At the time I thought it was odd, his willingness to go separate ways. Today I suspect the conversations were hard for him, too. He must have hated being so boring and vulnerable. He must have hated being the good-guy father he thought I wanted, instead of the bad-guy father he was.

I was on the run after those calls. When my father was merely gone, an empty cauldron to be filled with whatever spell I needed, I could do or be anything. The phone calls eroded that belief. I struggled with the dismal math of our relationship. If my father was nothing, how could I ever be something?

I had this idea that if I could just distinguish myself academically and land a job, I would be free of my father. I stayed with this idea, even as I started failing at baseball, moving from center field to left field to right field to the bench, where I lost part of my scholarship. I stayed with it through sessions with a school counselor and rounds of antidepressants that left my vitals feeling like the frozen center of a microwaved pizza. I stayed with it until, improbably, I graduated as valedictorian of my undergraduate business school, the first to get my diploma, the only undergraduate speaker at our graduation. When the hats dropped, I had a job at the world's biggest and oldest public relations company, with offices all over the world. I chose San Francisco, the West, where I had no family and no friends, and I would be free to invent myself.

But almost right away my father slipped through the mail slot. He must have been in some sort of a program, because he volunteered that he was mentally ill, bipolar, and schizophrenic. When I replied that he was being a hypochondriac, he sent me a doctor's note attesting to it all. He'd been living mostly off disability for years, he explained, and he furnished me with more paperwork to prove it.

Oh, I said. I see. You're scamming the government, posing as ill for the money?

No, no, no, he clarified in another letter. He told me again that he was crazy. He told me that all the men in our family have been crazy, and that none of them had a real chance in life. He warned me about "a pack of wolves" who don't care who you are or what you can be. He signed off, "Hope this letter isn't a burden." No, Dad, not at all. He added, "Don't let it be!"

A few days later, after I had settled into life again, I received the cover of *Civilisation*, Sir Kenneth Clark's 1969 history of the world. The title of the book and Clark's byline had been torn away, and on the back of the page my father explained his gesture.

Tony—

Meet Sparks, Pirate Extraordinaire, whose treasure is lost to every treasure hunter the world over for 300 years until his two sons—on down the line—crack the code held in the simple child's necklace of carved wooden figures that he wore the day his mother was murdered by the King's Assassin, Mad Dogo.

Belief and Hoorays!

Dad

A few weeks later, he wrote to say, "The Pirate Kings is writing itself. I never experienced such a wonderful power! My left hemisphere flashes and feels hot, like a magic lamp someone has rubbed, and a marvelous thing happens—theme, characters, conflicts and resolutions start to march in my mind's eye."

He followed with two weeks of raving paranoid madness. My mother, Charlie, Timber Tom, Willy, and others all danced out of his mind, making car alarms go off when he passed, pushing revolving doors into his heels. They pop up and smile, he said, brandishing pencil drawings and little red cans of gasoline, and once they even took over his favorite radio station, playing "Every Breath You Take (I'll Be Watching You)."

My father begged me to "intercede," to "ask Charlie, Ann, Tom and Willy to stop torturing me." In the margins, he asked for help six more times: "Please help me Tony," "Please help me Tony," "Please help me . . ."

I did not help.

I could not help.

I could not let him in.

After a lull, my father sent me a hundred-dollar bill, attaching a note.

It said, "The rest is in my heart."

At my lowest I took three different buses to end up at the Golden Gate Bridge, where I had a fluttery feeling I recognized from other times when I'd held an object at a great height, near a railing, say, a mishap away from losing it. There's a reason people throw things into oceans and ditches, out car windows and from the end of piers. It feels good, that destruction. It feels fine.

Instead of jumping, I moved to New York. I enrolled in a master's program, American studies, of course, the most romantic of all fields, and to pay for it I signed on for tens of thousands of dollars in student loans. It took all of an hour to fill out the forms online and click "Apply." I was approved in what felt like seconds, the money slammed into my student checking account.

My father still hung on the periphery of my life. During a rare phone conversation he tried to sell me his computer; the time before that, his shoes. I had no intention of paying the loans off. I planned to be dead before they came due. I planned to get low and dirty, and go down in a wash of glory, like a surfer falling slowly backward into the foam. Without realizing it, I was planning to go down like my dad.

Then I met a girl and in that timeless way, I thought, maybe I'd like to live a little longer. Maybe, for that matter, I'd like to buy a new suit and take her out for a nice dinner. I asked my mother about what my father had said about her having money, how certain he had been. There was money, she confirmed. But my father had lost it.

And still I didn't know where it had really come from, this lost pile of money. She said some of it had been buried but she never explained why. I started dreaming about it: buried treasure, my father's dough, the legend of the Pirate Kings. Maybe it was true. My mother was more encouraging this time. She could tell I was desperate, maybe, or maybe she was curious. "Who knows where the money went," she admitted. "There was a lot of it."

I stopped by unannounced and rang the buzzer with my name on it. All I could think about was the time on the boat in 1986, the last time my father had seemed whole rather than helplessly, hopelessly deranged, kneeling over a glass table, the Mets on TV.

To my surprise, his neighborhood was nice. The street had shiny meters and clean new awnings. Somewhere in my mind the old myth machine turned on. He really was swashbucklingly rich after all, I thought. The old dog.

Then I found his building. Just a block away from the shiny people, two blocks from a well-tended community garden, his was a dreary apartment building for ex-cons, the kind of place that brings down real estate prices and is quietly campaigned away by people with children. His name, my name, comes from a Czech word that means "Bought it all." I recognized the shaky block letters on the buzzer label.

No answer. Another resident was leaving, so I slipped in and sat in the lobby. Metallic-green floors, overpowering smell of ammonia, institution-strength metal doors. What was I doing? For years I'd worried about this guy dropping into my life. Here I was, dropping into his. I started to leave when the elevator opened, and he walked out.

He looked like a guy who had been on an all-night bus every night of his life. He had the Dokoupil look, as he would call it, or the remains of it, anyway. But I suppose a physical description of him would have to begin with his mustache, still woolly, and his cheeks, the color of dusty marble. He was a walking public service announcement for liver disease. And it was definitely him. He seemed to catalogue me warily, the way you note the presence of a dog off its leash.

"Are you Tony?" I asked.

"Yes."

"I'm Tony," I said.

"Okay."

"No," I said. "You don't understand. I'm Tony."

"Your name is Tony, too?"

"Yes. I'm Tony."

"Stop shitting me."

"No, I'm Tony."

No response.

"Your son?"

Here comes the bear hug, which I returned like a member of a prize-giving organization, the Publishers Clearing House of Estranged Children. He pushed me back into the wall. He was a smoker. He used Right Guard. He saved money on laundry. He was skinny except for his belly, which was fat in that way people appear to be fat when they're undernourished. His fingernails were thick and brown and yellow, and everything about him was raw: his eyes, his fingers, his voice. Yet he also seemed jolly, a bit slapstick, and his eyes were watering unnaturally. I found myself wondering if he was high.

His room was a studio with a shared bathroom down the hall. It was barren of furniture except for a bed with a body print on the mattress, night sweats in the sheets. There were a couple of hardback chairs, a desk. The walls and surfaces were cluttered with Christian iconography and plastic cups with cigarette scars.

But I could see where he got the goober voice, the "Hel-oh" that sounded like weakness to me. I could see why even his craziest letter came with a return-address sticker with a butterfly on it. He was trying to make himself as normal as possible. He had the For Dummies series—computers, novels, and screenplays—along with titles like *50 Ways to Hook the Reader*, *How to Sell Your Fiction*, *The Market Guide for Writers*. The first item on his to-do list was "teach oneself to use the computer."

"Pirate Kings" is written out in long form on paper stolen from the library. He can be memorable on the page. A man's face is "all rolls and hollows like a moving sea." But his manuscript is mostly just wildly annotated outlines, splashed with exhortations: "Yes!" "Yes!" "Develop!" "A sound and believable premise!" "Use it!"

He refused lunch, saying he couldn't handle crowds and showing me the pen-cap-size pills he took to stave off schizophrenic episodes. We went for coffee, his treat, he insisted, and then to his local library, where he introduced me to the bewildered librarians, their eyes assuming the same unfocused look of kids confronted with a chalkboard full of hard math. We were a head-scratcher, all right. I was fit, twenty-six, a graduate student in the big city. He was fat and unkempt, sixty, eyes wild in a way that made a person feel perverted by association.

Less than thirty minutes later, I excused myself. I did not even ask him about the money. A man in his sixties who should be living a life of nice meals, vacations, and sprees but instead shares a bathroom down the hall is emphatically not hoarding cash. I consciously went unconscious about my father, burying him in order to live.

And *still* no one said anything about marijuana.

We may have plowed the ground only to there if not for the fact that soon I expected to become a father myself. It was two years later when I heard the news: a weekend morning, lazy and sweet. Most dads would celebrate the chance to pass along their heritage, but I was keen to replant the family tree, to recast what it means to be a man in the Dokoupil family. To do that I knew I needed to see my father again. I scheduled a visit for June 2009, but I also decided to go armed with something I had never had before: the basic facts.

I contacted the National Archives and Records Administration, keeper of America's most important files. Of every document ever created by the federal government, only "1%–3% are so important for legal or historical reasons that they are kept by us forever," according to a statement on the NARA home page. I doubted the crimes of Anthony Edward Dokoupil were of such importance, but I asked anyway.

At the same time I ran my father's name through the world of digitized court records. The result was a few lawsuits, an old DUI, an old pickup for cocaine possession. Small-time stuff that put me in an odd sort of black mood, a disappointment driven by my father's all-too-good behavior. Then an e-mail arrived from Boston, a fourteen-page e-fax. I clicked the file open. My screen blinked and I could make out the smudged heading of a document, case #91-CR-10280: "The United States of America V. Anthony Doukupil [*sic*]."

I read what followed and I read it again. Then I e-mailed a friend who appreciates this sort of insanity.

"I just got my father's records," I began. "He was arrested for importing 35,000 pounds of marijuana in 1986 alone."

"Zounds!!!" came his reply, and I felt the same way. The job would have had a street value of more than $100 million in 2009. Never has a son been so happy to discover that his father was a federal felon.

I called my mother, who had always supported my reconnection with Big Tony, once she could be convinced that he was still alive.

"We were going to tell you," she insisted, cutting me off mid-sentence.

"I'm thirty," I said.

"That seemed about right. But then you got that journalist bug, and I thought, Oh boy, here we go."

My stepfather, Charlie, came on the line to tell us both to shut up.

"Phones are fucking ridiculous," he explained. "Never trust a phone."

We hung up.

He called back. The TV blared in the background and he talked over it. He said he had a few names and phone numbers to help me learn "the truth," whatever that meant, but first I needed to swear to tell people that my source was William Terry. "I don't know if he's alive or dead and I don't care," he said, "but I'd like to live the rest of my life. You understand?"

I told him I did.

"I don't think you do," he said. "Maybe you think this is ancient history. It isn't. It's serious shit. You don't want to cause a death do you? Because they'll kill your father. Now, I don't care. But I'm serious. I'm dead serious. Think about your mother." Then he added, by way of signing off, "Okay, I've had a belly full."

He handed the phone to my mother, who suddenly remembered the Yukon gold mine and the lost money. She said her memory was like "an antique dresser with sticky drawers" that had just come unstuck. She gave me a number for a man, she explained, who had a lot of my father's money and who could be compelled to give it back. "I wouldn't meet him alone," she advised. "He was a crazy son of a bitch." Then she was my mother again, telling me about her latest nature photos before ringing off to finish a game of Yahtzee.

In the movies people always get their cathartic moment. They get their "why" conversation, the key exchange they needed for closure. In real life that moment rarely happens. The people who caused you pain are long gone. The violent young man is replaced by a gentle old one who is as confused as you are by the actions of the person he sees in old pictures. But what if you could bring the young man back? What if you had no choice?

It was a drizzly day in late June when I took a train up to Boston to meet my father. I recognized him, standing at the end of the platform with the same mustache he's had since I was a kid. I sized him up again: beige Windbreaker, jeans, slicked-back hair. He was dressed up for this, but with the same red-rimmed eyes and ashen cheeks, he still looked like a man from a public service announcement.

"God, you look like a movie star," he said, and compared to him I suppose I did. In the dead silence of the car-rental kiosk, I could hear his breathing, quick and shallow.

We drove to a different subsidized apartment, a federal home for the elderly and disabled, half a mile from Harvard University. It was still spare and grimy, adorned with the same Christian iconography and cigarette-scarred plastic cups. It may even have had the same liter of Diet Pepsi in the fridge.

We sat at the card table in the center of the room, where my father clapped his hands and smiled. He said he was happy about the apartment and he bragged about his health and my physical inheritance. "My lungs are great, Tony. You're so lucky, you're going to live forever." He lit one of his off-brand cigarettes and in the fading light he began to tell me all the things I couldn't remember and never would have known.

Hurricane Andrew didn't kill my father because he had already been extradited to Massachusetts, where he was held in an overflow county facility with federal prisoners. Metal bunk. Metal desk. Metal can. Here's what he hated about prison: "pants with no pockets, open showers so you are cold on your back while washing your front, and a constant high noise level of babble and yelling and cursing, so you can't watch television enjoyably."

The DEA, FBI, and IRS pressed him about his missing money and why he hadn't hired a lawyer, like all his partners had. They asked him, in so many words, what the hell he was trying to pull, pretending to be broke. They accused him of having an alias, a silent partner, someone holding money for him. "I told them," my father recalled, "I don't own one sock, not even underwear."

My father was sort of honorable. He kept my mother out of it, and he kept his customers out of it. When there was bullying talk of booking everybody as part of a continuing criminal enterprise, he refused to cooperate against his old networks in Miami and Connecticut. But he was more than willing to pledge new and unknown details about "Willy T, the snitch and Charlie M, the snitch" as well as his other partners.

He was a rat, in other words, like hundreds of ex–pot barons moving through the judicial system. But he thought back to when he began in his line of work, when he and his best pals in the world shook hands and made their most solemn good-guy promises to button their lips and stand tall together, pirates for life. He broke the code and in the end it left a stain on his conscience that will most likely never go away. "I feel I have been a whore for you," he wrote in a copy of a letter to his lawyer, or possibly a draft of a letter never sent. "I feel my life will be in danger and that hasn't been addressed."

Even with cooperation, sentencing hearings are an uncertain business. Judges do not have to accept plea bargains, and drug cases are as likely as any to inspire flights of personal vengeance. In Virginia the judge sentenced Pierre, the marina owner in Urbanna, to sixteen years in prison for his role in a prior load of twenty-four thousand pounds of dope—"a shocking amount," he intoned from the bench, "heavens knows how many lives you wrecked by bringing those drugs into this country." (It did not help that his wife wrote to the judge that Panis "considers himself a pirate.") In Florida a judge sentenced Jimbo to five years for driving that U-Haul truck (Adventures in Moving, indeed). In a Massachusetts courtroom, John was called "a grave threat to the safety of the community," and sentenced to a hundred and thirty-five months, or more than eleven years.

By comparison, my father and his colleagues were lucky. If their crime had been committed a year later, it would have triggered a mandatory minimum sentence of more than a decade without parole. Instead they drew a strict civil libertarian judge who, while he happened to look like the severe blue eagle from the *Muppets*, was easy on gentleman dope dealers. No one got more than three years, even the guys who did not talk. My father did a year and a half in custody: six months time served, six additional months in a home for addicts and the insane, six more for violating the rules of the home.

He showed me his first post-prison résumé, which presented a man "able to manage multiple tasks, set appropriate priorities, and meet deadlines," all of which was true enough. His first straight job was as a medication officer at an old folks home, aka the drug guy behind the Plexiglas, still the dealer. Later he was an overnight security guard in the John Hancock Tower, "maintaining the safety and security of a 42-story office building," per a later résumé, king of the world's biggest stash house.

After talking for a couple of hours, we stepped out into a cool summer evening, hunting dinner in downtown Cambridge. We still made for an odd pair, I guess, because when we stopped at a bank to use the ATM, the guard came over to make sure I wasn't being bothered. My father claimed to have less than $5 in his pocket, so I bought him a pack of cigarettes and took him out to a decent seafood joint, where he slipped right back into the good life, ordering a strawberry daiquiri, white wine, a plate of mussels, and coffee with a splash of Sambuca for dessert. "When you're rich you can do anything," he said with a wink.

Reality returned the next morning with breakfast at a Dunkin' Donuts. Dad seemed to know most of the down-and-outers who wiled away their hours in the brightly lit space. I hate to say it, but he fit right in. His taste buds were so fried from drugs that he used ten packs of Sweet'N Low. His arms were shredded from needles. His teeth were stumps with visible rings and would never be otherwise unless licked clean by flames. With a face grooved and dented by prison fights and repeated falls after blackouts, he was the guy you move away from on the street, the guy I wanted to move away from then.

But of course, it's not so easy.

I needed to go inside that stripped-down, straightforward document from the National Archives. I needed to know what kind of man my father was. Because that July I had become a father myself. And I realized you can ignore your old man forever. You can turn over his pictures, decline his calls, and spend a lifetime pretending you were flown in by the stork. It doesn't change who you are.

10

Reunion

Massachusetts, Miami, and New York City, 2009–Present Day

My father did not waver when I asked him to act as a tour guide to his former haunts. We started tramping through New York City, loitering in the lobbies of the five-star hotels he used to frequent. We walked into the tasseled opulence of the Palace Hotel and walked back in time. A house detective picked us up at the door. Dad waved at the dick, a little toodle-oo move, and sure enough he followed us through the foyer and the dining area and watched as my father pawed toward the check-in counter.

Dad moved like a man with $5,000 in his boot, and when he leaned across the counter—raw-eyed and irregular despite his confidence—I cringed, but the check-in girl leaned toward him. To my surprise, the exchange carried on for a while. She laughed a little. Finally my father sauntered back to me, his legs working in those enlivening half circles, never straight lines. "Seven hundred and fifty dollars," he said, eyes half open. "Fucking rip-off."

It was a similar scene at the Plaza, where we took a seat in the lobby, and I was sure we were about to be brushed back outside. A waiter appeared, dropping menus in front of us, and standing until we made a move. The Diet Coke was $6. My father moved first. "We won't be having anything today," he said, holding out the menus. The waiter's pen hovered above the pad.

He said, "Excuse me?"

My father lifted his chin and managed to look down his nose at the waiter, who seemed to be losing air from somewhere in his lower back. The silence and the stare lingered until the little man could do nothing but tiptoe away, shooed off by a charity case in a purple thrift-store T-shirt. I didn't even know declining to order was an option.

And yet our proudest moment was our last of the day: a peek inside the Gramercy Park Hotel, scene of my father's most exuberant freak-outs and wildest parties, a place where he nettled the staff with endless late-night calls for more coffee and lubricant. The hotel had recently been redecorated, part of a quarter-billion-dollar renovation overseen by the painter and sculptor Julian Schnabel. The *Times* called the work "truly grand." My father sniffed around as though it were a ruined car.

"It's too bad they had to do this," he said, passing artwork by Andy Warhol and Damien Hirst. He paused by a massive fireplace in a baroque, heavy-beamed lobby, deriding it all as "some place in Vermont." On the way out we passed beneath a humongous chandelier suspended by bronze chains. My father gave it a verbal middle finger. "Those crystals aren't even real," he said, and I dragged him out before anyone heard more. Later I looked it up, however, and it turns out he's right. Schnabel designed the chandelier with cast-resin. My father knows his chandeliers.

For our first few days together, we were easy in each other's company. My father was full of far-seeing criminal wisdoms and tourist-board-ready exclamations. On Broadway he sauntered into the middle of the street and yelled down the canyon of buildings, hollering toward the horizon line: "I love being back in New York!" He only got on my nerves when his tone turned to one of regret. "Boy, I wish I had the money to live in the city," he said, as we walked a lane in the southeast corner of Central Park.

"You *did* have the money," I said.

"I did have the money," my father repeated. "But I had you and Ann."

"That's not where the money went."

"No, that's right. The money went like lightning. There was so much money I didn't know what to do with it. Like that $500,000 I buried—but what else was I going to do?"

"Put it in a safe-deposit box?"

"Jesus. I shoulda. I should have put it in a fucking safe-deposit box."

Part of me had not given up hope that my father had a pot of gold somewhere. I imagined that if I just asked him in the right way, he'd remember. He'd jerk upright as if bitten by a snake and we'd run off, driving to Long Island or the Catskills, where we'd dig up a carefully caulked, perfectly preserved Styrofoam cooler of cash. Or else we'd go find this lawyer together, rough him up like Charlie did, and demand our money. I asked him what kind of paperwork he got from the guy.

"He said he'd give me a certificate of deposit," my father said. "But he never did."

"Did you get a receipt at least?"

"No. I didn't get any receipts. I didn't ask for any. I never asked for papers. I had faith."

"In what?"

"He was Charlie's friend, so I thought he would be my friend, too."

"What the fuck were you thinking?"

"I know. It's a nightmare for me. It's crazy, isn't it? Six hundred and sixty thousand down the drain."

I asked him about the $750,000 from his last job, and he shrugged. "I was totally fried."

A few minutes later he patted all his stash spots, forgetting where he put his wad of taxpayer dollars. He found it and a government twenty fell from his pocket as he paid for a $2 food-cart coffee. People don't change but the world around them does, and the world today—or at least the America that is the only world my father has ever known—has reversed itself once again on marijuana, redefining my father's life in the process.

In the twenty years since my father was busted Americans have elected three pot-experienced presidents, approved use of medicinal marijuana in eighteen states, and voted to do what no other government ever has: create a commercial pot market. In Colorado and Washington State, as long as the federal government doesn't fight the will of the voters, pot will be sold, taxed, and regulated much like alcohol. It will be street legal not only for medicinal purposes but, as *Rolling Stone* recently enthused, "for getting high purposes."

This may be the end of pot prohibition; or merely the beginning of the end; or simply the beginning of the beginning of the end; or the last instant before another two-decade lockout because the door of reforms is never so close as when it's being slammed in your face. But it's certainly no longer a world of outlaws and pirates, a country of little boys in the summer before girls.

It's a business world: aboveboard, sober, boring. It's as though Blackbeard went to Harvard Business School, cut his beard, and came out fluent in decision theory and schooled in the complexities of Excel spreadsheets. I know because I took a break from my father to tour the new pot world in Colorado. My guides were self-described "social entrepreneurs," a "nerd herd" comprised of young men on good terms with a barber. A finance veteran, two children of the Ivy League, multiple lawyers, and the son of a police chief: They could have done anything with their lives. "My brother is a physician" is the kind of thing one hears them say, but they chose the pot business as a boom market, miracle cure, and social movement decades in the making and suddenly, thrillingly near.

"This is our Facebook," said one of my hosts, a founding member of a marijuana industry group that's buried the age of sandwich-board activism and instead strives to partner with law enforcement and politicians. In a high-rise in downtown Denver, I watched one of the group's meetings, flanked by a Pulitzer Prize–winning communications consultant, two state lobbyists, and a nationally known political operative. The guest of honor was a state senator who hungrily accepted campaign donations, a series of envelopes stuffed with cash.

"Huge thank you, everyone," the politician said, guiding the conversation back to the next legislative session and the kinds of legal changes this group would like to see. Here again, it's not what you'd expect from a band of outsiders. There's talk of youth drug-abuse prevention, a bill to define "drugged" driving. When the politician finally rises to leave, after more than an hour, the dealers in their pressed shirts and suit jackets clap heartily. "Thank you," the politician says, bowing slightly. "Thank you for what you do."

What they do is procure and distribute marijuana. And not via sailboats and street corners. Heading west toward the Rocky Mountains, Denver rises like a city in a snow globe, but before you reach the exits for downtown, there's a stark industrial ring, a hard-hat zone of freight trains, heavy equipment, and all-purpose warehouse space. This is the Silicon Valley of the American pot business, which is housed in at least a million square feet, more than all the office space in the city's tallest skyscraper.

I visited three of these warehouses, each as boring as a soundstage until the moment one actually sees the plants. One second you're in the gray, empty cold of a warehouse, your mind hypnotized by the dull hum of electricity. The next you're standing in a perfect simulacrum of summer sunshine with hundreds of gorgeous green plants gently waving, stirred by fans and soothed by classical music (or energized by hard rock, depending on what the master grower says the plant "likes").

It's always harvest time in some of these rooms. Always processing time in others. A magic garden with no sun or bugs. My father's pot was dirty: doused in ocean spray, soaked in fuel, infested with spiders. This is a beautiful, and explicitly professional, product: hundreds of acorn-size buds flecked with crystals of THC, the chemical without which these plants might as well be hotel ferns.

The old procurement side of the scam—Willy or John getting dope from darkest Colombia—has been replaced by a team of growers who act as botanical gods, replicating different seasons in different rooms, monitoring delivery systems that account for every gram of pot, every plant, all of it accessible to Colorado authorities twenty-four hours a day. If growing conditions slip, these tattooed gardeners (née smugglers) get a text message and respond not with dirty money and a new boat but with a tweak to the water line, maybe a few shakes of plant food.

The old distribution side of the scam—my father and Bobby selling the dope to everyday America—has been replaced by a retail storefront. Stash-house buddies have become young female "budtenders" (née dealers) who distribute the dope from glass apothecary jars. If there's a problem, the owner, who would have been my father in another life, appears on the scene with a clipboard and an official employee badge, threatening to take this up to human resources rather than cool everyone out with a box of Velveeta, frozen peas, and a six-pack.

The frisson of illegality isn't gone completely. Every morning outside the unmarked bottling factory, home to Dixie Elixirs, America's first multistate cannabis-infused-soda maker, men in suits hold the door for twenty-somethings in spiderweb-patterned skullcaps and sweatpants. At one of the warehouses I toured, the master grower, a six-figure hire, was wearing flannel pajama pants and a "420 Weed" T-shirt, as he threw out a doughnut box. Another tour was interrupted by the arrival of one of the staff trimmers, the wizard-bearded host of a Web show called *Tokin.* All the best talent is de facto black market talent, developed in violation of federal law.

And this tension between the shadowy roots of pot and the direct light of legalization pervades the industry. I saw fleets of contractors collecting checks, along with gardening wholesalers, business consultants, and software developers. But because the industry is still technically felonious under federal law, new businesses struggle for basic services. Banks and landlords hesitate to take their money. They can't get traditional loans, or insurance, or health coverage. Credit-card companies won't process transactions in their stores. Judges won't enforce their contracts. The IRS forbids normal business deductions, bankrupting many operations.

This in-between nature of the business is present in the very product, too. Does medicinal pot help people? Absolutely. It eases pain and nausea, generates appetite, encourages sleep, and generally comforts the seriously afflicted. Yet it's also a euphoric drug that parks itself in a part of the brain named after the Sanskrit word for "bliss." It's both a medicine and a drug—a medicine you like to take—which is why some patients with pot prescriptions have cancer or glaucoma, but the vast majority are young to middle-aged men with vague complaints of pain. "Skateboarders with bruises" is the running aside from critics.

The prescribing of medical marijuana is also a bit of a slapstick routine. Oh, you have cancer? Try this wonder medicine called Pineapple

Grenade or Alien Dog or Face Wreck. Oh, you have a doctor's recommendation? Try smoking this dab of hash with a butane torch, some foil, and what looks like a crack pipe. And then there are the festivals, so-called cannabis cups that blend the sobriety of a bar crawl with the crowd behavior of the Adult Video News Awards, all doctor-approved. Sometimes there's even a doctor on-site writing scrips.

The future can perhaps be glimpsed in pot companies expanding in an upscale direction, choosing clean generic brand names that would work for any bourgeois bohemian product. Names can grow, in other words, which is perhaps the biggest distinction between the new pot and the old: sheer size and visibility.

As state laws have softened, pot use has risen sharply. More than three million people started smoking it regularly in the past five years, and the rate of high-school experimentation is at a thirty-year high. One in fifteen high-school seniors are smoking daily or near daily. And when a kid first lights up at about age sixteen, it's usually not with a cigarette. Prohibition prevents an even more tremendous uptick; remove it and you can expect a doubling or even tripling of the existing market, a spike to levels far surpassing any on record, and this in a country that already consumes the plant at three times the global average.

My new friends in the boardroom are counting on it. Sure, they revel in their historic role, talking like the future subjects of a Ken Burns–style documentary, the pioneers who emerged from a dysfunctional prohibition. One framed the federal letter warning him that his store was too close to a school. Others brighten as they describe the signs of surveillance—the clicks on the phone, unmarked vans in the lane. They talked to me in part because they respect my father, a Rosa Parks of the legalization movement who in time will be honored appropriately along with his colleagues: friends of freedom who violated an unjust law.

They respect my father—they just don't want to end up like him. There are always exceptions but new pot barons are generally uninterested in social banditry; they are immune to the allure of pirates and codes, dive bars and profligate living. After the board meeting, in fact, I went out drinking with eight or ten of them and found myself not in one of Denver's evergreen-scented holes in the wall but the Churchill Bar, a smoking club inside the city's poshest hotel, the Brown Palace. There, as a pretty waitress delivered round after round of top-shelf conviviality and an electronic joint prototype appeared, it was easy to see my hosts in thirty years, when legalization is old news and my father is dead, sitting in the same woozy affluence—fatter, balder, and fabulously rich.

Our flight to Miami was my father's first takeoff since his extradition flight in 1992. Back then he was wearing an orange jumper, his feet chained together and his hands cuffed and then locked inside a black box, as though otherwise he might spontaneously procure and deal another seventeen tons of reefer. This time he wore an oversize blue knit shirt that has, in two-inch letters, POLO emblazoned across his heart. He began furiously chewing gum, mouth open wide enough to pop in a grape between each clench. His toes, exposed and wiggling in a pair of liquor giveaway flip-flops, looked like they were recently recovered from an archaeological dig.

"Where's the stewardess?" he asked me. I looked up from a magazine to see my father hit the orange Call button again, and again, and again. Finally a flight attendant came over, a concerned expression on her face, like my father might be having a heart attack.

"Is everything okay, sir?"

"Could I have a coffee, please?"

The flight attendant looked annoyed but also wary. This might be a corporate test, or else a revived season of *Candid Camera*. She leveled with him, gingerly.

"We don't have coffee prepared yet, sir. I'm sorry."

"Well, how long before the meal?" my father asked.

"No meal, sir." She gave him a wincing smile. "We'll be around with a drink cart soon enough. Meantime, would you like some peanuts?"

"Yes, thank you. And some coffee when it's ready."

My father downed the peanuts. When the coffee came he downed that, too. He'd assumed he'd get a plate of eggs, which is why he hadn't eaten in the airport. I could hear his stomach rumbling. He moved to hit the button again, and I grabbed his hand.

"Quit it."

"Why?"

"They don't give you multiple cups of coffee anymore."

"They don't?"

"No," I said. "What are you thinking?"

"They used to," he said, sinking back into a teenage sadness.

In Miami I got a glimpse of my father in his natural habitat, the place where he lived among his own kind, a group of righteous dope dealers that Timothy Leary once described as "the holiest, handsomest, healthiest, horniest, humorest, most saintly group of men that I have met in my life." And why? Because they are "the new Robin Hood, the spiritual guerrilla, a mysterious agent—who will take the place of the cowboy hero." When the legalization movement took off, my father was a supporter but his enthusiasm was tempered by a crisp, self-satisfied melancholy, an acknowledgment of the fact that legalization meant the final extinction of this old way of life.

But all that was far away as he was walking through Miami International Airport, recalling the spirit and thrill of his last triumphant arrival in the fall of 1986. Back then he was a hero to thirty million regular marijuana smokers in America, all of whom needed him and his kind to get their ticket to freedom and joy. He was their forty-year-old god, with a frisky bag of money at his side and the promise of extraterrestrial bliss until every dollar was spent. He could go anywhere in those days—the Mutiny, Tobacco Road, Sonesta Beach—secure in a certain elastic definition of fatherhood and fidelity, love and family.

The first thing we did was drive to the Sonesta, where I had booked us a room. My father hummed happily to himself during the trip down South Bayshore Drive in the rental car. The old Sonesta Beach Hotel was one of my father's favorite hangouts. But when we pulled up to the hotel, his mood blackened.

"What the hell is this?" he said.

At the front desk, we learned that this was the new Sonesta Bayfront, in Coconut Grove. We were given an address for the old hotel. We were not prepared for what it would look like. It turns out that the Sonesta Beach Hotel had been on an epic slide of its own. It was half destroyed by Hurricane Andrew, which left it windowless and closed for more than a year, and it never fully recovered. It had changed hands a few times, sold and resold. Big rehabs were hatched. And then, just a few months before we got there, the Sonesta was demolished, the tennis courts hacked up, the beach brushed clean.

When we arrived at the site, it was just a pile of rubble. My father put his hands on his head, and said, "Oh no. Oh no. Oh no." He stepped out of the car before it stopped rolling and, in his flip-flops, slipped in the construction muck as he walked to a perimeter fence and peered in at a mud pit. The picture could have run on front pages as a natural-disaster photo: Man in grief. It was not just the building they had flattened. It was my father. It was his "best times in the world."

So we returned to the new Sonesta, which was first class in every way, but I couldn't help notice that it had no poolside bar, no Geno waiting with a shot of rum for Dad, a virgin daiquiri for his son. There was a business center but no beach for father-son Wiffle ball, and I didn't see anybody wearing Speedos. As our first day in Miami faded to night, something heavy settled in my mind: Some of my own best times were gone as well.

For dinner we went to the rooftop restaurant, where we had a view of Biscayne Bay, which bristled with dozens of sailboats in half silhouette. It was Sailboat Bay, we suddenly realized, almost the same view as from the upper rooms of the Mutiny Hotel, where my father had so much fun he didn't come home.

The old Mutiny was right next door but it too had fallen on hard times, changing hands and suffering a series of reversals. A federal savings and loan foreclosed on the Mutiny, and when it reopened in 1999 the club was gone and so were the rooms, which once had functioned like themed porn sets. The "Gypsy Caravan," "Hot Fudge," and "Outer Space" rooms, along with a hundred and thirty-five other scenes of vigorous American history, were redone in a uniform British Colonial motif and sold as condos.

"All the good old times are fucking gone," my father said the next morning at breakfast on the hotel terrace. He took one last glance at the ghost of the old Mutiny, found a poolside lounge chair, and lay down, throwing his hand over his head in a death-to-sunlight sort of fashion. After I ordered us some omelets, he came over to join me, adding a white wine to the tab. He seemed bored, like he had seen it all before, only better.

In the afternoon we went to Miami Beach and took a gander at the lifeguard stands he used to sleep in, newly painted by the city. He took his shirt off for a dip in the sea, not far from Joe's Stone Crab in the heart of South Beach, surrounded by half-dressed young people. He had the biggest gut I could see. Hard-living old men return to a baby's shape: ab-less, curved, unsteady, walking with a T-shirt in hand that might just as well be a teddy. Men with his physique are on every boardwalk, every boulevard. They are your winos, your tramps, and every time I see one I see my father.

That night I heard him singing nonsense in the shower, and when he came out he laid on top of the covers in his Fruit of the Looms. It was strange to shake the hands of men with whom my father had counted money, courted women, and snorted coke. It was stranger to hug women who had worried over these men like my mother worried over my father, and who stayed with them nonetheless. The urge in Miami was even stranger. I wanted to have a thousand drinks with my father, paint the town, until he looked at me like an old picture of him, which would of course make time an illusion and turn us into the same man at last.

At one point my father looked in the drawer next to the bed, something he had done a thousand times or more. If it was a nice hotel, the drawer slid; a shitty hotel, the drawer stuck. This one slid and my father peered in. Just a Bible inside. The new Sonesta didn't stock the yellow pages. No girls tonight.

I realized then—in my strange state of disappointment—that I didn't lose my father to drugs or addiction or anything quite so shameful. I lost him to work, to passion, strange to say, a drive not so different from another man's drive to put his name on a door, his stamp on a building. Evidence of fatherless children is everywhere once you become alive to life's trade-offs, and you learn that there is no such thing as balance, none possible, and for many, my father included, none really desired.

The next morning we drove to Gulliver, and it was my turn for a melancholic survey. The classrooms were empty for the summer, the main office locked. With the possessive confidence of an alumni I jumped a waist-high playground fence and walked the school's open-air hallways. Same tropic-hospital smell, same vague rustling in every bush. The sprinklers were on, black plastic periscopes poking up along the walkways, spritzing my ankles. The same spindly-legged birds owned the fields and blue crabs patrolled the walkways. In the distance, I could hear the heavier artillery, the big, clanging metal sprinkler heads that had drenched me the last day of fourth grade, my last year in the school. Had no one shut them off since I left?

I had to squint as I entered the school's breezy limestone amphitheater, snug in the center of campus. Here Florida's brightest school officials responded to the drug-fueled floating orgy of greater Miami. We heard from former junkies and fallen athletes, and once from "Punchy," a robot with tank treads for feet, glowing red eyes, and boxing gloves for hands. He zoomed and twirled like Johnny Five from *Short Circuit*, playing "Ice Ice Baby" from hidden speakers in his head.

I noticed a new-looking mural along the outside wall of what used to be my second-grade classroom. It's a collage of Florida characters: politicians shaking hands, teachers leading class, architects with plans rolled up under their arms, and various people in uniform, firefighters, police. Then there's something else. Like Lenin's head in Diego Rivera's old mural in Rockefeller Center, there's a lazy gringo in this hall of the learned. He has a brush mustache, sombrero over his eyes, and he's lying in a hammock. He looked like an "Indian chief" to me.

"You were happy here," my father said, when I came back to the car. My blood boiled. The idea that he had any insight into how I felt. This man who abandoned me. This man who made his own Vizcaya, then torched it for fun. I wanted to level him with a question, remind him how much he had missed.

"How would you know?" I asked.

"I know because I used to park over there," my father said. He pointed to a spot where the bushes break and the playground was visible from the road. "I used to watch you swing. I know because I used to watch you play. That's how I know." I loved him then, at least a little bit, but back in the car my father volunteered that he was going to heaven, and he reminded me that his was a victimless crime, and that if he had the chance to do it again he would live his life exactly the same way.

"All of it?" I said.

"In a second," he said.

And right about then I felt something release.

We had driven over the causeway to find the Monkey Jungle, one of the only father-son haunts we had left to visit. It was gone, another casualty of Hurricane Andrew. So I headed down an interesting side road, passing dry pines, then mangroves, then a greedy water line that left just a few feet of land, and a row of colorful shacks, fishermen's lean-tos and the like, festively repainted like the lifeguard stands. A school bus threw shade on some old men selling drinks. We bought Diet Cokes and walked out on a dock, revealing a perfect view of the Miami skyline.

My father started in again about money and wishing he could live in Miami, and I realized that he was enjoying this trip too much. He loved the high life. He loved to lose it. And he didn't give a shit about the damage that remained. Evidently, he never even thought about it, never had the creeping feeling that maybe he made the wrong choices, that his life was all wrong, all of it, wrong, wrong, wrong. His own father went crazy because he could never see what really happened after the bombs fell. My father never even cared to look.

"Do you think there was something romantic about pissing your life away?" I asked him.

"Looking back, it wasn't romantic."

"Yeah, I know. Sure. That's what you're supposed to say. But seriously. Was it literary for you to live the low life?"

"Tony," he said, with a shrug, "I've liked my life. I liked the drugs and the girls and the money. I liked living like a pirate, outside the real world, never doing anything but dabbling and talking."

"I've liked my life." I repeated it back to him slowly. He was like a tongue on a sore tooth, a finger in a scab. I hated him for having it both ways. "You wouldn't change a thing?"

"I wouldn't have walked out on you and Ann."

"But you had that chance. You made a choice."

"I chose drugs."

"Yes, you chose drugs. So you can't go through the motions of regret, not if you don't really feel them."

"I regret . . ." He stopped. "I regret that I pissed it all away."

"Bullshit," I said. "That's what I mean. You don't. Obviously you don't. You had to piss it all away or you wouldn't be an outlaw."

"That's good, Tony. You're a pretty smart kid, you know that? I think you hit it on the head."

We stood in silence.

"I also think I was angry inside. You think that's bullshit?" he asked.

"I think you made your choice."

"I thought I was going to die not being with you. It felt like a stone in my stomach, like having a rock inside me, a heavy rock, and the dope didn't take it away, and the prostitutes didn't make it better."

"If it was so bad, then why didn't you stay with me?"

"I did the coke to dull the pain."

"If the pain was so bad, why not alleviate it by staying?"

"I have no explanation. I don't know," he said. "I know the coke didn't work."

The world of drugs and crime is stupid with paradox, but I find the compassion paradox the most galling. How could a person so compassionate, so empathetic—a man who couldn't bear to be around people in casts, would throw up if he saw vomit, would give away his last dime—also be so insensitive, so hurtful. He abandoned his family, hit his wife, allowed a another man to father his son. I had to ask: Had he really thought he was up for fatherhood?

"Yeah."

"Really?"

"Yeah."

"How could you think that?"

"It just seemed like the next step."

"That's not the question. Why did you think a drug-dealing, drug-taking smuggler would be a good dad?"

"I guess I was delusional."

At the hotel in Miami, on our last night, I looked up old news reports of Carolin Mines using a more powerful archive than Google. Shares were frozen in 1987, it turned out, after the company admitted to misleading press releases. Previous reports of a mega-lode of gold, it said, were not "to be relied on." It went bankrupt the following year, when I was eight. Later I called the old phone numbers my mother gave me. I quizzed Connie about burial spots on her lawn. Nothing turned up. The money is gone, all right. It's gone, fair and square.

We parted ways again in New York. I headed for my family in Brooklyn, he headed to Chinatown for an all-night bus to Boston. That night, for the first time, I looked at the darker side of my father's story without looking away. I glanced through pictures from the trip, toggling between the reality of the picture, my father's reality, and my own. To everyone else who saw him bathing in the sea on that Saturday on Miami Beach, he was surely a bum. To me he was a bum who was once a millionaire, and that's a very different thing. It gave him the air of an elite performer who has gone soft in retirement. I am a son, and a son sees what he needs to see.

Or maybe it is just that I have my father's eyes, not their blue tint but their double vision. I see the horror; I see the glory. I am a little blond boy abandoned by a father who still describes his time drug dealing, and not his time raising a son, as "the most exhilarating and wonderful years of my life," "absolute heaven." I am a starry-eyed adult who understands my father's reasons, even if I do not find them compelling. When I look at my own son, as my father must have looked at me, I think my father is heartless for leaving. When I look at the man who left, I think he is human for doing so.

"I loved you," my father said at one point, interrupting one of my interrogations. "I would die for you. But I was what I was. I was a scammer and a smuggler and I was a good one. That's it. That consumed me. I never thought about doing anything else."

This is also the part where I might scold my father for losing his bearings. But he's actually hard to hate. He spent his adult life in the deepest streams of American romanticism, living as the sensitive junkie, the intelligent hobo, the moral criminal. His life was a way of exploring the world, of giving himself enviably extreme experiences. Americans love traditional success but we are ambivalent about what results from it: daily planners, insurance premiums, savings accounts, tomorrows as mild as today. In the end, whenever it comes, my father will have skipped all that and lived exactly the life he wanted: an earth-kissing existence of near triumph but never greatness.

God help me, I love this about my father. It means everything, in fact, because for as long as I can remember, I've been afraid of becoming him. I thought I would lose control and go skidding into his state of being. But my father wasn't out of control. He wasn't driven by demons. If he chose his life, I can choose mine.

When I told my father that he would soon have a grandson, he was of course overjoyed. When my son is older, I figured, I'd tell him about his grandfather, but I assumed they would never meet. The time for bonding was over, I said, even though my father seemed oblivious as ever. Were we thinking of calling him Anthony, he asked. "No, Dad," I said. "I don't think so."

I was right about the name. The one we chose is clean and capacious, well-suited for a lawyer or a writer, anything, really, but a drug dealer. But I was wrong about my father never meeting his grandson. My father has made a few trips to Brooklyn. In fact, it's no longer clear which Dokoupil is the more haggard one: me or my father. My son emerged with a ferocity that can only described as Braveheart-like, and so it has been a hard few years. Nightlife doesn't destroy one's body nearly as much as fatherhood does, if honestly pursued.

My father holds nothing back on his trips to see us. When he met my wife, a woman far classier than myself, he pointed to a picture of me on the wall, a head shot taken in a photo booth overseas. "It looks like a mug shot!" he said. "Jesus, you should shave more, Tony. You look like a criminal." Later my wife put on a white shirt with ruffles, declaring herself ready for dinner. My father was all compliments. "Oh, my, that's gorgeous. You look like a pirate girl."

During the meal he filled us in on his current life, which he still lives as though for the benefit of some unseen camera. He rides around Harvard on a classic English bicycle, a three-speed, which he keeps in the easiest gear, collapsing in the grass near the Charles River, where he likes to watch the girls run. He lives well, for a man on the dole. He goes to yoga four days a week at the senior center and circle time at the Quaker House. He owns a juicer and a computer, where he's back at it with "Pirate Kings." He says, "I've got the whole book down in my mind now." He remains hard to stay angry at because his monstrousness is limned by likable idiocy.

The other day on the way to his Quaker meeting he was stopped by a kid with a clipboard, an activist collecting signatures for marijuana reform. My father signed and at group he spoke out in favor of legalization, which won him a shoulder tap and a handshake from a libertine hippie in his old folks home, who invited my father over for a homegrown joint, something Dad had never tried.

It "touched all the pleasant memories," he told me, and knocked him flat with its strength. One puff, two puffs. Pot today is four, five times stronger than it was in my father's time, each bud fuzzy and sparkly and wet as a stamp pad. He goes back for more every month, gets lit up, thinks a little, smiles a lot. He still likes his life. He wouldn't change a thing.

I once told him about an essay I cowrote about how to make men more involved as fathers.

"And that's possible?" he says.

"Yes, Dad. That's possible," I say.

"Well you certainly didn't learn anything from me."

We can laugh at it now but it can also get uncomfortable.

"Where's that knife you found the other day?" my wife asked one night. She and my mother were on the living-room floor trying to put together a toy garage for our son.

"This one?" I said.

"Yeah."

"It's my dad's pot knife."

"What do you mean?"

"He opened bales with it."

My mother snorts, but my wife waves away the conversation. "Can we not, please? Thank you."

Not long after, my wife and I were sitting in a coffee shop, our son asleep on my chest. My father was with us, and we were talking about the old days, until my downstairs neighbor walked in with his three-year-old son. My wife and I shut up instinctively. But my father plowed on, shaking his blocky head about "the hookers, the hookers, I couldn't stay away from the hookers. The hookers were my downfall."

He continues to have a keen if not exactly insightful sense of his own story. One day I watched him pick up *The Pearl*, a thin Steinbeck novel, in a box of free books. It's about a poor skin diver who tries to provide for his infant son by selling the world's biggest pearl, then loses the boy and the money in the evil that swirls around the object. Sound familiar?

"That's a good one," my father said, pushing it on me, and reaching for James Michener's *The Drifters*, a world of "dreams, drugs, and dedication to pleasure," per the jacket copy. He pocketed it as we walked on.

As a grandparent, he is a lot like he was as a parent. He brings gifts and plays endless chasing games, exactly as he played with me. One day we walked to the park, and as we watched my son play, my father was undeniably the same man he has always been. "It gets pretty boring, huh?" he said.

A few minutes later he looked long and hard at my son, who was not quite two years old and still ate wood chips if you didn't watch him closely. "Do you think he will be a genius?" my father asked, with complete honesty. "I think he's going to work in research and development. I think he's going to be somebody."

Maybe.

But my son is another little blond boy, just as I was and as my father was. Beyond an eerie physical resemblance, there is an energy, a mischievous charisma that scares and delights at the same time. On swings in the park he throws his head back in bliss and closes his eyes, watching the sunspots on his eyelids. Bedtime is a struggle, but he falls off his scooter with stoicism, even gusto. His favorite hat is a pirate hat. His third birthday was pirate themed.

At a coffee shop in our neighborhood, mid-winter, my boy arrived in an orange flap hat, thick-frame checkered sunglasses. There were smiles from the other tables as he sat down and solemnly removed his personal belongings from his pockets: rock, rubber band, rock, another rubber band, a temporary tattoo. Then he leaned back and waited for his muffin, sunglasses still on, a familiar death-to-sunlight affect in his body language.

Then there's the way he talks, this boy of mine. "I make my pee a waterfall," he said in the bathroom one day. "My penis is as big as the moon," he added a couple of mornings later.

Do I think he's going to work in research and development?

In the early 1980s, a Coast Guard officer, plying the seas between Miami and the Caribbean, trying to disrupt marijuana shipments, had a similar thought. "It's discouraging," he said, "to think that one day we'll look back at the dopers like we look back at the rumrunners. Who knows? One of their grandsons may become president."

Would it be so.

Acknowledgments

Before I can thank the many people who made this book possible, I must first offer a bow to my father's side of the family, which sometimes had trouble understanding my desire to spotlight our blackest of black sheep but eventually accepted it with grace. I'm sorry I didn't get the chance to grow up among you. I wish I knew Frances most of all.

I also need to offer a bow to my mother, who endured questions about a past it was sometimes hard to relive, or even acknowledge, and yet who never turned away once I asked her to look. Thank you for understanding why I needed to write this book and for supporting it. I only wish there was something I could say to ease your mind. Maybe this: There will be no sequel.

This work would have been impossible without the memories of many people who lived through the great stoned age and its unending aftermath. There is no way to thank them properly for their generosity without outing them for their excesses. But they should know that I know and that I'm grateful for their recollections.

I'm also grateful to the many people who gave me assistance with the facts and the feel of the years described. They include former Assistant U.S. Attorney Paul Kelly; DEA special investigator Damian Farley; DEA agent Joe Desmond; former "drug czar" Peter Bourne; the staffs of the National Archives in Boston, St. Louis, and Atlanta; the late public defender Owen Walker; along with Andrea Lofgren, David Bienenstock, Christopher Harwood, Richard Stratton, Keith Stroup, and Robert Platshorn, among many others who scramble the boundaries between friend and family member, participant and onlooker, source and scholar. Thank you all.

A huge thank you to Tom Watson, one of the greats, who first suggested that I write about my father and who did more than most to teach me how to write in the first place. Thank you to Andrew Jackson (or was it Thomas Jefferson?) for distracting Jon Meacham long enough to allow Tom to smuggle the original article into the old *Newsweek*. Thank you to Tina Brown for giving me the time and space to write long, including the time off to write a draft of this book. Thank you to my new bosses, Hillary Frey and Gregory Gittrich, for granting me the delayed start I needed to rewrite and finish it.

Good editors are so rare that I feel especially privileged to have had three of them on this book. My friend and former colleague Jennie Yabroff read numerous early drafts and made them so much better, especially on a sentence-to-sentence level. Alison Callahan, formerly of Doubleday, amazed me with her sense of structure and story, and without her support this first-time author would have been lost. Gerry Howard inherited the book but has treated it as one of his own, and for that I'm grateful.

Thank you to Alison Rich and her team and to everyone at Doubleday for championing the project. Thank you to James Melia for doing the work of an EA with unflagging charm and exceptional taste. And of course a deep bow to my agent, Amanda Urban, who started me on this path of book writing and put me in better company than I probably deserve.

During the years it took to write this book, I benefited from the insight, aid, encouragement, conversation, and company of too many friends and colleagues to name. I'm grateful to them all, but a special blessing on the heads of Devin Gordon, Bret Begun, Mark Miller, Marc Peyser, Susanna Schrobsdorff, Ted Moncreiff, Sarah Blustain, Andrew Blum, Andrew Romano, David Cutler, and Nick Iovacchini. Thank you to Seth Wenig for an author photo that erased the haggard look of authorship.

Nobody put more into this book than my wife, Dani, who endured my absences and preoccupations and, despite a raging day job of her own, kept much of our family life spinning and our children in clothes. There are no words.

About the Author

Tony Dokoupil is a senior writer for NBC News. He was a senior reporter with *Newsweek*, where the article that led to this book first appeared. Dokoupil holds a master's degree in American studies from Columbia University and lives in Brooklyn with his wife and children.